Straight Choices

Straight Choices

The psychology of decision making

**Benjamin R. Newell, David A. Lagnado
and David R. Shanks**

Psychology Press
Taylor & Francis Group
HOVE AND NEW YORK

First published 2007 by Psychology Press
27 Church Road, Hove, East Sussex, BN3 2FA

Simultaneously published in the USA and Canada
by Psychology Press
270 Madison Avenue, New York, NY 10016

*Psychology Press is an imprint of the Taylor & Francis Group,
an Informa Business*

Copyright © 2007 Psychology Press

Typeset in Times by RefineCatch Limited, Bungay, Suffolk
Printed and bound in Great Britain by TJ International Ltd,
Padstow, Cornwall
Cover design by Lisa Dynan

British Library Cataloguing in Publication Data
A catalogue record for this book is available from the British Library

Library of Congress Cataloging-in-Publication Data
Newell, Benjamin R., 1972–
    Straight choices : the psychology of decision making / Benjamin R.
        p.; cm.
    Includes bibliographical references and index.
    ISBN-13: 978–1–84169–588–4 (hardcover)
    ISBN-10: 1–84169–588–2 (hardcover)
    1. Decision making. 2. Learning, Psychology of. I. Lagnado, David
A., 1962– II. Shanks, David R. III. Title.
BF448.N49 2007
153.8'3 – dc22

2006037993

ISBN: 978–1–84169–588–4

To Richard, Joss, Sandra and Zoila Eve, Tracy Ray, and Ella, Will and Miranda

Contents

Preface

> Choose life. Choose a job. Choose a career. Choose a family. Choose a . . . big television; choose washing machines, cars, compact disc players, and electrical tin openers. Choose good health, low cholesterol and dental insurance. Choose fixed-interest mortgage repayments . . .
>
> (from John Hodge's screenplay of *Trainspotting*)

So begins Renton's soliloquy in the adaptation of Irvine Welsh's (1996) well-known novel *Trainspotting*. Renton's outburst emphasizes what we all know to be true: life is filled with a dazzling array of choices. How can we hope to deal with this overload of information and make good decisions? How can we ensure that our choices remain 'straight'?

In *Straight Choices* we present a scholarly yet accessible introduction to the psychology of decision making, enhanced by discussion of relevant examples of decision problems faced in everyday life. We provide an integrative account in which clear connections are made between empirical results and how these results can help us understand our uncertain world. An innovative feature of *Straight Choices* is the emphasis on an exploration of the relationship between learning and decision making. Our thesis is that the best way to understand how and why decisions are made is in the context of the learning that precedes them and the feedback that follows them. Decisions don't emerge out of thin air but rather are informed by our prior experience, and each decision yields some information (did it work out well or badly?) that we can add to our stock of experience for future benefit. This novel approach allows us to integrate findings from the decision and learning literatures to provide a unique perspective on the psychology of decision making.

The book is divided into 15 easily digestible chapters and the material is presented in as non-technical a manner as possible, thus making the book highly appropriate and accessible for any students with an interest in decision making – be they students of psychology, economics, marketing or business. The book should also appeal to more senior scholars of decision making, or indeed any cognitive psychologists who are seeking an up-to-date review of current research and are interested in the novel learning-based perspective that we provide.

Throughout the book we have also tried to emphasize the practical applications of much of the research on decision making. We hope that by reading this book you will gain a greater understanding of the psychology of how – and how well – we make decisions and that you will apply that understanding to improve your own decision making.

Ben Newell, David Lagnado and David Shanks
Sydney and London, September 2006

Acknowledgements

It is, of course, impossible to acknowledge all the people who have influenced our thinking about the issues discussed in this book, but conversations with the following people have had significant impact: Peter Juslin, Peter Todd, Tim Rakow, Nigel Harvey, Arndt Bröder, Richard Tunney, Maarten Speekenbrink, Magda Osman, Tilman Börgers, Nick Chater, Steven Sloman, Alastair McClelland, Clare Harries and Dan Lan.

Very special thanks are due to Peter Ayton and John Maule for comprehensive, insightful and very helpful criticism of an earlier draft of the manuscript. We would also like to thank the editorial team at Psychology Press for their excellent assistance throughout the publication process.

Ben Newell would like to thank, first and foremost, his co-authors for 'agreeing' to be cajoled into writing this book with him. The project began when the three authors were based at University College London but only really started to take shape after Ben left for the University of New South Wales and started to bombard the two Davids with multiple emails entitled 'book'. Writing the book has been a very pleasurable and educational experience and Ben is glad to have shared that experience with two such wonderful colleagues. Ben also thanks his research assistants Tamara Cavenett and Brooke Hahn for their help with editing. The support of the Australian Research Council (Discovery Project DP 558181) and the UK Economic and Social Research Council is also gratefully acknowledged.

David Lagnado would like to acknowledge the support of the Leverhulme Trust/ESRC Research Programme 'Evidence, Inference and Enquiry', and in particular Nigel Harvey and Philip Dawid for their excellent guidance of this interdisciplinary project. Special thanks also to Aimable Jonckheere for many thought-provoking discussions.

David Shanks would like to thank the UK Economic and Social Research Council, who for several years have provided funding for the Centre for Economic Learning and Social Evolution at University College London, and which has provided inspiring interaction between psychologists, economists, biologists and mathematicians.

1 Falling off the straight and narrow

The cult film *Donnie Darko* begins with the hero Donnie narrowly surviving (or does he?) a bizarre accident. Donnie is lying in his bed in his suburban family home when he is woken by a strange voice. The voice 'leads' him down the stairs, out of the house and into the street. Moments later a horrendous screeching noise signals the arrival of an aeroplane's jet engine crashing through the roof of the house. The engine completely destroys Donnie's bedroom.

Most of us would agree that being killed by a falling jet engine is an extremely unlikely, freak occurrence. Indeed, if we were asked the question 'Which is more likely: being killed by falling aeroplane parts or being killed by a shark?' the majority of us would probably think a shark attack more likely (Plous, 1993). But we would be wrong. According to *Newsweek* ('Death odds', 1990) we are 30 times more likely to be killed by falling aeroplane parts than by sharks. The reason (or reasons) why we tend to err in answering this question is just one of the many intriguing, challenging and fundamentally important issues that are addressed in this book. Understanding the psychology of how – and how well – we make decisions can have a significant impact on how we live our lives (and how to avoid freak deaths).

Even for a decision as simple as buying a book (a decision that you may well be contemplating right now) we can engage in a series of quite complex thought processes: noting the attributes of different alternatives (cost, appearance, recommendations), comparing different alternatives by making 'trade-offs' on these attributes (e.g., this one is cheaper but it wasn't recommended), and deciding how to allocate our limited resources (e.g., money for books or beer). These processes, and many more besides, can be investigated in systematic ways to discover what leads us to make the decisions we do, how we should make decisions given the preferences we have, and to find out why our decision making sometimes goes awry.

Our approach and the plan of the book

In this book we provide a novel perspective on judgment and decision making along with an accessible review and integration of many of the key research findings. Our perspective is novel in that we view judgment and decision making as often exquisitely subtle and well tuned to the world, especially in situations where we have the opportunity to respond repeatedly under similar conditions where we can learn from feedback. We argue that many of the well-documented errors or biases of judgment often occur in one-shot decision situations where we do not have the chance to learn adequately about the environment. Focusing on errors in these one-shot situations can be a very fruitful research strategy, as the 'heuristics and biases' approach that has dominated the field has demonstrated (Kahneman, Slovic, & Tversky, 1982). However, the downside of this approach is that it can lead to an overly pessimistic view of human judgment and decision making (Gigerenzer, 1996). Our perspective aims to reclaim the original reason for emphasizing errors, namely that errors can be thought of as quirks akin to visual illusions. Like visual illusions they arise in a system that is in general extremely accurate in its functioning.

Take the sharks versus falling aeroplane parts example. In a one-shot decision about the likelihood of death we might choose sharks erroneously. One explanation for such a choice is that we base our decision on the ease with which we can recall instances of people being killed by sharks or by falling aeroplane parts. Shark attacks are likely to be easier to recall – presumably because they receive wider coverage in the media – and so we answer 'sharks'. In general using the ease-of-recall or 'availability' heuristic will serve us well, but in certain situations, particularly when we are insensitive to the distribution of information in the environment (i.e., insensitive to the fact that shark attacks receive more media coverage than falling aeroplane parts), we make errors (see Tversky & Kahneman, 1974). One of the key messages of our approach is that being given the opportunity to learn about information in the environment through repetition and feedback often gives rise to exceptionally accurate judgments and decisions.

This message is pursued most directly in chapters 7 'Associative thinking', 11 'Learning to choose, choosing to learn' and 12 'Optimality, expertise and insight', although the theme of learning runs throughout the book. Some readers might find these chapters a little more challenging than the others but we encourage you to persevere. Chapters 1 and 2 introduce many of the concepts that will be relevant to our exploration of judgment and decision making, through considering some practical decisions (e.g., What medical treatment should I adopt?) and by giving a brief historical overview of the field. Chapters 3 and 4 take us on a journey through the stages of judgment from the discovery of information to the role of feedback. Chapter 5 presents some formal ways of appraising our probability judgments and then in chapter 6 we look at how people actually make judgments. In a similar fashion, chapter 8 presents formal methods for analysing decisions and then chapter 9 examines how people actually make decisions and choices under uncertainty. Chapter 10 extends this analysis to examine the influence of time on decisions. The final three chapters provide some insights into the role that emotion plays on our decisions (chapter 13), the way groups make decisions (chapter 14) and an investigation of some of the more practical methods for implementing what we have learned about decision making in the laboratory to the world outside (chapter 15). The book can be read as a whole – cover to cover – or if you have particular interests then the chapters are, for the most part, self-contained enough to enable you to dip in and choose the parts that appeal. Our aims are twofold: to introduce you to this exciting field, and to help you improve your own decision-making skills.

Decisions, decisions . . .

We are faced with a plethora of decisions, choices and judgments every day and throughout our lives: what to have for lunch, where to go on holiday, what car to buy, whom to hire for a new faculty position, whom to marry, and so on. Such examples illustrate the abundance of decisions in our lives and thus the importance of understanding the how and why of decision making. Some of these decisions will have little impact on our lives (e.g., what to have for lunch); others will have long-lasting effects (e.g., whom to marry). To introduce many of the relevant concepts, in this first chapter we consider three important decisions that we might face in the course of our lives: (1) Which medical treatment should I choose? (2) Is this person guilty or innocent? and (3) How should I invest my money? For each situation we examine some of the factors that can influence the decisions we make. We cover quite a bit of ground in these three examples so don't worry if the amount of information is rather overwhelming. The aim here is simply to give a taste of the breadth of issues that can affect our decision making. There will be ample opportunity in later chapters to explore many of these issues in more depth.

Which medical treatment should I choose?

Barry and Trevor have just received some devastating news: they have both been diagnosed with lung cancer. Fortunately their cancers are still in relatively early stages and should respond to treatment. Barry goes to see his doctor and is given the following information about two alternative therapies – radiation and surgery:

> Of 100 people having surgery, on average, 10 will die during treatment, 32 will have died by 1 year and 66 will have died by 5 years. Of 100 people having radiation therapy, on average, none will die during treatment, 23 will die by 1 year and 78 will die by 5 years.

Trevor goes to see his doctor, who is different from Barry's, and is told the following about the same two therapies:

Of 100 people having surgery, on average, 90 will survive the treatment, 68 will survive for 1 year and 34 will survive for 5 years. Of 100 people having radiation therapy, on average, all will survive the treatment, 77 will survive for 1 year and 22 will survive for 5 years.

Which treatment do you think Barry will opt for, and which one will Trevor opt for? If they behave in the same way as patients in a study by McNeil, Pauker, Sox, and Tversky (1982) then Barry will opt for the radiation treatment and Trevor will opt for surgery. Why? You have probably noticed that the efficacy of the two treatments is equivalent in the information provided to Barry and Trevor. In both cases, radiation therapy has lower long-term survival chances but no risk of dying during treatment, whereas surgery has better long-term prospects but there is a risk of dying on the operating table. The key difference between the two is the way in which the information is presented to the patients. Barry's doctor presented, or *framed* the information in terms of how many people will *die* from the two treatments, whereas Trevor's doctor framed the information in terms of how many people will *survive*. It appears that the risk of dying during treatment looms larger when it is presented in terms of mortality (i.e., Barry's doctor) than in terms of survival (i.e., Trevor's doctor) – making surgery less attractive for Barry but more attractive for Trevor.

This simple change in the framing of information can have a large impact on the decisions we make. McNeil et al. (1982) found that across groups of patients, students *and* doctors, on average radiation therapy was preferred to surgery 42 per cent of the time when the negative frame was used (probability of dying), but only 25 per cent of the time when the positive frame (probability of living) was used (see also Tversky & Kahneman, 1981).

Positive versus negative framing is not the only type of framing that can affect decisions about medical treatments. Edwards, Elwyn, Covey, Mathews, and Pill (2001) in a comprehensive review identified nine different types of framing including those comparing verbal, numerical and graphical presentation of risk information, manipulations of the base rate (absolute risk) of treatments, using lay versus medical terminology, and comparing the amount of information (number of factual statements) presented about choices.

The largest framing effects were evident when *relative* as opposed to *absolute* risk information was presented to patients (Edwards et al., 2001). Relative and absolute risks are two ways of conveying information about the efficacy of a treatment, however, unlike the previous example they are not logically equivalent. Consider the following two statements adapted from an article about communicating the efficacy of cholesterol-reducing drugs (Skolbekken, 1998, see also Gigerenzer, 2002):

(1) 'Savastatin is proven to reduce the risk of a coronary mortality by 3.5 per cent'.

(2) 'Savastatin is proven to reduce the risk of a coronary mortality by 42 per cent'.

A person suffering from high cholesterol would presumably be far more willing to take the drug Savastatin when presented with statement 2 than when presented with statement 1. Moreover, a doctor is more likely to prescribe the drug if presented with statement 2. But is this willingness well placed?

In statement 1 the 3.5 per cent reduction in risk referred to is the *absolute risk reduction* – that is, the proportion of patients who die without taking the drug (those who take a placebo) minus the proportion who die having taken the drug (Gigerenzer, 2002). In the study discussed by Skolbekken (1998) the proportion of coronary mortalities for people taking the drug was 5.0 per cent compared to 8.5 per cent of those on a placebo (i.e., a reduction of 3.5 per cent). In statement 2 absolute risk has been replaced by the *relative risk reduction* – that is, the absolute risk reduction divided by the proportion of patients who die without taking the drug. Recall that the absolute risk reduction was 3.5 per cent and the proportion of deaths for patients on the placebo was 8.5 per cent, thus the 42 per cent reduction in the statement comes from dividing 3.5 by 8.5.

Table 1.1 provides some simple examples of how the relative risk reduction can remain constant while the absolute risk reduction varies widely. Not surprisingly, several studies have found much higher percentages of patients assenting to treatment when relative as opposed to absolute risk reductions are presented. For example, Hux and Naylor (1995) reported that 88 per cent of patients assented to lipid lowering therapy when relative risk reduction information was provided, compared with only 42 per cent when absolute risk reduction information was given. Similarly, Malenka, Baron, Johansen, Wahrenberger, and Ross (1993) found that 79 per cent of hypothetical patients preferred a treatment presented with relative risk benefits compared to 21 per cent who chose the absolute risk option. As Edwards et al. (2001) conclude, 'relative risk information appears much more "persuasive" than the corresponding absolute risk . . . data' (p. 74), presumably just because the numbers are larger.

So what is the best way to convey information about medical treatment? Skolbekken (1998) advocates an approach in which one avoids using

Table 1.1 Examples of absolute and relative risk reduction

Treatment group		Placebo group		Relative risk reduction (%)	Absolute risk reduction (%)
Survivals	Mortalities	Survivals	Mortalities		
9000	1000	8000	2000	50	10
9900	100	9800	200	50	1
9990	10	9880	20	50	0.1

Source: Adapted from Skolbekken (1998).

'value-laden' words like risk or chance, and carefully explains the absolute risks rather than relative risks. Thus for a patient suffering high cholesterol who is considering taking Savastatin, a doctor should tell him or her something like: 'If 100 people like you are given no treatment for five years 92 will live and eight will die. Whether you are one of the 92 or one of the eight, I do not know. Then, if 100 people like you take a certain drug every day for five years 95 will live and five will die. Again, I do not know whether you are one of the 95 or one of the five' (Skolbekken, 1998, p. 1958). The key question would be whether such a presentation format reduces errors or biases in decision making.

Is this person guilty or innocent?

At some point in your life it is quite likely that you will be called for jury duty. As a member of a jury you will be required to make a decision about the guilt or innocence of a defendant. The way in which juries and the individuals that make up a jury arrive at their decisions has been the topic of much research (e.g., Hastie, 1993). Here we focus on one aspect of this research: the impact of scientific, especially DNA evidence on jurors' decisions about the guilt or innocence of defendants.

Faced with DNA evidence in a criminal trial many jurors are inclined to think, 'science does not lie'; these jurors appear to be susceptible to 'white coat syndrome', an unquestioning belief in the power of science that generates misplaced confidence and leads to DNA evidence being regarded as infallible (Goodman-Delahunty & Newell, 2004). Indeed, some research confirms that people often overestimate the accuracy and reliability of scientific evidence (in comparison with other types of evidence, such as eyewitness testimony or confessions), thus assigning it undeserved probative value. For example, mock jurors rated blood tests as significantly more reliable than testimony from an eyewitness (Goodman, 1992).

Is it simply because we have so much trust in science that DNA evidence is so compelling, or are there other reasons? Consider the 2001 trial of Wayne Edward Butler in which he was convicted of murdering Celia Douty in Brampton Island, Queensland, Australia in 1983. Police had suspected Butler for a long time but it was not until DNA profiling was used that a case was brought against him. The victim's body had been found covered by a red towel stained with semen. DNA profiling techniques unavailable in 1983 established the probability that the semen stains were Butler's, and on the basis of this evidence he was charged. At trial, a forensic expert told the jury that the probability of someone else having a DNA profile that matched the one obtained from the semen (i.e., the random match probability, RMP) was *one in 43 trillion*. Extreme probabilities such as this make it appear that there is no margin of error – the defendant must be guilty! It is not only the fact that DNA evidence is grounded in the scientific method that makes it appear more objective and even foolproof, but it is also the manner in which DNA evidence is presented – the probabilities cited by the DNA experts – that makes this evidence so very influential and persuasive to jurors.

Clearly, these numbers sound compelling, but what does an infinitesimal RMP like 1 in 43 trillion really mean? Assuming that no errors occurred in the laboratory processing and that the probability of a random match can be stated with some legitimacy, what should a conscientious juror conclude? Often people interpret the probability not simply as the likelihood that another person will have the same DNA as that found on the towel, but as the probability that the defendant was not guilty. The leap from a 'match probability' to an inference about the guilt of the defendant is dubbed the 'prosecutor's fallacy' (Thompson & Schumann, 1987) and its commission has been observed in many trials (Koehler, 1993).

The most well-known example of the prosecutor's fallacy is the case of *People v. Collins* (1968). In this case the prosecution secured a conviction by erroneously calculating a 1 in 12 million probability that a random couple would possess a series of characteristics (a female with a blond ponytail, a man with black hair and a black beard) and then, again erroneously, equating this incorrect probability with the probability that the accused couple did not commit the robbery. Fortunately, the original conviction was overturned in the appeals court and a stern warning was given about the dangers of a 'trial by mathematics' (Koehler, 1993).

More recent work has examined the extent to which jurors understand the match probabilities that are often presented in trials. For example, Koehler, Chia, and Lindsey (1995) gave students written summaries of a murder case that included evidence about a DNA match between the defendant and a blood trace recovered from the victim's fingernails. One group reviewed two items of information: (1) a random match probability of 1 in 1,000,000,000, and (2) the probability of 1 in 1000 that a human error had occurred leading to an incorrect match. A second group was told simply that the combined probability of error from random matches and laboratory mistakes was 1 in 1000. Both groups studied the evidence then provided verdicts (guilty or not guilty).

What is your intuition about the result? If you are like the students in the experiment then you will have found the evidence about the '1 in a billion' random match probability compelling and be more likely to judge the defendant 'guilty' faced with this number. In fact, Koehler et al. (1995) found that almost three times as many guilty verdicts were recorded in the group given that figure. This pattern of results was replicated with jurors. Figure 1.1 displays the results from the two participant populations.

What is wrong with this inference? Why shouldn't we be more convinced by the one in a billion figure? The answer lies in how we should correctly combine both the random match probability and the human error probability. Koehler et al. (1995) use a baseball analogy to illustrate the problem: consider a baseball infielder who makes throwing errors less than one time in a million, but makes fielding errors about two times in a hundred. The chance of the

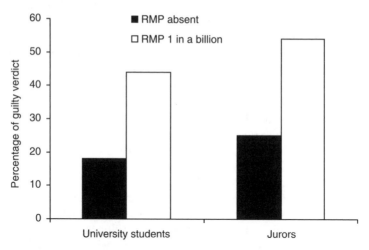

Figure 1.1 Percentage of guilty verdicts. RMP = Random match probability. (Drawn using data reported in Koehler, Chia, & Lindsey, 1995.)

player making an error on the next attempt either because he drops it or because he makes a bad throw is at least two out of a hundred. If he makes an error it will almost certainly be a fielding error – but it is still an error. The important point is that even if the player reduces his throwing error rate to one in a hundred million or one in a billion it will not be reflected in his overall error rate. So as Koehler et al. (1995) point out 'a baseball talent scout should be no more impressed by the infielder's throwing ability than a legal factfinder should be upon hearing the vanishingly small random match probabilities' in DNA evidence at trial (p. 211). In both cases the lower bound threshold for error estimates is set by the greater probability – fielding errors in the case of the infielder and laboratory errors in the case of DNA evidence.

The example illustrates that the human error rate – the DNA laboratory error rate – is the number that really matters. Even if there is only a one in 43 trillion probability of a random match, if the lab conducting the analysis makes errors of the order of one in a hundred or a thousand samples, then the random match probability is essentially irrelevant. Forensic experts often know this. Koehler's experiments show that, unfortunately, jurors may not, and can make flawed judgments about the probative value or weight to accord to DNA evidence as a result.

Consistent with the medical studies discussed above, there are ways of portraying information to jurors that can improve the decisions they make. One such modification is the presentation of DNA evidence in natural frequency formats (e.g., 1 in a 1,000,000 rather than probability formats (e.g., .0001 per cent). In chapter 6 we discuss why such changes in format have a facilitative effect on decision making, but for now we briefly review a study relevant to the legal domain.

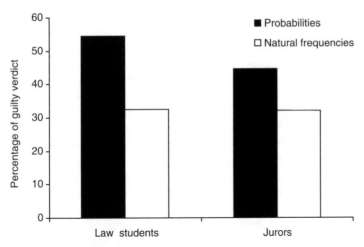

Figure 1.2 Percentage of guilty verdicts made by the two samples. From Lindsey, S., Hertwig, R., & Gigerenzer, G. (2003). Communicating statistical DNA evidence. *Jurimetrics, 43*, 147–163. Copyright 2003 by the American Bar Association. Reprinted with permission.

Lindsey, Hertwig, and Gigerenzer (2003) presented jurors and law students with a sexual assault case that included expert testimony on DNA matching evidence linking the suspect and the crime scene. One group received all information in a probability format, while a second group received identical information presented in a frequency format. Figure 1.2 displays the percentage of guilty verdicts by the two groups of participants who received the different formats of expert numerical evidence.

The results depicted in Figure 1.2 clearly show that the *same statistical information* presented in different formats has a strong impact on the decisions made by students and jurors. When frequency formats were used there were significantly fewer guilty verdicts. Once again, it is sobering to think that such a minor format change can have a major influence on both students' and jurors' decisions.

The results of the studies briefly reviewed here, along with many others, indicate that jurors' decisions can be influenced strongly by variations in the presentation of scientific evidence. In the light of these findings, as Koehler and Macchi (2004) conclude: 'it might be appropriate to present statistical evidence to jurors in multiple ways to minimize the influence of any particular bias' (p. 545).

How should I invest my money?

Imagine you have just won a substantial sum of money on the lottery (if only!) and you are faced with the enviable problem of deciding how best to invest your new found wealth. Although you might be tempted to hide the cash under your mattress, you might also consider putting the money in the stock market – but what stocks should you invest in?

The problem you face is to work out how to 'beat' the notoriously unpredictable stock market. Unfortunately, modern theories of finance claim that players in the financial market are well informed, smart and greedy and that it is therefore impossible to make money for nothing in the long term. This general idea is often described as the Efficient Markets Hypothesis (Batchelor, 2004). However, against the background of this rather pessimistic outlook, one extremely simple rule of thumb for investment choice might be able to help you: invest in the stocks of the companies that you recognize.

Borges, Goldstein, Ortmann, and Gigerenzer (1999) claim that such recognition-based investment decisions can lead to much higher returns than stocks selected by financial experts. This 'stock selection heuristic' states simply that when picking a subset of stocks from all those available for investment one should choose those objects in the larger set that are highly recognized.

Given this formulation, it is clear that the heuristic is only useful for people who recognize some but not all of a given set of stocks. If you do not recognize any stocks you cannot pick highly recognized ones, and similarly if you are an expert and recognize all stocks the heuristic cannot be used. You need what Ortmann, Gigerenzer, Borges, and Goldstein (in press) describe as a 'beneficial degree of ignorance'.

How well can such a simple rule perform? Borges et al. (1999) put their recognition heuristic to the test in the following way. Germans and Americans were asked to indicate the companies they recognized from those listed in the Standard & Poor's 500 and from 298 additional stocks trading on German stock exchanges in December 1996. Four categories of participant were interviewed: Munich pedestrians, Chicago pedestrians, University of Munich finance students, and University of Chicago finance students. The former two groups were described as 'laypersons', the latter two 'experts'. The recognition responses of these four groups were then used to construct stock portfolios of highly recognized companies (those recognized by 90 per cent or more of the participants in a group) for both domestic recognition (companies from the respondent's own country) and international recognition (foreign companies). This resulted in eight recognition-based portfolios. Over a 6-month period (December 1996 to June 1997) these high recognition portfolios were compared against portfolios of 'unrecognized' companies (those recognized by 10 per cent or fewer of the participants in a group), market indices, mutual funds and chance portfolios (constructed by selecting companies at random).

Figure 1.3 displays the data from the two German groups (experts and laypeople) on the domestic stocks. It can be seen clearly that the portfolios of highly recognized stocks produced much higher returns over the 6-month period than those of the unrecognized stocks. Even more impressively, the high recognition companies outperformed the market index and the managed

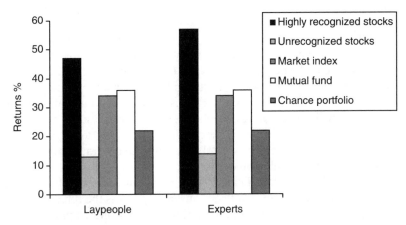

Figure 1.3 Performance of the portfolios by German laypeople and experts in the German domestic market. From data reported in Borges, B., Goldstein, D. G., Ortmann, A., & Gigerenzer, G. (1999). Can ignorance beat the stock market? In G. Gigerenzer, P. M. Todd, & the ABC Research Group (Eds.), *Simple heuristics that make us smart* (pp. 59–72). New York: Oxford University Press. Copyright 1999 by Oxford University Press. By permission of Oxford University Press, Inc.

mutual funds. The data for all the groups showed similar patterns – the recognized stocks always outperformed the unrecognized ones – however, recognition did not outperform the market index or mutual funds for the US domestic recognition markets.

These results appear to suggest we can go from 'recognition to riches' (Ortmann et al., in press) and that ignorance can indeed be beneficial. And it may not only be in the financial domain that ignorance can be good for you. For example, Goldstein and Gigerenzer (2002) reported that German students made slightly more correct inferences about the relative sizes of American cities than US students – despite the US students recognizing more of the cities. Goldstein and Gigerenzer suggest that this counter-intuitive 'less-is-more' effect occurs because the German students were able to rely more often on the recognition heuristic (simply inferring that a recognized city is larger than an unrecognized one) than the US students. The US students, because of their higher rate of recognition, were forced to rely on other knowledge about the cities, which in some instances appeared to lead them to an incorrect inference.

Ayton and Önkal (2004) report a similar less-is-more effect in the sports domain. They asked groups of Turkish and English students to predict the outcomes of English football matches and found that despite the Turkish students' low levels of recognition for the teams, their accuracy in predicting the results barely differed from the knowledgeable English students (62.5 per cent compared to 65.5 per cent respectively). We return to the recognition heuristic in chapter 3 and scrutinize the claims about the benefits of ignorance, but for now let us return to the question of what to do with your money.

Even if you are not fortunate enough to win the lottery, a financial decision that you will probably have to make at some point in your life is how to save for your retirement. As Benartzi and Thaler (2001, 2002) have noted there is a growing worldwide trend towards giving individuals some responsibility in making their own asset allocation decisions in defined contribution saving plans. Such devolvement of responsibility raises the question of people's ability to make these decisions. For example, if you were asked to allocate your contributions among money markets, insurance contracts, bonds funds and stock funds, how would you do it?

According to Benartzi and Thaler (2001) many investors simply use a '1/n strategy' in which they divide contributions evenly across the funds offered in the plan. In their first experiment Benartzi and Thaler offered participants a plan with a bond fund and a stock fund and found that the majority of participants opted for a 50:50 split between the funds – consistent with the use of a 1/n strategy. In a follow-up study, two multiple plans were compared – one with five funds comprising four stock and one bond fund, the other also with five but comprising four bond and one stock fund. The question was: do these different combinations of stock and bond funds lead to different allocations of contributions? In the plan dominated by bond funds, participants allocated 43 per cent of their contributions to the single stock fund. However in the plan dominated by stock funds, participants allocated 68 per cent of their contributions to the stock funds. This result shows that a simple change in the composition of the two plans gives rise to a 25 per cent shift in the amount allocated to the riskier stock funds. Put simply, when more stocks funds were offered, more of the available resources were allocated to them. The result implies that participants' attitudes to risk (i.e., exposure to fluctuations in the stock market) are highly contingent on the way in which options are presented (see Hilton, 2003, and chapter 9).

The '1/n strategy' is a special case of a more general choice heuristic described by Read and Lowenstein (1995) as the 'diversification heuristic'. The idea is that when people are asked to make several choices simultaneously they tend to diversify rather than selecting the same item several times. Simonson (1990) demonstrated the use of such a heuristic in an experiment in which he offered students the opportunity to choose three items from a selection of snack foods (chocolate bars, crisps, etc.) to be eaten during class time each week. One group was told at the start of the first class that they had to select snacks for the following three weeks, while another group was given the opportunity to select a snack at the beginning of *each* class. Simonson found that 64 per cent of the participants in the simultaneous choice condition chose three different items, whereas only 9 per cent of those in the sequential condition did so. The results are consistent with the idea that people seek variety when asked to make simultaneous choices (Read & Lowenstein, 1995).

This rather naïve diversification strategy might be useful in many circumstances but is it appropriate for investment decisions? Benartzi and Thaler (2001) conclude that using a diversification heuristic 'can produce a reasonable portfolio [but] it does not assure sensible or coherent decision-making' (p. 96). For example, an employee with little confidence in his or her ability to invest wisely might assume that an employer has compiled a selection of options that is sensible for his or her plan. However, the plan might offer a large number of higher risk stock options, leading the employee to invest too aggressively (i.e., too heavily in stocks), which may be inappropriate for that person (Benartzi & Thaler, 2001).

Summary

These examples drawn from the medical, legal and financial arenas clearly show that our decisions can be greatly influenced by the way in which information is presented. Subtle differences in the way numbers are represented or options are displayed can affect the decisions we make – often in ways of which we are completely unaware. As we noted at the start of the chapter our aim was to illustrate the breadth of situations in which understanding how we make decisions is relevant. The details of why some of these effects arise will be explored in the coming chapters. By investigating, systematically, these types of framing and representational issues and understanding the reasons behind the effects you will have a better chance of keeping your decision making on the straight and narrow. But what is 'the straight and narrow'? – what makes a decision correct or incorrect, good or bad? We turn to these questions in chapter 2.

2 Decision quality and an historical context

'Choose always the way that seems best however rough it may be.' This quote, attributed to the Greek philosopher Pythagoras, implies that there is always a best course of action one should take to ensure a 'good' decision. Indeed the title of this book suggests a 'straight road' to good quality decisions. But what makes a decision 'good' or 'bad'?

Intuitions about decision quality

Research by Yates, Veinott, and Patalano (2003) took a very direct approach to assessing decision quality by simply asking participants to think about two good and two bad decisions they had made in the past year. The participants, who were university undergraduates, had to rate the decisions on scales of 'quality' (goodness/badness) and 'importance', in both cases making the judgments 'relative to all the important decisions you have ever made'. An impact score was then calculated by multiplying the importance and quality ratings, and further information was elicited about the two decisions (one bad and one good) with the highest impact scores.

Table 2.1 displays the results from the initial questioning of the participants. Two aspects of the data are worth noting: (1) good decisions were rated as higher on the quality dimension than bad ones, but were also further from the 0 neutral point, suggesting that good decisions seemed to be better than the bad decisions were bad; (2) participants rated their bad decisions as significantly less important than their good decisions. A further interesting finding was that it took participants less time to come up with their bad decisions (53 seconds on average) than their good decisions (70 seconds). Yates et al. (2003) speculate that this pattern of data suggests that in general people think their decision making in the past was, 'for the most part, just fine' (p. 54).

In other words, the fact that the badness and importance of bad decisions are rated as less extreme than the goodness and importance of good decisions suggests a certain degree of cognitive dissonance on the part of the participants. It is as if participants engage in post hoc re-evaluations of past decisions along the lines of, 'Well it did not work out too bad in the end' (e.g., Festinger, 1957; Wicklund & Brehm, 1976). Such a 'rose-tinted spectacles'

Table 2.1 Ratings of the quality and importance of real-life decisions

	Good decisions	Bad decisions
Quality (scale: +5 extremely good, 0 neither good nor bad, −5 extremely bad)	+3.6	−2.4
Importance (scale: 0 not important at all, 10 extremely important)	7.7	5.6

Source: Adapted from data reported in Yates, Veinott, and Patalano (2003).

view of the past would lead to bad decisions being recalled more quickly, perhaps because their extreme 'badness' makes them particularly distinctive and unusual (Yates et al., 2003). This positive retrospective bias also has implications for trying to improve decision making through the use of decision-aiding techniques: if people are more or less content with the way decisions have turned out in the past, they will be less likely to seek help with current decisions (Yates et al., 2003).

In the Yates et al. study, once participants had recalled and rated their decisions they were asked for specific details about the context in which the decisions were made and why particular decisions were classified as good or bad. The resulting explanations were then coded both by the experimenters and by naïve coders. This coding procedure revealed a number of 'super-categories' for goodness and badness respectively. By far the most often cited reason for a decision being classified as good or bad was that the 'experienced outcome' was either adverse or favourable. Eighty-nine per cent of bad decisions were described as bad because they resulted in bad outcomes; correspondingly 95.4 per cent of good decisions were described as good because they yielded good outcomes. Other super-categories that received some weight were 'options' in which 44 per cent of bad decisions were thought to be bad because they limited future options (such as a career path), and 'affect' in which 40.4 per cent of good decisions were justified as good because people felt good about making the decision, or felt good about themselves after making the decision.

The results of this coding procedure point to the conclusion that a decision maker's conception of quality is multifaceted, but is overwhelmingly dominated by outcomes: a good decision is good because it produces good outcomes, bad decisions yield bad ones (Yates et al., 2003). How far does such an intuitive conclusion get us in understanding what makes a decision good or bad? Can an outcome really be an unambiguous determinant of the quality of the decision that preceded it?

A formal approach to decision quality

The following example (proposed by Hastie & Dawes, 2001) illustrates why we cannot rely solely on outcomes to evaluate decisions. Imagine someone asked you to make an even-money bet on rolling two ones ('snake eyes') on a pair of unloaded dice. Given that the probability of rolling two ones is actually 1 in 36, taking an even-money bet would be very foolish. That is, you would think it was a 'bad' decision to take the bet. But what would happen if you *did* take the bet and subsequently *did* roll the snake eyes? Would your decision to take the bet now be a 'good' one because the resulting outcome was positive? Clearly not; because of the probabilities involved, the decision to take the bet would be foolish regardless of the outcome. This example suggests that the quality of a decision is determined not only by its outcome but also by the probability of that outcome occurring.

What else might affect quality? Consider this version of the 'snake eyes' scenario: you have no money and have defaulted on a loan with a disreputable company. If you do not repay your debts the company will send their heavies round to rough you up. Now do you take the bet, and if you do is it a good decision? The situation is very different: if taking the bet is the only way to avoid physical harm it is probably in your best interest to take it. Thus not only is the quality of a decision affected by its outcome and the probability of the outcome, it is also affected by the extent to which taking a particular course of action is beneficial (has value) for a given decision maker at a given point in time (Hastie & Dawes, 2001).

With these three aspects of decision quality in mind we are beginning to approach the classical definition of what makes a decision 'good' or, more specifically, what makes it rational. The origin of the notion of a rational choice can be traced to an exchange of letters between Blaise Pascal and Pierre Fermat, two seventeenth-century French mathematicians with a keen interest in gambling. Their discussions of various gambling problems led to the development of the concept of mathematical expectation, which at the time was thought to be the essence of a rational choice (see Hacking, 1975; Hertwig, Barron, Weber, & Erev, 2004). Put simply, a choice was thought to be rational if it maximized the *expected value* for the decision maker. Expected value is defined as the sum of the product of the probability of an outcome and the value of that outcome (typically a monetary outcome) for each possible outcome of a given alternative. In the case of the snake eyes example, the expected value of an even-money gamble with a £10 stake is therefore $(1/36 \times £10) + (35/36 \times £0) = £0.27$. Because this is less than the cost of the stake, it is clearly a poor gamble. Defined this way, expected value was thought to offer both a descriptive and prescriptive account of rationality, but it soon became clear that it was neither (Gigerenzer & Selten, 2001).

In 1713 Nicolas Bernoulli, a Swiss mathematician, proposed the following monetary gamble (known as the St Petersburg Paradox) as an example of how the notion of expected value failed to capture how people actually made choices. Imagine your friend has an unbiased coin and asks you to play a game in which (a) the coin is tossed until it lands on tails, and (b) you win £2 if it lands on tails on the first toss, £4 if it lands on tails on the second toss, £8 if tails appears on the third toss, and so on. The question your friend asks is:

How much would you be willing to pay to play the game? You, along with most people given this problem, would probably not be willing to pay more than a few pounds. However, according to the expected value theory, such behaviour is paradoxical because the expected value of the gamble is infinite. Why? Because on the first toss there is a 0.5 probability of obtaining a head, which would give an expected payoff of £1 (i.e. 0.5 × £2). On the second toss, the probability reduces to 0.25 (one head followed by a tail) but the payoff is still £1 (i.e., 0.25 × £4), and so on. The calculation is as follows:

$$\text{EV (Expected Value)} = (0.5 \times £2) + (0.25 \times £4) + (0.125 \times £8) + \ldots +$$

$$(0.5)^n (£2)^n + \ldots$$

(where n is the number of coin tosses). So if you kept playing you could end up with an infinite amount of money (in other words, the expected value of the gamble is infinite). The fact that people do not offer large amounts of money to play therefore presents a problem for expected value theory. To accommodate this 'paradoxical' finding, Daniel Bernoulli (Nicolas's younger cousin) modified the theory by exchanging the notion of expected 'value' with expected 'utility'. The latter incorporates two important caveats that are of high psychological relevance: (1) that the utility of money declines with increasing gains and (2) that this utility is dependent on the amount of money a person already has. Bernoulli (1954) suggested that the relation between utility and monetary value could be captured by the logarithmic function shown in Figure 2.1.

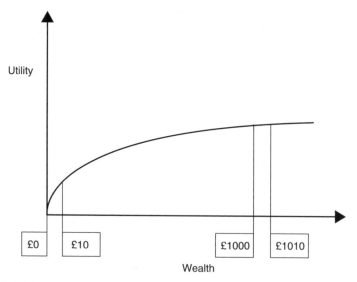

Figure 2.1 A logarithmic function showing the relation between utility (or happiness) and monetary value (or wealth).

To illustrate this idea, imagine that following the previous 'snake eyes' scenario, you failed to roll two ones and the heavies came over to rough you up. You are left with nothing, starving and living on the street. Consider the following three 'lucky breaks' that could then befall you: (1) you find an unaddressed envelope on the street containing a £10 note, (2) you find an envelope containing £1000, or (3) you find an envelope containing £1010. How would you feel in these three situations? Presumably pretty happy in all three cases, but the interesting question is how your happiness would differ as function of the numerical differences in wealth. Remember you have nothing, so finding £10 would be a real bonus (perhaps enough to stave off immediate hunger pangs); finding £1000 would be incredible, but would there be any difference to your happiness in finding £1000 or £1010? – probably not. This idea is illustrated in Figure 2.1. The lower section of the curve is steep and so a small change in wealth (£10) leads to a sharp rise in utility (or 'happiness'). The curve then begins to flatten out so the increase in wealth from £10 to £1000 results in a significant rise in utility, but it is not as steep as the rise from £0 to £10. Finally, by the time you have £1000 the additional £10 makes an almost imperceptible difference to your utility. The important thing to note is that this increase from £1000 to £1010 is identical in terms of wealth to the £0 to £10 change, but very different in terms of utility.

The discussion and analysis of these various gambling problems formed an important precursor to contemporary research on decision making. They provided ways of thinking about why a choice would be good, bad, rational or irrational, however it was not until the late 1940s and early 1950s that the field began to develop into the one we recognize today. In the next section of this chapter we provide a taste of the recent history of judgment and decision-making research.

A brief history of judgment and decision research

The treatment we offer here on the historical context of judgment and decision-making research will be necessarily rather brief. Interested readers should consult Goldstein and Hogarth (1997) for a more comprehensive coverage, or Doherty (2003) for another brief perspective. Our aim here is simply to highlight some of the historical setting for the areas of research that we consider in this book, and to indicate where topics will be covered in more depth.

Goldstein and Hogarth (1997) suggest that the recent development of judgment and decision-making research can be traced to two groups of psychologists: one group interested in 'decisions', the other in 'judgments'. A decision can be defined as a commitment to a course of action (Yates et al., 2003), thus researchers with an interest in decision making often ask questions such as, how do people choose a course of action? How do people decide what to do when they have conflicting goals and the consequences of a decision are uncertain? Do people choose rationally? A judgment, on the other hand, can be defined as an assessment or belief about a given situation based on the available information. As such, psychologists with an interest in judgment want to know how people integrate multiple sources of information (many of which might be imperfect or probabilistic indicators) to arrive at an understanding of, or judgment about, a situation. Judgment researchers also want to know how accurate people's judgments are, how environmental factors such as learning and feedback affect judgment ability, and how experts and novices differ in the way they make judgments. The origin of both approaches can be traced to the late 1940s and early 1950s. First we plot the trajectory of research into decisions.

Decisions

In 1947, the second edition of von Neumann and Morgenstern's *Theory of Games and Economic Behavior* was published. Unlike the first, 1944, edition, this version contained an appendix with a theorem for assessing decision making according to the principle of maximizing expected utility. Von Neumann and Morgenstern were interested in the mathematical rather than the behavioural implications of their theorem, but an added result of this axiomatization of expected utility was that it provided researchers with a 'set of rules' for testing the rationality of people's choices. Thus what began with Pascal's musings about how people would respond in various gambling situations grew into a fully fledged theory of rational choice.

Savage (1954) developed von Neumann and Morgenstern's work further by incorporating the notion of subjectivity into the maximization of expected utility. Savage proved that a person whose choices satisfy all the axioms of the theory, chooses as if he or she were maximizing his or her expected utility, while assigning subjective probabilities to the possible outcomes of a choice. These ideas are covered in much greater depth in chapter 8, but for now to give a flavour of these axioms or 'rules for rational choice' we will illustrate one axiom – that of *transitivity* – with the following simple example:

> Suppose Barry prefers Strawberry lollipops to Lemon, and Lemon to Lime *but* Lime to Strawberry. Assuming Barry is not indifferent in his choice between any of these alternatives he should be willing to pay something to swap a less preferred flavour for a more preferred one. Barry is given a Lemon lollipop. Because he prefers Strawberry to Lemon he should be willing to pay something (20p perhaps?) to have Strawberry instead. But he prefers Lime to Strawberry so he should be willing to pay something to substitute these. Finally, he should also pay to substitute Lime for Lemon because he prefers the latter to the former.

As you can probably see, because of his 'intransitive preferences' Barry ends up back where he started (with a lemon lollipop) but he is now 60p out of pocket! The axiom of transitivity states quite simply that if one prefers outcome A (strawberry) to outcome B (lemon) and outcome B to outcome C (lime) then one should prefer A to C. Because Barry showed the opposite final preference – preferring C (lime) to A (strawberry) he violated the axiom of transitivity and found himself in a 'money-pump' situation that would ultimately bankrupt him.

Expected utility theory (EUT) was developed within the discipline of economics but has had a strong and lasting influence on psychological investigations of decision making. As Juslin and Montgomery (1999) note, its principal influence has been twofold: First, the subcomponents of EUT–utility functions and subjective probabilities – have been used to conceptualize how decisions are made, and second, EUT has provided the normative yardstick against which human decision behaviour is measured.

However, just as Nicholas Bernoulli had proposed the St Petersburg Paradox as a problem for expected value theory, it was not long before objections were raised to the von Neumann and Morgenstern/Savage version of EUT. Several researchers posed problems in which the observed behaviour clearly violated one or more of the axioms of the theory. Many of these violations became known as 'paradoxes' like the St Petersburg Paradox we discussed earlier, however, as Gigerenzer and Selten (2001) note such findings are not *logical* paradoxes, they are labelled paradoxical purely because the theory is so 'at odds with' (Gigerenzer & Selten, 2001, p. 2) what people do when confronted with the problems. Indeed, when Daniel Ellsberg, a famous critic of rational choice theory, addressed a meeting of the Society for Judgment and Decision Making in 2002 he expressed his dismay at the fact that his work had been labelled paradoxical – it is what people do, he told the audience – where is the 'paradox' in that!

These early objections to EUT as a descriptive theory of choice were followed in subsequent decades by increasing amounts of evidence showing that people systematically violate the axioms of rational choice theory (e.g., see Kahneman & Tversky, 2000 for a review). Broadly speaking, the evidence that human behaviour contradicted EUT had three major impacts on the development of judgment and decision-making (JDM) research. First, it inspired some researchers, most notably Herbert Simon, to raise serious doubts about the applicability of EUT to human choice. The main thrust of Simon's argument was that given human cognitive limitations in processing information, and environmental limitations on the availability of information, it was inconceivable that a 'real person' could implement anything approaching the full-scale rational choice theory when making decisions (Simon, 1955, 1956). Instead of being 'fully rational', Simon proposed that humans should be viewed as being 'boundedly rational'. The idea was that by capitalizing on the structure of the environments in which they found themselves and through the intelligent use of their limited cognitive resources humans could make decisions that were 'good enough' if not strictly optimal. The key to achieving bounded rationality was the use of simple heuristics such as 'satisficing' whereby a person chooses an alternative that surpasses a pre-specified aspiration level, even if that alternative is not the optimal choice. Simon's ideas have had a huge impact on JDM research, recently in the work of Gigerenzer and colleagues (e.g., Gigerenzer, Todd, & the ABC Research Group, 1999) of which we will hear more in chapter 3.

The second effect of the accumulation of evidence showing violations of EUT was to encourage researchers to examine other areas of decision-making behaviour (Goldstein & Hogarth, 1997). Ward Edwards (1968) was particularly influential in expanding the area of study to include probabilistic judgment. Rather than using EUT as the normative yardstick, Edwards compared people's judgments to those mandated by mathematical principles and the laws of probability. Edwards' early work examined questions such as whether people updated their beliefs about the probability of an outcome given some evidence in the ways dictated by Bayes' theorem (a formal theory that specifies how beliefs *should* be updated). His findings, that typically people did not provide Bayesian estimates, laid the groundwork for subsequent investigations of probability judgment by Amos Tversky and Daniel Kahneman (e.g., Tversky & Kahneman, 1974). Their research programme named for the *heuristic* processes that they identified (e.g., availability, representativeness, anchoring) and the characteristic *biases* evidenced through the use of these heuristics, has been perhaps the most influential in the history of JDM research. Chapters 5 and 6 provide a detailed coverage of Bayes' theorem and the heuristics and biases approach.

The third and final impact of the observed violations of EUT was to inspire researchers to modify the theory so as to make it a better descriptive theory of choice. Perhaps the most influential of these modified theories is Prospect Theory, proposed by Kahneman and Tversky (1979a). As we will explore in chapter 9, the central insight of prospect theory is in demonstrating that although our choices involve maximizing some kind of expectation, the utilities and probabilities of outcomes undergo systematic psychological or cognitive distortions when they are evaluated. These distortions have major implications for predicting choice under uncertainty.

Judgments

Research into the psychology of judgment was inspired in its early days by an analogy with visual perception (Doherty, 2003; Goldstein & Hogarth, 1997). Hammond (1955) argued that principles of perception proposed by Brunswik (1952, 1956) could be applied to the study of judgment. The main ideas in the Brunswikian approach to perception are that an object in the environment (a 'distal' stimulus) produces multiple cues through the stimulation of the perceiver's sense organs. These 'proximal' cues are necessarily fallible (due to the probabilistic nature of the relation between the cues and the environment) and therefore only imperfectly indicate the true state of the external environment. Thus perception is a constructive process, involving inferences drawn on the basis of incomplete and ambiguous sensory information.

Hammond's important contribution was to show that judgment could be viewed in the same way. Beginning with clinical judgment, Hammond and his colleagues went on to demonstrate that Social Judgment Theory, as it became known, could be applied to a wide range of situations involving multi-attribute judgment (Doherty, 2003). The main 'tool' of the social judgment theorist is the lens model. (We describe studies that have used this tool in more detail in chapter 3 and examine the learning mechanisms underlying performance in such studies in chapter 11.) In essence the lens model is a metaphor for thinking about how a 'to-be-judged' criterion in the world (e.g., whether a patient is psychotic or neurotic) relates to the judgment made in the 'mind' of the judge. It has been used by Brunswikians to guide their research programme and, through the use of the 'lens model equation' (Tucker, 1964) to aid in the analysis of data.

An important distinction between research on decisions and research on judgments is that in the former the focus has been on the extent to which people's beliefs and preferences are coherent, while the latter is concerned with the correspondence between subjective and environmental states (Hammond, 1996; Juslin & Montgomery, 1999). Judgment theorists are not necessarily concerned by behaviour that does not conform to normative yardsticks like EUT or Bayes' theorem, they are interested in whether a judgment is accurate in the sense that it reflects the true state of the world.

Early and highly influential work investigating the accuracy of judgment in the 'real world' was published by Paul Meehl (1954) in a book entitled *Clinical versus Statistical Prediction: A Theoretical Analysis and a Review of the Evidence.* In the book Meehl described how judgments made by experts – usually clinicians – were often inferior in terms of accuracy to simple statistical models provided with the same information. We describe these studies in more detail in chapter 3, here we simply note that this controversial finding led to a surge of interest in understanding how people combine information from multiple sources to make judgments. This interest, in conjunction with the methodological and theoretical advances made by Hammond and colleagues in the application of Brunswik's principles, ensured the swift development of this important and fruitful branch of judgment research (see Hammond & Stewart, 2001 for a review).

Although not enjoying the same high profile as research into decisions and preferential choice (perhaps because of its lesser overlap with other disciplines such as Economics), research in the 'correspondence' tradition of judgment continues to be fertile and influential. Brunswik's ideas have been taken into more mainstream psychological writings through the work of the Swedish psychologists Berndt Brehmer, Mats Bjorkman and Peter Juslin (e.g., Juslin & Montgomery, 1999) as well as by Gerd Gigerenzer and his group (e.g., Gigerenzer, Hoffrage, & Kleinbölting, 1991). Hillel Einhorn, Robyn Dawes and Robin Hogarth, among others, have been instrumental in furthering our understanding of the processes underlying clinical and statistical judgment (e.g., Dawes, 1979; Einhorn & Hogarth, 1981). We examine much of this work in the chapters that follow.

Summary

Simple introspection can help us to understand what makes a decision good or bad ('What are some good decisions I have made, what are some bad ones?'). Such intuitive approaches tend to focus on outcomes – good decisions produce good outcomes, bad decisions bad outcomes. However, sole focus on outcomes does not provide an unambiguous index of decision quality. Researchers have found it useful to consider three main aspects of decisions: outcomes, probabilities and the value or utility of an outcome to the decision maker. From early musings about how these three aspects of quality related to preferences between monetary gambles, a theory of rational choice was developed, which proposed a set of rules or 'axioms' that a person should follow in order to act in a rational manner. Research into decisions and choice followed a path of comparing human behaviour with these axioms and has produced many important insights into when and why decisions depart from normative standards. Research into judgment has taken a different approach by focusing on when and how people combine information from multiple sources to make judgments and whether these judgments correspond to the true state of the world. In the next two chapters we explore this research by examining the stages involved in making a judgment.

3 Stages of judgment I: Discovering, acquiring and combining information

Imagine you are walking down the street with a friend and you pass a shiny, new car parked at the side of the road. Your friend, who is interested in buying a new car, asks you how much you think the car would cost. You are faced with a judgment – how do you go about estimating the cost of the car? You might start by looking at the make – you know that a Mercedes or BMW is likely to be more expensive than a Hyundai. Then perhaps you might look at the 'trim' – does it have alloy wheels, a sunroof, chromium fittings, and so on? You might take a look through the windows – are there leather seats, a navigation system? Once you have gathered what you think is enough information you combine it to make a global judgment about the cost. You tell your friend, 'About £20,000'; he replies that in fact the car only costs £15,000 (he has been doing some research in preparation for buying a car). You take this information on board, and perhaps revise your thinking about how much the various features of the car that you considered contribute to its overall value, so next time someone asks you about the value of that car (or a similar one) you will be able to make a better judgment.

This example serves to illustrate some of the key processes involved in making judgments:

(1) *Discovering information*: How do we know where to look? How do we know that the make of a car is a good indicator of cost?
(2) *Acquiring and searching through information*: How much information should we acquire and in what order should we look for it? Should we look at the make first or whether the car has a navigation system?
(3) *Combining information*: How should we put the information together to make a global judgment about the cost of the car?
(4) *Feedback*: Once we have made the judgment, how do we use information about the difference between our estimate and the actual cost of the car?

In this chapter we consider the first three of these stages in turn and in the next chapter we examine the role of feedback in more detail. The idea is that the processes encapsulated by these stages remain common across a vast range of situations from estimating the price of a car, to deciding whether to take up a job, or even (arguably) choosing a person to marry! Our approach focuses on the experimental analysis of these stages, so first we examine a framework for judgment that has provided the basis for the majority of the studies we consider.

Conceptualizing judgment: The lens model

Our interaction with objects and events in the world is necessarily indirect. Our internal perceptions of external events are mediated through our sense organs – light, sound, odours are all transduced into electrical signals and interpreted by the brain. Egon Brunswik, an Austrian American psychologist, conceptualized judgment processes as being transduced in a similar fashion through a 'lens of cues' that divides the events and objects in the real world from the psychological processes in the mind of the person making a judgment (Hammond & Stewart, 2001). Figure 3.1 is a diagrammatic representation of this relationship. The left hand side of the diagram represents the 'real world' in which the criterion or to-be-judged event exists. The right hand side represents the mind of the judge and in between is the lens of cues through which the judge attempts to 'see' the true state of the world. The arrows on the left hand side indicate that the criterion is associated (possibly causally associated) with the various signs or cues in the environment, which comprise the lens. The arrows on the right hand side represent the way in

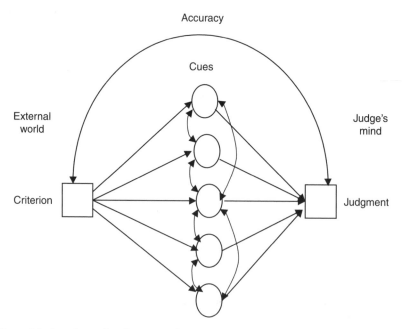

Figure 3.1 A schematic diagram of Brunswik's lens model for conceptualizing judgment.

which the judge utilizes information from the cues and integrates them to form a judgment. The arrows connecting the cues indicate that there are relations among the cues themselves; in other words, they are not independent. The overarching line connecting the criterion and the judgment represents the judge's accuracy in estimating the to-be-judged criterion. Applied to our example of judging the cost of a car, the actual price is the criterion to be judged, the trim, make and other features of the car are the 'cues', and the judgment is your estimate of the price.

Using this basic framework, researchers have developed ingenious methods for inferring how judges utilize information from multiple imperfect cues in the environment to make decisions about uncertain outcomes. The framework has been used in many of the domains we examined in chapter 1 – legal, medical and financial situations and has sometimes been successful in influencing policy decisions in those areas (e.g., Hammond & Adelman, 1976).

As well as these applied studies, which have focused on the way existing, identifiable cues in the environment are used in judgments (e.g., Dawes & Corrigan, 1974), a wealth of experimental research that focuses on *learning* novel cue–outcome relations has also been conducted. The principal technique used in these experimental studies is multiple-cue probability learning (MCPL). As its name suggests, MCPL at its most fundamental involves learning to predict an outcome on the basis of the values of multiple cues in situations where the relation between the outcome and the cues is probabilistic. This means that cues in the environment vary in their 'validity' or their 'goodness' for predicting the outcome. (Validity is a term that is often used slightly differently by different researchers but the key idea is that it is a measure of how 'good' a cue is for predicting an outcome: a cue with a validity of 1 is perfect, a cue with validity of 0 is useless.) Most of the studies reviewed in this chapter have used this cue-learning paradigm in one form or another. The first aspect of cue learning we consider is how people discover relevant cues in the environment.

Discovering information

Dawes and Corrigan (1974) famously claimed that when making decisions involving multiple sources of information 'the whole trick is to decide what variables to look at and then know how to add' (p. 105). Later in the chapter we consider the usefulness of 'knowing how to add', but first we examine the intriguing 'trick' of deciding what to look at.

The majority of MCPL tasks present participants with a predetermined 'short-list' of the cues that can be used for the required judgment or decision. For example, for predicting a person's credit rating participants might be provided with information concerning 'average monthly debt' and 'average number of creditors' (Muchinsky & Dudycha, 1975); or for predicting a particular disease participants might be given a patient's temperature and blood pressure (Friedman & Massaro, 1998). However, by providing this set of explicitly identified cues, Klayman (1984, 1988a) has argued that MCPL studies are excluding a very important aspect of decision making in complex environments – namely the process of cue discovery.

Klayman (1988a) defines cue discovery as identifying a set of valid predictive cues, and uses the following example (1984) to illustrate this process:

> Suppose . . . you are a planner who wants to develop a model of patterns of usage for a certain train station. At first, you may have only base-rate information about the average number of people who pass through the station in a week. As you study the station, you may add the factor 'time of day' to your model. With further study you may incorporate more subtle factors (e.g., seasonal changes, effects of local economic conditions). As your model becomes more complete, your predictive accuracy increases.
>
> (Klayman, 1984, p. 86)

Klayman (1988a) suggests that the key process here is the discovery of new valid predictive cues and their incorporation into one's 'mental model' of the situation. A few MCPL studies have examined aspects of cue discovery by including cues in the environment that have *no* predictive value. For example, in a two-cue MCPL task Muchinsky and Dudycha (1975) provided participants with one cue that had a validity of .80 or .60 and a second that manifested no predictive validity (.00). Thus a large element of learning for the participants involved discovering which of the two cues had predictive value and learning to ignore the other cue. However, these tasks still provided participants with explicitly defined cues and thus missed out perhaps the most important aspect of cue discovery – inferring through interaction with the environment what the cues themselves might be.

To examine this problem directly Klayman (1984, 1988a) used a modified MCPL task in which participants had not only to discover which cues among a set were valid, but also what the cues in an environment were. Participants were presented with a computer-controlled graphic display in which geometric figures appeared in various locations (see Figure 3.2). On each trial a figure appeared that could be one of three shapes (square, triangle or circle), sizes (small, medium or large) and shadings (crosshatch, narrow stripe or wide stripe). An asterisk then appeared on the screen and a straight line or trace was drawn out from that asterisk. The participants' task was to learn to predict whether a particular trace would stop before it reached the edge of the display or simply go 'off the screen', and if it were to stop, where they thought it would do so (see Figure 3.2).

The element of cue discovery was introduced because participants soon learned that the explicitly identified cues (shape, size and shading) were not the only variables that were relevant to the behaviour of the trace. Over trials it became apparent that other variables such as the height of the shape on the

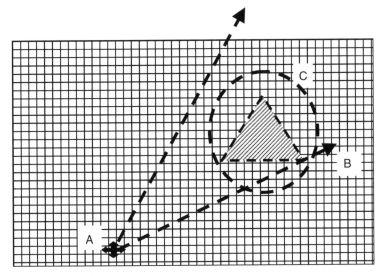

Figure 3.2 Adapted example of a display screen used to study cue discovery. From Klayman, J. (1988). Cue discovery in probabilistic environments: Uncertainty and experimentation. *Journal of Experimental Psychology: Learning, Memory, and Cognition, 14,* 317–330. Copyright 1988 by the American Psychological Association. Adapted with permission. Note: A straight line or trace is drawn from the origin (A) in any direction. The place that the trace stops (B) is determined by, among other factors, how close it passes to the 'area of influence' (C). Note that in the experiments the letters did not appear on the display but grid coordinates not shown here were presented.

screen and the proximity of the trace and the shape also played a role in determining where the trace would stop.

Klayman (1988a) reported two key results from these studies. First, participants were able to discover which cues were valid both among the explicit cues (e.g., size was a valid cue, shading was not) and from the inferred cues (e.g., when travelling in a more leftward direction the trace went farther). This process of discovery took a long time – an average of about 700 trials dispersed over 7 days – but by the end of this period participants had discovered about three or four of the valid cues.

Second, the experiments showed that participants who were free to design their own screens and locate the shapes and trace origins anywhere on the display, did better than participants who just observed a random selection of trials. Within the former intervention or 'experiment' group there was wide individual variability in the degree and quality of experimentation engaged in, and there was a strong association between the quality of experimentation and success in discovering predictive cues. 'Good' experimenters only changed one variable between trials when testing a hypothesis, and achieved more accurate predictions more rapidly than the 'bad' experimenters who changed a number of variables between consecutive trials.

Since Klayman's studies there have been disappointingly few follow-up investigations of cue discovery. It is disappointing because the studies leave many interesting questions unanswered. For instance, what types of cue might be easier or harder to discover? Why is the opportunity to experiment important? Would passive observation of another person's experimentation yield the same benefits or does one have to be actively involved in testing hypotheses (Klayman, 1988a)?

Advances in the formal modelling of causal relations (Pearl, 2000) have stimulated renewed interest in the role of intervention and experimentation in learning (Gopnik, Glymour, Sobel, Schulz, Kushnir, & Danks, 2004; Rehder, 2003; Steyvers, Tenenbaum, Wagenmakers, & Blum, 2003). Lagnado and Sloman (2004a), for example, used a trial-by-trial-based learning paradigm in which participants obtained probabilistic data about causally related events either through observing sequences (e.g., *seeing* a high fuel temperature and a low combustion chamber pressure leading to the launch of a rocket) or through intervention (e.g., *setting* temperature or pressure to either high or low and then observing whether a rocket launched or failed). The results showed a clear advantage for interveners in terms of their ability to subsequently select the causal model likely to have generated the data (from an array of possible models).

As a result of this renewed interest in the role of experimentation, some recent work has begun to ask questions similar to those posed by Klayman (1988a). Although not examining cue discovery per se, these studies have compared intervention and observation strategies in multiple-cue judgment tasks. Thus far the evidence suggests that intervention can be beneficial (e.g., Enkvist, Newell, Juslin, & Olsson, 2006) but the improvements found with intervention do not appear to be as dramatic as those seen in causal reasoning tasks. One key difference is that in the causal literature the focus has been on learning causal relations that connect events (e.g., Lagnado & Sloman, 2004a, 2006; Steyvers et al., 2003), but in multiple-cue judgment the task is generally to predict the criterion. Therefore, the causal reasoning tasks may more strongly invite representation in terms of causal models, which can be tested through intervention. It seems clear that a fruitful avenue for future research will be to identify what tasks and instructions promote strategies of learning that are benefited by the opportunity to intervene.

Acquiring information

Before making any major decision we often attempt to gather information in the hope that it will lead to a better decision. If we are lucky, we will already know 'where to look' and will not have to go through the process of discovering relevant sources of information, but often we still have to work out how much information to look at, and in what order. Before buying a new car, a consumer may take time and effort to consult *What Car?* magazine to check the specifications of different models. An employer might ask potential employees for letters of reference, test scores, or examples of competence before making a job offer. In both cases this behaviour can be described as 'pre-decisional acquisition of information' – a strategy engaged in in the hope of reducing the risk of making an erroneous decision (Connolly & Thorn, 1987). But how much information should we acquire before making a decision? Acquiring too much can be extremely costly; acquiring too little can lead to excessive risks of making the wrong decision. Such situations are ubiquitous in day-to-day life and though the trade-off between the costs and benefits of acquiring further information is conceptually simple, in practice computing an optimal function for acquisition can be extremely complex (see Gigerenzer et al., 1999).

The study of information acquisition has found that people generally respond in the appropriate direction to changes in task characteristics such as the cost or diagnosticity of information. However, the magnitude of response is typically less than normative principles specify (Fried & Peterson, 1969; Hershman & Levine, 1970; Lanzetta & Kanareff, 1962; Pitz, 1968; Van Wallendael & Guignard, 1992). Relative to the prescriptions of normative principles (e.g., Edwards, 1965; Marschak, 1954; Stigler, 1961; Wendt, 1969), findings regarding the scale of acquisition are equivocal: obtaining too much, too little and about the right amount of information are all observed (Hershman & Levine, 1970; Kaplan & Newman, 1966; Pruitt, 1961; Tversky & Edwards, 1966). Recall from chapter 2 that the 'normative principles' are those derived from formal models such as expected utility theory.

A series of studies by Terry Connolly and colleagues (Connolly & Gilani, 1982; Connolly & Serre, 1984; Connolly & Thorn, 1987; Connolly & Wholey, 1988) provide an illustrative set of investigations of information acquisition in laboratory multiple-cue environments. In a representative experiment (Connolly & Thorn, 1987, Experiment 1), participants played the role of a production manager whose task was to set a production quota for a manufacturing plant. Participants were told that if production was set too high or too low the company would incur damaging losses. To help them set their quotas participants could buy reports of the firm's orders from the various distribution centres. On each trial participants made whatever purchases they wished and then set a production quota.

The principal finding was that the majority of participants underpurchased the reports (compared to the mathematically optimal amount). This was true regardless of whether there were two, four or six reports offered. Some learning was evident in that as the experiment progressed participants tended to buy more 'good' reports (those that were stronger predictors of the actual quota) than 'bad' reports, but there was still considerable deviation from optimal purchasing at the end of the experiment. In general, participants purchased only about half of the good reports, and although the underpurchase saved acquisition costs the consequent penalties more than offset the savings. In fact, the costs incurred ranged to almost twice those incurred by an optimal policy (Connolly & Thorn, 1987). Interestingly, in post-experimental interviews participants were able to distinguish between the good and bad sources of information, but this knowledge seemed not to prevent them underpurchasing the good reports.

What are we to make of this suboptimality in balancing the costs and benefits of information purchase? One possibility is that participants were not given enough time in the environment to develop an optimal strategy. As we will see in chapter 11, often thousands of trials are required before optimizing is achieved – even in simple choice games. In the Connolly experiments, typically only 40 trials were used. Given extended training perhaps participants would learn more readily about the differential validity of information sources (Connolly & Serre, 1984). However, in the experiment described above, participants had learned to distinguish good from bad sources and yet their purchase was still suboptimal – why? One plausible explanation is that information costs are immediate and certain, whereas the payoff for making a correct decision is delayed and uncertain (Connolly & Thorn, 1987). In other words the participants were 'risk-seekers' preferring to gamble rather than methodically go through all the available information.

This underpurchase suggests that participants simply could not face the extra effort (and immediate cost) involved in acquiring and thinking about extra information. But then, if one is not going to look at everything, how does one decide on the order to look through the information that is available?

Ordering search

In many investigations of search behaviour, order is simply determined by people's preferences. To illustrate this, consider the often-used apartment-renting scenario (e.g., Payne, 1976). In this task participants are given access to information (the attributes) about a number of apartments (the alternatives, or options). The attributes might include information concerning the rent, proximity to work, shops, noise level, and so on. Participants are allowed to search through the attributes and alternatives in their own preferred order. A participant who values a quiet neighbourhood highly might choose to examine this attribute for all the alternatives first, whereas a highly budget-conscious participant might choose to examine the rent first. In contrast some participants might decide to examine all the attributes for a particular apartment before looking at another apartment. What are the advantages of adopting a predominantly alternative-wise or attribute-wise search strategy?

Payne, Bettman, and Johnson (1993) suggest that deciding how to decide involves a trade-off between the *accuracy* of a decision and the *effort* involved in making the decision. They proposed thinking of the strategies available to a decision maker as points in two-dimensional space, with one dimension representing the relative accuracy of the strategies and the other dimension the amount of cognitive effort required to complete the strategies. Conceptualizing trade-off in this way makes it possible to see what combinations of accuracy and effort are entailed by particular strategies. The strategy ultimately selected from that set would depend on the relative weight placed by the decision maker on the goal of making an accurate decision versus saving cognitive effort.

If you have limitless time, and do not mind expending a good deal of cognitive effort you might decide to use an *alternative-based* strategy. Such strategies consider each alternative (i.e., an apartment) one at a time and make a summary evaluation of the alternative before considering the next one in a choice set. An example of an alternative-based strategy is the weighted additive linear rule. This rule entails placing a 'weight' or degree of importance on each attribute (e.g., cost is most important, space second most important, etc.) then examining each alternative one at a time and calculating an overall 'score' by adding up the weighted value of each attribute. Such a strategy, although prescribed by rational theories, is obviously effortful and time consuming.

As we saw in chapter 2, Herbert Simon (1956) introduced the concept of 'bounded rationality' in acknowledgement of the strains put on a decision makers' cognitive capacity through engaging in such computationally difficult and time-consuming processes. The term bounded rationality highlights the interconnectedness of the limitations of the mind and the structure of the environment. Simon argued that because of these limitations people 'satisfice' – or look for 'good enough' solutions that approximate the accuracy of optimal algorithms (like the weighted additive linear rule) without placing too heavy a demand on the cognitive system (e.g., working memory, processing capacity).

How would such a satisficing strategy be used to search through alternatives? A 'satisficer' searches the alternatives in a non-specified order and the first alternative examined that exceeds a predetermined aspiration level is chosen (e.g., the first apartment considered that has the combination of rent below £1000 per month and being within walking distance of work). As Payne, Bettman, and Luce (1998) note, a major implication of the satisficing heuristic is that choice depends on the *order* in which alternatives are considered. If alternatives A and B both exceed the aspiration level but alternative A is considered first it will be chosen. Such a choice would be made even if B were preferable on any or all of the choice criteria (e.g., apartment B was cheaper).

So how do people deal with this trade-off in real-world decisions? Fasolo, McClelland, and Lange (2005) considered this question in a study examining pre-decisional search in a consumer choice task. They argued that difficulties arise for consumers when products available for choice have conflicting attributes (e.g., quality and convenience) one product might be high in convenience but low in price, whereas another might be low in convenience but high in quality. The greater these attribute conflicts become, the harder the decision for the consumer. To investigate the effect of attribute conflict on choice, Fasolo et al. gave participants a task in which they were asked to recommend to a friend one digital camera from a selection of five models. Each model was described along the same eight attributes (optical zoom, resolution, image capacity, etc.) and participants were able to access information about each attribute via a computer-based 'information board'. (The 'board' was a screen containing an 8 by 5 grid of boxes, the contents of which were revealed when the cursor was placed over a particular box.) The 'friend' provided a memo indicating that all the attributes were equally important – this was to ensure participants knew they needed to consider each attribute.

Fasolo et al. (2005) found that when there was a high degree of conflict, participants tended to search more by alternatives than by attributes, whereas when conflict was low attributes were searched predominantly. Search was also more extensive under high conflict conditions, perhaps reflecting participants' inability to remember the conflicting implications of different attributes. Furthermore, when conflict was high, participants rated the decisions as more difficult, were more dissatisfied with their decision, and had lower confidence in their choice, than when conflict was low.

The results are consistent with intuitions about consumer choice – when we begin searching for a product we can easily exclude items from our choice set that do not match our criteria – a product that is too expensive might also be too large. However, when we near the end of our search and have winnowed down the set to a few likely alternatives, we may find a number of conflicting attributes (one camera has a resolution of 3.5 mega pixels but poor memory capacity, another the opposite attributes) so we need to consider each alternative very carefully. As Fasolo et al. point out, the results suggest that more could be done to help decision makers in their search for information – especially in internet-based shopping where information boards of the type used in Fasolo et al.'s experiment are often displayed.

Combining information

Research examining the processes of information discovery and acquisition has revealed several important insights about how we discover predictive cues in the environment and how we might trade off the cost and benefits of acquiring information. But arguably the most difficult aspect of decision making is working out what to do with the information we have. Once the search is over and we have all the information we think we need for a decision, what should we do with it? How should we put it all together?

A decision strategy that advocates combining all information, can be described as *compensatory*. This is because the acquisition of successive pieces of information can influence the judgment that is made. Consider the car example again: your estimate of the price might be high when you note that the car is a Mercedes but then lowered when you notice that the car has poor trim (no leather seats or alloy wheels – perhaps it is a bottom-of-the-range

Mercedes). So your initial estimate based on the make is *compensated* by the information you subsequently acquired. In contrast, a *non-compensatory* strategy relies on less information (sometimes only one piece – perhaps the make of the car) and ignores the possible influence of other information in the environment.

In both cases, whether we have acquired many or few pieces of information we need to know how to put what we have together to make a decision. In this section we examine methods that advocate combining all available pieces of information with those that advocate simpler and more frugal combination methods. As we shall see, some of the findings for both classes of models are counter-intuitive and remarkable.

Compensatory strategies

According to Dawes and Corrigan (1974), once we have worked out what variables to look at, simply 'knowing how to add' (p. 105) is sufficient for combining information. But what does it mean to say that we should 'add' up information – what are we adding? Back to the car example again: one strategy would be to adopt the weighted linear additive rule described above. Imagine assigning a weight (a score between 0 and 10) to each of the attributes you'd identified, where 0 meant 'no importance' and 10 'very important'. You might give 7 to the make, 3 to alloy wheels, 6 to a navigation system, and so on. Your overall judgment about the price would then be based on the sum ('weighted additive') of these attributes – the greater the sum, the higher your estimate of the price. For example, if the car had alloy wheels this would contribute +3 to the sum, if it did not then you would subtract 3 (–3) from the sum. This might seem rather complicated so an alternative compensatory strategy would be to consider all the attributes but to assign *equal* weights to all of them (e.g., now the presence of alloy wheels would add 1 (+1) and their absence would subtract 1 (–1) from the sum). How accurate would our judgments be if we adopted these types of strategy?

As we noted briefly in the section on the history of judgment research in chapter 2, important insights into the accuracy of these types of strategies were made by Paul Meehl (1954). He described how comparisons of the judgments made by expert clinicians (psychologists and psychiatrists) and those derived from statistical models (like the weighted additive rule) that used only the empirical data (the left side of the lens model shown in Figure 3.1) revealed consistently that either the statistical models made more accurate predictions or the two methods tied for accuracy. In other words, a rule that simply adds statistically optimal weights (derived via multiple regression analyses) in a linear fashion will in most cases outperform the considered and deliberated judgments of experts. The basic pattern of findings first reported by Meehl (1954) has been corroborated by a series of other studies in diverse contexts (e.g., Dawes, Faust, & Meehl, 1989; Einhorn, 1972; Goldberg, 1968; Grove & Meehl, 1996; Werner, Rose, & Yesavage, 1983). A meta-analysis of 136 studies in the areas of medicine, mental health, education and training found that on average statistical techniques were 10 per cent more accurate than experts, statistical techniques were superior to experts in 47 per cent of studies and the reverse was true in only 6 per cent of studies. For the remaining 47 per cent the two methods tied for accuracy (Grove, Zald, Lebow, Snitz, & Nelson, 2000). This consistent pattern of findings has led some researchers to conclude that, 'Whenever possible, human judges should be replaced by simple linear models' (Hastie & Dawes, 2001, p. 63).

But how can a simple statistical model outperform human predictions? Dawes et al. (1989) list several factors that can contribute to this superior performance. First, a statistical method will always arrive at the same judgment for a given set of data. Experts, on the other hand, are susceptible to the effects of fatigue or changes in motivation/concentration, the influence of changes in the way information is presented (as we saw in chapter 1), and recent experience. In a well-known study of diagnostic ability, Brooks, Norman, and Allen (1991) demonstrated that physicians' diagnoses of dermatological conditions were greatly affected by the similarity between current and recently experienced examples. This effect of specific similarity lasted for at least a week and reduced accuracy in diagnoses by 10–20 per cent – a reduction that was both statistically and clinically significant.

Second, experts are often exposed to skewed samples of evidence, making it difficult to assess the actual relation between variables and a criterion of interest. Dawes et al. (1989) give the example of a doctor attempting to ascertain the relation between juvenile delinquency and abnormal electroencephalographic (EEG) recordings. If, in a given sample of delinquents, a doctor discovers that approximately half show an abnormal EEG pattern, then he or she might conclude that such a pattern is a good indicator of delinquency. However, to draw this conclusion the doctor would need to know the prevalence of this EEG pattern in both delinquent *and* non-delinquent juveniles. The doctor is more likely to evaluate delinquent juveniles (as these will be the ones that are referred) and this exposure to an unrepresentative sample makes it more difficult to conduct the comparisons necessary for drawing a valid conclusion.

Dawes et al. (1989) also note that this tendency to draw invalid conclusions on the basis of skewed samples is compounded by our susceptibility to confirmation biases. Several studies have documented our propensity to seek out information that confirms our existing beliefs rather than information that might disconfirm them (e.g., Klayman & Ha, 1987; Wason, 1960). Thus once an expert has drawn an invalid conclusion, the belief in that conclusion is likely to be reinforced by a bias in the information that is subsequently attended to.

These reasons and many others (see Dawes, 1979; Dawes et al., 1989) contribute to the superiority of statistical methods over experts and together they make a strong case for adopting the statistical technique in a variety of situations. There is, however, an important distinction that needs to be made before jumping to strong conclusions about replacing humans with statistical models. Einhorn (1972), echoing an earlier review by Sawyer (1966), made the point that although 'mechanical combination' – the term used to describe the statistical mode of combining information – had been shown to be superior to 'expert combination', there is still potentially an important role to be played by the expert as the *provider* of information to be put into the mechanical combination.

To illustrate the point Einhorn makes a distinction between a *global* overall judgment made about a criterion and the *components* that go into that judgment. Global judgments are a combination of the components and this combination can be performed either statistically or via an expert. To explore the relation between components and global judgments Einhorn focused on an issue that had close personal significance for him – the diagnosis of Hodgkin's disease – a form of lymph cancer that he died from in 1987. The global judgment in the study was the severity of the disease in a group of patients. The components were judgments about the relative amount of nine histological characteristics that had been identified by the three pathologists in the study as relevant for determining disease severity. Biopsy slides taken from 193 patients diagnosed with the disease were shown individually to the three expert pathologists. All of the patients used in the study had already died, making it possible for Einhorn and colleagues to examine retrospectively how accurately the pathologists' analysis of the severity of the disease predicted survival time. The analysis of the global judgments conformed to the standard view that experts were poor at combining information: none of the judgments correlated significantly with survival time, and indeed for some judges the relationship was in the opposite direction – higher severity ratings associated with a longer survival time.

However, when Einhorn examined the components of the global judgment (judgments of the histological signs) he found a more encouraging picture. Ignoring the global judgments and just examining the relation between the components and survival time revealed stronger correlations. For example, for one judge the amount of variance explained jumped from 0 per cent when his global judgment was used to almost 20 per cent when only the components were used. Although overall the correlations were not that high, they were statistically reliable and significantly more accurate than the global judgments. The findings led Einhorn (1972) to conclude that the 'use of expert information or judgment can be a very useful method for getting input for a mechanical combination process' (p. 102). Dawes et al. (1989) echo this conclusion, noting that only human observers may be able to recognize particular cues such as mannerisms (e.g., the 'float-like' walk of certain schizophrenic patients) as having true predictive value. However, they emphasize that 'a unique capacity to observe is not the same as a unique capacity to predict on the basis of integration of observations' (p. 1671) and thus suggest that greater accuracy might be achieved if the expert identifies the important cues through observation and then leaves it up to a statistical model to combine these observations in an optimal way.

Experts seem to be good at identifying the components necessary for accurate judgments, but are poor at combining those components. Presumably, one of the reasons for this poor performance in combination is an inability to weight the components in an optimal way – as a statistical model does (Einhorn, 1972). But which aspect of the judgment process is more important – identifying the information or combining it using an optimal weighting scheme? Dawes (1979) demonstrated convincingly that the former part of the process is the crucial one. He showed that it is not even necessary to use statistically optimal weights in linear models to outperform experts' global judgments – *any* linear model will do the job! Dawes used several data sources to construct linear models with weights determined randomly except for the sign (positive or negative), arguing that the direction in which each cue predicted the criterion would be known in advance in any prediction context of interest. Surprisingly, these *random linear models* outperformed human judges in contexts ranging from predictions of psychosis versus neurosis, to faculty ratings of graduate students on the basis of indicators of academic performance. On average the random linear models accounted for 150 per cent more of the variance between criteria and prediction than the expert judges. For mathematical reasons, converting the random weights into *unit weights* (by standardizing and prescribing a value of +1 or −1 depending on the direction of the cue – this is the same as the *equal weight* strategy we discussed in relation to the car example earlier) achieved even better performance – an average of 261 per cent more variance. Models of this latter type have subsequently been described as conforming to 'Dawes' Rule' (see also Einhorn & Hogarth, 1975 for a detailed discussion of unit weighting schemes).

Non-compensatory strategies

The preceding examples illustrate that models that 'mechanically' combine all the relevant information before making a decision can be very accurate. However, such an exhaustive integrative process is not always appropriate or achievable (see Simon, 1956; chapter 2). As we saw in the section on acquiring information, the work of Payne and colleagues (e.g., Payne et al., 1993), among others, has highlighted the importance of the trade-off between the accuracy achieved by searching through and integrating all sources of information and the cost in terms of the cognitive effort and time involved in that process. How good can our decisions be if we base them on less information?

The fast-and-frugal heuristics of Gigerenzer and colleagues (e.g., Gigerenzer et al., 1999) provide an exemplary approach to such 'ignorance-based decision making' (Goldstein & Gigerenzer, 2002). Gigerenzer et al. (1999) view the mind as containing an 'adaptive toolbox' of specialized cognitive heuristics suited to different problems (e.g., choosing between alternatives, categorizing items, estimating quantities). The heuristics contained in this adaptive toolbox capitalize on what proponents describe as the 'benefits of cognitive limitations' (e.g., Hertwig & Todd, 2004) – the observation that the bounded nature of human cognition can, in certain environments, give rise to advantages in terms of frugality and speed of the decision process *without* suffering any concurrent loss in the accuracy of judgments and decisions.

To illustrate why this somewhat counter-intuitive situation might arise, we consider one of the most prominent heuristics in the adaptive toolbox – 'Take-the-Best' (TTB). TTB is a heuristic designed for binary choice situations. Such situations are extremely common in everyday life – for example, choosing between two job candidates, choosing between two stocks, two cars, two routes to travel on, and so on. TTB exemplifies non-compensatory decision making by simply using the 'best' piece of information applicable in a given situation. TTB operates according to two principles. The first – the recognition principle – states that in any given decision made under uncertainty, if only one among a range of alternatives is recognized, then the recognized alternative should be chosen (Goldstein & Gigerenzer, 2002). We heard about this recognition principle or heuristic in chapter 1 when we discussed its use as an investment tool (e.g., Borges et al., 1999). The second principle is invoked when more than one of the alternatives is recognized and the recognition principle cannot provide discriminatory information. In such cases, people are assumed to have access to a reference class of cues or features. People are then thought to search the cues in descending order of feature validity until they discover a feature that discriminates one alternative from the other. Once this single discriminating feature has been found, the search is terminated (the 'stopping rule') and the feature is used to make a decision (the 'decision rule'). Figure 3.3 illustrates the processing steps of the TTB algorithm.

TTB has been applied to tasks involving almanac questions such as, 'Which has the larger population, Hamburg or Leipzig?' (e.g., Gigerenzer & Goldstein, 1996). The reference class accessed to answer such a question is assumed to include cues such as 'Is the city the capital?', 'Does it have an airport/university/football team?', and so on. Assuming both cities are recognized, as soon as a cue is discovered that has different values for the two cities (e.g., Hamburg has a soccer team in the major league – positive evidence – but Leipzig does not – negative evidence) the search stops and this single cue is used to infer (correctly in this case) that Hamburg has the larger population.

TTB is a special case of a lexicographic strategy (e.g., Fishburn, 1974), so called because cues are looked up in a fixed order, like the alphabetic order used to arrange words in a dictionary. Many such strategies have been developed to explain behaviour in preference problems – most notably perhaps Tversky's (1972) Elimination by Aspects (EBA), which tends to consider the most important cue first, retrieves a cut-off value for that cue and eliminates

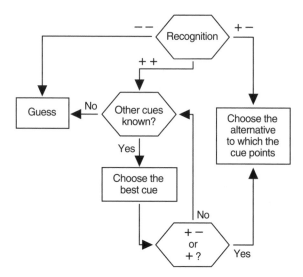

Figure 3.3 A flow chart of the processing steps of the Take-the-Best heuristic. A '+'
indicates a positive cue value; '–' indicates a negative cue value and '?'
indicates that the cue value is unknown. For example, if one knows that
one city has a football team (+) and either knows for sure that the other
does not (–) or is uncertain as to whether it has (?), then according to TTB
one uses this single piece of discriminating information to make a judgment. From Gigerenzer, G., & Goldstein, D. G. (1996). Reasoning the fast
and frugal way: Models of bounded rationality. *Psychological Review, 103,*
650–669. Copyright 1996 by the American Psychological Association.
Adapted with permission.

all alternatives with values worse than the cut-off. It continues to do this by
considering the second most important attribute (and so on) until only one
option remains. TTB is similar to elimination by aspects but the latter uses a
probability function to determine 'cue importance', whereas TTB uses cue
validity (see Bergert & Nosofsky, in press, for discussion of how TTB and
EBA are related).

To test the performance of this simple decision heuristic, Gigerenzer and
Goldstein (1996) set up a competition between TTB and a range of compensatory decision rules. The task used in the competition was the German
cities task in which the aim is to determine which of a pair of cities has the
larger population. The environment comprised the 83 German cities with a
population over 100,000 and nine cues, each with its own validity (where
validity was defined as the probability that the cue will lead to the correct
choice if cue values differ between alternatives – see Newell, Rakow, Weston,
& Shanks, 2004, and Rakow, Newell, Fayers, & Hersby, 2005, for a discussion
of other ways to conceptualize cue validity).

Each decision strategy in the competition had its own method for utilizing
cue information and arriving at a decision. TTB only knows the order of

the validities of the cues and it simply searches down this order until it finds a cue that has different values for the two alternatives, then stops the search and chooses the alternative to which the cue points (see Figure 3.3). Importantly, if one city is recognized but the other is not, the search is terminated and the recognized city is chosen without looking at any of the other nine cues. The other decision strategies in the competition were all compensatory because they looked up all the cue values. Note that these strategies look up 10 cues in all – the nine cues and recognition information, which is treated as 'just another cue' by the compensatory strategies. Table 3.1 presents each strategy along with a brief description of how each one combines cue information.

These six strategies were pitted against each other in a competition involving 252,000 simulated individuals. Such a large number was used to ensure that the simulation included 'people' with varying degrees of knowledge about German cities and thus enabled the simulated people to invoke the recognition heuristic. The results of the competition are summarized in Table 3.2. What is immediately surprising about the results is how well TTB does by using such a small amount of information in comparison to the strategies that use all available information. Although weighted tallying does as well as TTB it uses over three times as much information on average (10 compared to 3 cues) and thus Gigerenzer and Goldstein (1996) judged TTB to be the overall winner of the competition.

Why do weighted linear and unit weight linear strategies perform relatively poorly, when we know them to be highly robust in many situations (e.g., Dawes, 1979)? The answer lies in the information carried by recognition. Through simply integrating recognition information along with the other

Table 3.1 Description of the strategies used in the German cities task competition in Gigerenzer and Goldstein (1996)

Strategy	Cue combination method
Take-the-Best	Searches cues in validity order and bases choice on the first cue that discriminates between alternatives.
Tallying	Tallies up all the positive evidence and the alternative with largest number of positive cue values is chosen.
Weighted tallying	Weights each cue according to its validity (only looks at positive information).
Unit weight linear	Assigns positive and negative weights depending on cue value (same as 'Dawes' Rule').
Weighted linear	Cue values are multiplied by their respective validities (often viewed as optimal rule for preferential choice under the idealization of independent cues; Keeney & Raiffa, 1976).
Multiple regression	Creates weights that reflect validities of cues and covariance between cues (interdependencies). (Viewed as optimal way to integrate information – neural networks using the delta rule determine optimal weights by the same principle as multiple regression; Stone, 1986 – see chapter 11).

Table 3.2 Results of the competition between Take-the-Best and five compensatory strategies

Strategy	Knowledge about cues	Frugality (number of cues looked up)	Accuracy (% of correct predictions)
Take-the-Best	Order	3	65.8
Tallying	Direction	10	65.6
Weighted tallying	Validities	10	65.8
Unit weight linear	Direction	10	62.1
Weighted linear	Validities	10	62.3
Multiple regression	Beta-weights	10	65.7

Source: Compiled from data reported in Gigerenzer and Goldstein (1996, 1999).

cues, these strategies can violate the recognition heuristic by choosing the unrecognized alternative and therefore make a number of incorrect inferences. This is because in the German cities environment most cities have more negative cue values than positive ones (i.e., the answers to the 'Does it have an airport/university/soccer team?' questions are more often 'no' than 'yes'). This means that when a recognized city is compared with an unrecognized one the sum of its cue values will often be smaller than that of the unrecognized city. It follows that the overwhelming negative evidence for the recognized city will lead the unit weight and weighted linear models to choose erroneously the unrecognized city. The tallying models do not suffer from this problem because they ignore all negative evidence and thus have the recognition heuristic 'built in' (Gigerenzer & Goldstein, 1996).

There are other mathematical reasons why TTB outperforms the more compensatory strategies. Interested readers should examine the work of Martignon and Hoffrage (1999, 2002) and Hogarth and Karelaia (2005) for more detailed accounts of how TTB capitalizes on the structure of environments to ensure its good performance (e.g., whether information in an environment is structured in a compensatory or non-compensatory way). For now though we turn to the question of whether these clearly 'fast' and 'frugal' heuristics are also adopted by people when making decisions.

Empirical tests of fast-and-frugal strategies

There is no doubt that the simulation data described above demonstrate the impressive speed and accuracy of fast-and-frugal strategies like TTB. The simplicity of these strategies also, according to Gigerenzer and Goldstein (1996), makes them 'plausible psychological mechanisms of inference . . . that a mind can actually carry out under limited time and knowledge' (p. 652). However, as Bröder and Schiffer (2003) eloquently pointed out, 'plausibility is a weak advisor in the scientific endeavor' (p. 278) and empirical evidence, if it is attainable, should always be preferred. The evidence that documents the formal properties and efficiency of a number of fast and frugal heuristics (Czerlinski, Gigerenzer, & Goldstein, 1999; Goldstein et al., 2001; Martignon & Hoffrage, 1999) needs to be complemented by empirical validation demonstrating that people do indeed use these heuristics in the environments in which they are claimed to operate (see Chater, Oaksford, Nakisa, & Redington, 2003).

For example, Oppenheimer (2003) asked whether there is any evidence that recognition is indeed used in a non-compensatory manner. Recall that much of the success of TTB in the German cities competition was due to the search being stopped as soon as only one of a pair of cities was recognized – is this really what people do when faced with such a task? Oppenheimer (2003) reasoned that if knowledge other than recognition really was ignored then the recognition heuristic predicts that individuals would judge a recognized city as larger than an unrecognized city *even if the recognized city were known to be small*. Oppenheimer (2003) tested this counter-intuitive prediction in an experiment in which he paired cities that were recognizable (due to their proximity to the university where the study was conducted) but known to be small (e.g., Cupertino), with fictional cities that, by definition, could not be recognized (e.g., Rhavadran). On average participants judged the local – recognized – city to be larger on only 37 per cent of trials. This result, which contrasts starkly with the prediction of the recognition heuristic, led Oppenheimer (2003) to conclude: 'people clearly are using information beyond recognition when making judgments about city size' (p. B4). Subsequent investigations of the recognition heuristic in both artificial and real-world environments have all failed to find evidence for the non-compensatory use of recognition. It appears that in most inference tasks recognition is simply used as one cue among many others (Bröder & Eichler, 2006; Newell & Fernandez, 2006; Newell & Shanks, 2004; Richter & Späth, 2006).

In a series of studies, Newell and colleagues (Newell & Shanks, 2003, 2004; Newell, Weston, & Shanks, 2003; Newell et al., 2004; Rakow et al., 2005) sought empirical validation of fast-and-frugal heuristics using a simple MCPL-type task. They used a share prediction task in which participants aimed to make money by investing in the company that ended up with the higher share price. Each trial consisted of a choice between two companies. To help them make their decisions participants could buy information about four cues or indicators of each company's financial status (e.g., *Is it an established company? Does the company have financial reserves?*). The cues were binary, such that the answer to each question (uncovered by clicking on a 'Buy Information' button) was either 'YES' or 'NO'. This information board set-up allowed several kinds of data to be obtained, such as the order in which participants bought information, the amount of information they bought, and the final choice made. This allowed examination of people's adherence to the search, stopping and decision rules of both the recognition heuristic and TTB.

In the experiments a number of different factors were varied to examine their effects on the adoption of different decision strategies. The factors included the cost of information, the familiarity of companies, the number of cues in the environment (2, 4 or 6), the underlying structure of the task (deterministic or probabilistic) and the provision of hints concerning the validity ordering of the cues. The reason for changing these factors was to try to design environments that were strongly constrained to promote the use of TTB or recognition. Despite these attempts, in all the experiments the overall pattern of results was similar: simply stated, some of the people used the heuristics some of the time. In all experiments, a significant proportion of participants adopted strategies that violated all or some of their rules – especially the stopping rule. Indeed, in the two experiments reported in Newell et al. (2003) only a third of participants behaved in a manner completely consistent with TTB's search, stopping and decision rules.

A key finding was that a large number of participants sought more information than was predicted by the frugal stopping rules of the heuristics. That is, they continued to buy information after recognizing only one of a pair of companies or after discovering a cue that discriminated between the two companies. Newell (2005) has argued that the large individual differences in the amount of evidence acquired before a decision is made are more consistent with a weighted-evidence threshold model than a fast-and-frugal heuristic. One way of explaining individual variability is to suggest that all participants use an evidence-accumulation strategy, but that some participants require greater amounts of evidence than others before making their decisions. Lee and Cummins (2004) found that such an evidence-accumulation model accounted for 84.5 per cent of the decisions made by participants in a similar cue-learning task – more than that accounted for by either TTB or a compensatory strategy alone.

The results of these and several other empirical investigations of the fast-and-frugal heuristics (e.g., Bröder, 2000, 2003; Bröder & Schiffer, 2003; Juslin, Jones, Olsson, & Winman, 2003a) demonstrate that the heuristics are clearly not universally adopted by participants – even under conditions strongly constrained to promote their use. Some other investigations have provided evidence that TTB or some similar non-compensatory heuristic may be one of the strategies that people adopt in certain situations. For example, Dhami and Ayton (2001) reported that a close variant of TTB (the Matching Heuristic) provided a better fit than two compensatory mechanisms for a substantial minority of lay magistrates' judgments of whether defendants should be granted bail in the English legal system. Dhami and Harries (2001) found in a medical context that this same matching heuristic did as well as a logistic regression in capturing doctors' prescription decisions. Conclusions drawn on the basis of the matching heuristic may be a little premature however: Bröder and Schiffer (2003) noted that free parameters in the heuristic led it to be the best fitting model even for data sets generated randomly! This superior fit to random data suggests that the model is doing something beyond what a psychological model should do (i.e., overfitting; Cutting, 2000).

The picture painted by the empirical data suggests mixed support for fast-and-frugal heuristics. There is some evidence that people use 'something like' TTB some of the time (Bröder, 2000, Bröder & Schiffer, 2003; Dhami & Ayton, 2001; Dhami & Harries, 2001; Rieskamp & Hoffrage, 1999) but equally a growing body of evidence suggesting wide individual differences and a poor fit with their constituent rules (Bröder & Eichler, 2006; Juslin & Persson, 2002; Newell & Fernandez, 2006; Newell & Shanks, 2003, 2004; Newell et al., 2003, 2004; Oppenheimer, 2003; Rakow et al., 2005).

It is clear that examining the benefits and use of compensatory and non-compensatory 'fast-and-frugal' strategies in decision making will continue to be a fruitful area for research and debate, especially as the techniques used for assessing behaviour become more sophisticated (e.g., Bergert & Nosofsky, in press; Rieskamp & Otto, 2006).

Summary

When we make judgments and decisions we must first discover the relevant information in the environment, search through and acquire that information and then combine it in some manner. A useful metaphor for conceptualizing these processes is provided by the lens model framework of Egon Brunswik. In this framework a judge is thought to view the world through a lens of 'cues' that are probabilistically related to the true state of the environment. One experimental technique borne out of this metaphor is multiple-cue probability learning (MCPL). Experiments using this technique have examined the processes underlying the discovery, acquisition and combination of information.

The few studies that have examined cue discovery suggest that discovering valid cues in the environment takes many hundreds if not thousands of trials, but that the opportunity to experiment or intervene during the learning process enhances this discovery, especially in environments with causal structures. Cue search and acquisition can be guided by simple preference or objective cue validity and is influenced by the trade-off between the cost and benefit of obtaining more information, although not always in the way specified by normative analyses.

In studies of information combination a contrast is drawn between methods that combine all relevant information – compensatory – or fewer pieces of information – non-compensatory. A wealth of evidence suggests that statistical methods for combining information outperform human methods, but humans are useful for identifying the relevant components for combination. Some simple non-compensatory heuristics such as Take-the-Best are almost as accurate as more complex compensatory strategies (e.g., a weighted additive rule) despite using far fewer pieces of information. However, the psychological plausibility of such simple heuristics has been questioned because of a lack of clear empirical evidence indicating that people actually employ such techniques in their judgments and decisions.

The take-home message from this journey through the stages of discovery, acquisition and combination is the importance of experience in environments for improving our judgments. In keeping with our emphasis on the importance of learning, we have seen how the discovery of cues, and the adoption of different strategies for information acquisition and combination are affected by our exposure to the environment and our opportunities to learn. However, one aspect of the data we have reviewed so far that might seem inconsistent with this view is the finding that experts – who have by definition had a great deal of experience in the relevant environments – are outperformed by statistical models. We will return to this interesting issue when we cover expertise in more detail in chapter 12, but for now we need to consider the final 'stage' in the process of making judgments and decisions – how do we use feedback to help us learn?

4 Stages of judgment II: Feedback effects and dynamic environments

'If at first you don't succeed then try, try again.' We have all been told to persevere or 'keep at it' if we get something wrong the first time. The assumption is that through repeated efforts we will improve and eventually succeed – we will learn from our experience. But what aspects of our experience do we learn from? Is it enough to simply be told that we were right or wrong, or do we need to be told *why* we were right or wrong? Or at least be given the information that helps us to infer where we went wrong?

The effects of feedback have been investigated in a wide range of judgment and decision-making tasks (e.g., see Harvey & Fischer, 2005 for a discussion of the role of feedback in confidence judgment, probability estimation and advice-taking tasks), but in keeping with the focus of chapter 3, in the first part of this chapter we examine primarily the evidence from multiple-cue probability learning (MCPL) tasks. In the second part of the chapter we take a more integrative view by considering how all the separate stages of judgment are combined. We note that the environments in which we make decisions are typically not controlled by 'static' rules ensuring that properties of the environment remain constant (as they are in many laboratory tasks), but are usually dynamic and require us to anticipate and learn to control changes in those environments. Feedback is particularly important in these situations and so we consider attempts to investigate how feedback interacts with the other stages of decision making in real-time 'dynamic' tasks. We also look at ways in which our understanding of the stages can be used to analyse decisions made in real-world naturalistic settings, such as those made by fire-fighters.

Learning from feedback

Learning from feedback is often thought of as a single process; however, there are a number of different ways in which feedback may be used to learn a task. First, as the section on cue discovery in chapter 3 made clear, one needs to work out what the important variables are in a task (Klayman, 1988a, 1988b). To improve your performance, it seems essential to 'know what to look at' before you can construct any kind of 'mental model' of how your interactions with a system affect its behaviour. As Klayman has argued, though this initial process of discovery seems to be a prerequisite for understanding how feedback operates, it is perhaps the least understood aspect of learning from experience.

Once the relevant cues have been discovered, or have been given to you (as is often the case in laboratory experiments) you need to work out the best way to use the information provided by the cues. Brehmer (1979) has argued that there are three components involved in ascertaining this 'best way'. First, you need to learn about the functional relation between each cue and the criterion that you are predicting. (Does an increase in the amount of a particular hormone always indicate an improvement in the health of a patient – i.e., a linear function; or does either too much or too little of the hormone indicate poor health – i.e., an inverted U function.) Second, the decision maker needs to learn the optimal relative weighting to ascribe to different pieces of information. (Is the result of Test A a stronger predictor of the presence of a disease than Test B?) Finally, if multiple cues are involved, the decision maker has to consider relations among the cues and determine the best way to integrate them – for example, via a simple additive rule or via some more complex interactive or multiplicative function.

Simply right or wrong: Outcome feedback

Having an assignment returned with FAIL written on it tells you that you did something wrong, but will that experience help you to write a better assignment next time? Probably not: in order to improve you need some information about *why* the assignment was poor. Did you concentrate on the wrong topics, or write too much on irrelevant details and too little on relevant ones, or perhaps fail to construct a coherent argument with the information available? Perhaps this is forcing the analogy too far, but each of these failures maps onto the ways outlined above in which feedback can help learning – that is, identifying the important variables (or topics), weighting them appropriately, and then integrating them correctly. Is the intuition about the ineffectiveness of simple outcome feedback for improving performance borne out by laboratory studies?

The 'received wisdom' in answer to this question is 'yes'. Outcome feedback alone does not appear to improve performance, or as Brehmer (1980) stated in the title of a paper on the subject 'In one word: Not from experience'. As we shall see a little later, this may be overstating the case somewhat but first we will address the evidence for this rather pessimistic conclusion.

In a typical MCPL task, outcome feedback is the provision of the true value of the criterion after participants have made their estimate on each trial. For example, if the task were predicting a person's salary on the basis of their weight, age, and the car they owned, a subject might predict £35,000 and then be given outcome feedback informing them that the correct answer was £50,000. Such feedback typically only leads to improvements in performance when the environment is very simple (two or three cues that are positively linearly related to the criterion) and when feedback is combined with a long series of trials (Balzer, Doherty, & O'Connor, 1989; Brehmer, 1980; Hammond, 1971; Hammond & Boyle, 1971; Klayman, 1988b; Todd & Hammond, 1965). If the functions relating the cues to the criterion are negative or, worse, non-linear, then learning is further impeded (Deane, Hammond, & Summers, 1972; Slovic, 1974). Finally, if the cues themselves are intercorrelated, then learning is typically disrupted (Lindell & Stewart, 1974; Schmitt & Dudycha, 1975).

What is it about the paucity of outcome feedback that makes learning from it so difficult? As Harvey and Fischer (2005) note, two competing explanations have been proposed. Brehmer (1980) in the paper referred to above suggests that the difficulty arises because 'people simply do not have the cognitive schemata needed for efficient performance in probabilistic tasks' (Brehmer, 1980, p. 233). He argues that people tend to form deterministic rules about the relations between cues and criterion – assuming for example that being over 50 always leads to a salary greater than £40,000 – and that when these rules break down (because the cues and outcomes are only probabilistically related) people discard the rules rather than considering that they may be probabilistic in character. Thus under Brehmer's interpretation it is not the paucity of the outcome feedback per se that is the problem, rather it is an inability on the part of the subject to learn *any* complex probabilistic task.

In contrast, Todd and Hammond (1965) suggested it is simply that outcome feedback in most MCPL tasks does not provide the information participants require in order to improve their performance. Specifically, it gives them no information about how to appropriately weight the cues available. If their estimate of a person's salary is too high is this because too much weight has been put on the car the person owns, or on the person's age (see Harvey & Fischer, 2005)? Similarly, in writing your essay, did you fail because you concentrated on the wrong topics altogether or because you spent too long on irrelevant details of those topics?

In an effort to distinguish between Brehmer's (1980) and Todd and Hammond's (1965) competing explanations, Harries and Harvey (2000) compared performance in a typical MCPL task with that in an 'advice-taking' task. The underlying probabilistic structure of the two tasks was identical, but the 'cover story' given to subjects differed. Both groups were required to predict sales of a consumer product. In the MCPL group sales were predicted on the basis of four pieces of information (number of sales outlets, competitors' promotional spending, etc.) each of which varied in predictive validity. For the advice-taking group, instead of the pieces of information, subjects were presented with sales forecasts from four 'advisors' who differed in their forecasting ability. In both conditions the actual numbers presented to participants were identical; the only difference was that in the MCPL condition the numbers were given labels corresponding to different sales indicators, whereas in the advice group *all* the numbers were labelled as sales forecasts.

Thus the crucial difference between these two tasks was that in the advice-taking task the cues (forecasts) and criterion (sales) all referred to the *same* variable, whereas in the MCPL task the cues (number of outlets, etc.) referred to different variables from that specified by the criterion and by the outcome feedback (i.e., sales volume). Thus in the advice task, outcome feedback informed participants not only about the error in their judgment, but also about the error in each forecast provided to them. As a result, participants were given information directly about how much they should rely on each cue – the aspect of feedback that Todd and Hammond's analysis suggested was essential for improvements in performance.

Note that both the advice and the MCPL tasks were relatively complex and probabilistic, so according to Brehmer's interpretation outcome feedback should have been equally ineffective in both. Contrary to this interpretation, however, Harries and Harvey found that learning in the advice task was much faster than in the MCPL task. Even at the end of the experiment performance was poorer in the MCPL task. The results appeared to lend strong support to Todd and Hammond's arguments but were inconsistent with Brehmer's (1980) pessimistic conclusion that people are just not capable of learning from experience in probabilistic tasks.

Feedback or feedforward?

Harries and Harvey's (2000) results provide some interesting evidence about how people perform in advice and MCPL tasks, but was the difference they found really a result of the way in which people learned from their experience in the task? A surprising finding in the Harries and Harvey study was that the advantage for the advice-taking group was evident on the very first trial of the experiment. This advantage could therefore not have been the result of the more effective use of feedback, rather it must have arisen because 'the expectations about the task that people generated after reading the experimental instructions were more useful in the advice-taking task' (Harvey & Fischer, 2005, p. 122). This interpretation is consistent with the idea that people used a feedforward mechanism in which information in the environment was used to guide performance on the task – even before they began to make predictions.

Bjorkman (1972) made a similar point in a discussion about the interaction between feedback and feedforward mechanisms in multiple-cue probability learning. Bjorkman (1972) suggested 'feedforward refers to task information transmitted to the subject by instructions, whereas feedback refers to the trial-by-trial information provided by task outcomes' (p. 153). The idea is that feedforward provides information that would otherwise have to be learned by feedback. As such the cognitive load placed on working memory is reduced, allowing for overall better performance on the task. Information provided via feedforward is also more consistent and accurate than that provided by feedback, because it is not subject to the various sources of error and bias that affect the trial-by-trial accumulation of information.

Therefore, it is perhaps not surprising that performance in the advice-taking task was superior to that in the MCPL task. Given the framing of the task in terms of 'advice-taking' one can speculate that participants' mental models might have led them to (correctly) estimate a sales value within the range of those provided by the advisors. In contrast, in the MCPL version, their mental models may not have imposed such a constraint on their judgments (Harvey & Fischer, 2005).

Evidence from a number of MCPL studies also supports the contention that it is the structure of the learning environment – and what that structure *affords* to participants' – 'mental models' – that is important for performance in MCPL tasks. For example, Muchinsky and Dudycha (1975) showed that participants' performance in an MCPL task was significantly superior when cue names were changed from the abstract 'Cue 1' and 'Cue 2' to meaningful labels such as 'average monthly debt' and 'average number of creditors'. Even greater improvements in performance are seen when the labels provided to the cues are congruent with participants' prior conceptions of how cues and outcomes are related in the 'real world'. For example, in the Muchinsky and Dudycha study, when the criterion 'credit rating' was negatively related to monthly debt (incongruent), performance was inferior compared to when the two were positively related (congruent).

Adelman (1981) found similar effects in an MCPL task that compared the level of achievement (the correlation between criterion and prediction in the lens model framework – see Figure 3.1) reached with either cognitive (detailed information about the task structure) or outcome feedback in three conditions that varied the congruence between task properties implied by the task content (or cover story) of the task and the actual task properties. When the task content was neutral (i.e., cues were presented simply as Cue 1, Cue 2, etc.) provision of cognitive feedback led to higher levels of achievement than outcome feedback alone. However when task-congruent labels were used such as 'expectations for academic achievement', and 'social success' for predicting grade point averages (GPA), there was no difference between the outcome and cognitive feedback groups – both performed at a similarly high level. Finally, when the task content was incongruent with the actual task properties (i.e., labelling 'academic achievement' as 'social success') the level of achievement with cognitive feedback was as low as with outcome feedback.

Note that in the Adelman study the cognitive feedback consisted of information such as the relative weights of cues, the function forms associated with cues and levels of predictability – all forms of information that are perhaps more appropriately described as feed*forward*. Thus, again, it seems that rather than *learning* from experience it is simply being able to *use* appropriate information that is responsible for higher levels of achievement. Close analysis of Adelman's data reveals that there is some evidence for learning (i.e., an improvement across blocks of trials) but the improvements tended to be modest and to level off relatively quickly, after 60–90 trials. Furthermore, when the task content was congruent achievement levels in both feedback groups started at a similarly high level, whereas when task content was neutral the advantage for the cognitive feedback group was seen in the very first block of trials.

But does the provision of relative weights, function forms and validities that typically comprise cognitive feedback always help participants? A series of studies by Castellan (Castellan, 1973, 1974; Castellan & Edgell, 1973; Castellan & Swaine, 1977) suggests not. For instance, Castellan (1974) compared the effects of four different types of feedback on performance in a two-cue binary outcome environment. On each trial participants were shown either a square or a triangle made up of either horizontal or vertical lines and had to predict whether the event '>' or '<' would occur. Participants were given one of four types of feedback in addition to outcome feedback: simple percentage correct, cue-event validity coefficients, cue-response utilization coefficients, or a combination of the last two forms. Castellan's (1974) general conclusion was that no form of feedback enhanced performance, and in fact *all types of feedback* except percentage correct led to a decrement in performance – a conclusion that was echoed in later studies (e.g., Castellan & Swaine, 1977).

How can we reconcile these findings with those of Adelman (1981) and many others showing the usefulness of cognitive feedback (e.g., Balzer et al., 1989)? The principal difference between the studies was that the Castellan ones used binary cues and binary outcomes whereas the Adelman study used continuous cues and outcomes. Why might the cognitive feedback be unhelpful in the former case? Perhaps the correlation information used to convey the relations between cues and outcomes was simply not *usable* by participants in the Castellan studies. Indeed, one of the experimenters involved in running the studies recalled that even he found it impossible to understand how to *use* the feedback (Stephen Edgell, personal communication). One potential explanation for this difficulty in use is that the cognitive feedback was given separately for each cue (e.g., the validity of the line orientation cue, and the validity of the shape cue) even though the cues themselves were presented as a configuration (e.g., a triangle containing horizontal lines). Such presentation might have made it very difficult for participants to work out the relative contribution of both shape and line orientation to the outcome. In contrast, in the Adelman study and many of the other studies that have examined the effects of cognitive feedback, separate cue validities may have been more usable because they apply to easily discriminable cues, such as expectations for academic achievement and social success.

Work by Peter Juslin and colleagues lends some weight to this conclusion (Juslin et al., 2003a). Participants were required to classify fictitious 'frogs' as harmless or dangerous based on their level of 'toxicity'. The toxicity could be inferred from four visual cues (e.g., length of legs, colour of back, etc.)

that combined to construct a schematic frog. Participants were provided with either simple outcome feedback ('Harmless' or 'Dangerous') or cognitive feedback relating to the toxicity of the whole frog (e.g., 'The toxicity is 57 per cent) rather than the relative contribution to toxicity given by the constituent features. Participants given this 'combined cognitive feedback' performed significantly better in the classification task than those just given the outcome feedback. Although these results are supportive of the idea that Castellan's participants found cognitive feedback hard to use because it was presented separately for each cue, to be more confident about the importance of combined versus separated cognitive feedback a direct comparison of these two conditions would be required.

The picture that emerges from this research is that the extent of learning from feedback depends on how easily the feedback can be interpreted in a way that gives judges information about how to improve their performance (Harvey & Fischer, 2005). Performance is also affected by the amount of information a participant can glean from the instructions, the framing of the task and expectations derived (presumably) from real-world experience – all elements of 'feedforward'. This notion of the interplay between feedback and feedforward is consistent with the idea that participants build a 'mental model' of the task with which they are engaged. Development of this model is influenced both 'top-down' via feedforward information and 'bottom-up' via feedback. If feedforward information matches with the feedback gained from engaging in the task, then feedback can be used to refine the feedforward and in turn to improve performance. If there is a mismatch between expectations and experience in the task then the feedforward information is rejected, and improvements must be sought through feedback (Harvey & Fischer, 2005; Klayman, 1988b).

Decision making in dynamic environments

As we noted in the opening paragraphs of this chapter, the vast majority of research in the cue-learning tradition has focused on static environments in which cue–criterion relations remain constant. These static environments contrast with the 'real world' where we often need to keep track of numerous changing variables. In such situations our ability to adapt and use both feedback and feedforward information quickly is crucial. What do we know about judgment and decision making in these dynamic environments?

A few early cue-learning studies incorporated elements of dynamic environments. Changes to environments such as a shift in the relative weights of cues in the middle of learning, or a cue that was non-predictive becoming valid, and vice versa, have been employed (e.g., Dudycha, Dumoff, & Dudycha, 1973; Peterson, Hammond, & Summers, 1965; Sniezek, 1986). The findings from these tasks have in general mirrored those of the static environments (Klayman, 1988b). However, these rather minor changes to the environment do not really capture what is meant by a dynamic decision task.

Brehmer and Allard (1991) defined dynamic decision tasks as having three important characteristics: (1) they require a series of interdependent decisions; (2) the state of the task changes over time, both autonomously and as a consequence of the decision maker's actions, and (3) the decisions have to be made in real time. One class of tasks that exhibit some of these characteristics is the complex control or judgmental control tasks that were studied intensively by Donald Broadbent and colleagues in the late 1970s and 1980s (e.g., Broadbent & Aston, 1978; Broadbent, Fitzgerald, & Broadbent, 1986; and Berry & Broadbent, 1984, 1988; Hayes & Broadbent, 1988). In these tasks participants aimed to control the interaction of several variables simultaneously to produce predictable outputs. For example, Berry and Broadbent (1984) used a 'sugar production task' in which the output variable was the volume of sugar produced by the factory and the input variable was the number of workers in the factory. Participants played the role of the manager and were required to reach and maintain the optimum sugar output level by varying the number of workers. The relationship between the number of workers and the output levels was not a simple linear one, but was determined in part by the response that participants made on the previous trial. Participants were able to perform relatively well in these tasks, despite having very little verbal knowledge of the underlying relationship of the variables governing the system. Frensch and Funke (1995) contains detailed evaluation of performance in these tasks.

However, the complex control tasks arguably only satisfy Brehmer and Allard's (1991) first and second characteristics of dynamic tasks. Interdependent decisions were required and the state of the task changed as a result of the participants' action, but the environment did not change autonomously and the task was self-paced so no 'real-time' changes occurred.

In order to satisfy all three characteristics Brehmer and Allard developed a dynamic environment in which participants played the role of a fire chief faced with the problem of extinguishing forest fires (see also Brehmer, 1999). The scenario was as follows: The chief receives information about the location and extent of the fires from a spotter plane. On the basis of this information he sends out fire-fighting units, which then report back on their progress in putting out the fires. Using these progress reports, the chief issues new instructions to those (and perhaps other) units, and continues to do so until the fires have been extinguished. Such an environment encapsulates all the characteristics of dynamic environments identified by Brehmer and Allard (1991): a series of decisions is required; the decisions are interdependent because sending a unit to one location precludes using it at another location; the state of the fire can change autonomously (as a result of weather conditions) or as a result of the unit's efforts; finally, time is crucial because if units are sent too early they will have no fire to fight, and if too late the fire may be too severe to tackle (Brehmer, 1999).

Using this cover story Brehmer and colleagues developed a computer simulation called 'NEWFIRE' in which they monitored the performance of novice participants (i.e., those with no expertise in fire-fighting) playing the role of the fire chief (e.g., Løvborg & Brehmer, 1991). Participants' goals were to prevent the fire from spreading and to extinguish the fire as quickly as possible. The simulation software allowed the experimenter to control a range of factors in the environment: the size and number of fires, the weather conditions, the location of the base (where the chief coordinates from), the speed at which the fire-fighting units move, and so on. Importantly, the simulation is 'clock-driven' – it continues to run without waiting for the participant to respond.

The principal findings from research using the 'NEWFIRE' environment was that although participants may not perform optimally, their behaviour is 'at least reasonable in the sense that it gets the job done' (Brehmer, 1999, p. 10). For example, Brehmer, Løvborg, and Winman (1992; cited in Brehmer, 1999) set up environments in which two fires had to be tackled. One fire near the base only required one unit to extinguish it; the other required four fire-fighting teams, because it was further from the base and would spread in the time it took for units to reach it. However, rather than taking this time consideration into account, participants fought both fires in roughly the same way. Although this was non-optimal because too many units were sent to the closer fire and too few to the distant one, the fires were still extinguished and the 'job was done'. Brehmer (1999) concluded that this and other similar results demonstrate that when participants cannot work out the optimal way to perform a task they find a reasonable way instead.

The conclusion that people simply perform 'reasonably' may seem trivial and rather uninteresting. However, Brehmer (1999) argued that this conception of decision making provides a more useful interpretation of how *actual* decisions are made. Much of the research in the judgment and decision-making literature has focused on comparisons between actual decision behaviour and the behaviour prescribed by normative models. The general conclusions drawn from this research are often characterized as suggesting that we are incompetent and irrational decision makers. This pessimistic conclusion results, Brehmer argues, from too narrow a sample of decision problems (e.g., gambles) and a fixation on normative theories. To understand 'real-life' decision making we need to move away from thinking about optimality and examine what people actually do when confronted with decision problems. Investigating dynamic environments represents a step in this direction, but a more radical method for examining real-life decision making – such as decisions made by actual fire chiefs – has come to be known as 'naturalistic decision making' and it is to this that we turn in the final section of this chapter.

Naturalistic decision making (NDM)

A report of flames in the basement of a four-storey building is received at the fire station. The fire chief arrives at the building: there are no externally visible signs of fire, but a quick internal inspection leads to the discovery of flames spreading up the laundry chute. That's straight-forward: a vertical fire spreading upward, recently started (because the fire has not reached the outside of the building) – tackle it by spraying water down from above. The fire chief sends one unit to the first floor and one to the second. Both units report that the fire has passed them. Another check of the outside of the building reveals that now the fire has spread and smoke is filling the building. Now that the 'quick option' for extinguishing the fire is no longer viable, the chief calls for more units and instigates a search and rescue – attention must now shift to establishing a safe evacuation route.

This vignette, adapted from Klein (1993) and obviously similar to the task used by Brehmer and colleagues, is typical of the kinds of situation that have been analysed in the development of models of naturalistic decision making (NDM). NDM emphasizes both the features of the context in which decisions are made (e.g., ill-structured problems, dynamic environments, competing goals, high stakes, time constraints) (Orasanu & Connolly, 1993) and the role that experience plays in decision making (Pruitt, Cannon-Bowers, & Salas, 1997). Zsambok provides a succinct definition stating 'NDM is the way people use their experience to make decisions in field settings' (Zsambok, 1997, p. 4).

Cognitive task analyses of fire-fighters' reports such as the one described in the vignette are a key aspect of the NDM methodology. The fascinating aspect of these task analyses, according to Klein (1993), is the *lack* of decisions. The chief sees the vertical fire and he knows what to do straight away – there is no process of generating varieties of options or of attempting to 'maximize utility' by picking the best option. Even when the course of action is negated by the spread of the fire, the chief knows instantly what to do next – switch to a search and rescue strategy. The chief never seems to *decide* anything.

Observations such as these led to the development of perhaps the proto-typical model that falls within the NDM framework: the recognition-primed decision-making model or RPD (Klein, 1993, 1998). In its current form the RPD has three variations (Lipshitz, Klein, Orasanu, & Salas, 2001). In the simplest variation a decision maker 'sizes up' a situation to recognize which course of action makes sense and then responds with the initial option that is generated or identified. The idea is that a skilled decision maker can typically rely on experience to ensure that the first option generated is a feasible course of action. In a second variation of RPD the decision maker relies on a story-building strategy to mentally simulate the events leading up to the observed characteristics of a situation. Such a strategy is invoked when the situation is not clear and the decision maker needs to take time to carry out a diagnosis. Finally, the third variation explains how decision makers evaluate single courses of action by imagining how they will play out in a given situation.

This mental simulation allows the decision maker to anticipate difficulties and amend the chosen strategy.

Expertise plays a key role in all three of these variations. Expertise is required for recognizing the 'typicality' of the situation (e.g., 'it's a vertical fire'), to construct mental models that allow for one explanation to be deemed more plausible than others, and for being able to mentally simulate a course of action in a situation (Lipshitz et al., 2001). This latter skill – mental simulation – has been documented in chess masters and is often described as 'progressive deepening' – playing a move out in the mind, to see how it would work (deGroot, 1965). Mental simulation in the RPD is also closely related to the *simulation heuristic* (Kahneman & Tversky, 1982a), by which people build a simulation or story to explain how something might happen, and disregard the simulation as implausible if it requires too many unlikely events. In fact, as Klein (1993) points out, the RPD model could be described as a combination of the *representativeness* and *availability* heuristics for recognizing the typicality of a situation, and the simulation heuristic for diagnosis and evaluation of a situation. (We discuss these heuristics and others in more detail in chapter 6, and in chapter 7 we explore the idea of mental simulation.)

The RPD model has been applied to a variety of different experts and contexts, (e.g., infantry officers, tank platoon leaders, and commercial aviation pilots). Consistent with the initial studies of the fire-fighters, RPD has been shown to be the most common strategy in 80–95 per cent of these environments (Lipshitz et al., 2001). These are impressive results, suggesting that the RPD model provides a very good description of the course of action followed by experienced decision makers, especially when they are under time pressure and have ill-defined goals (Klein, 1998).

The descriptive power of RPD is not in question, but can RPD be used to generate testable hypotheses? Some evidence for the confirmation of predictions of the RPD model has been found in the analysis of chess players (Calderwood, Klein, & Crandall, 1988; Klein, Wolf, Militello, & Zsambok, 1995). For example Klein et al. (1995) asked whether skilled chess players could generate reasonable moves as the very first one they considered in a chess problem (in much the same way as the fire chief seems to know what to do straightaway when confronted with fire situations). Klein et al. gave chess players four chess boards displaying different configurations of pieces. For each board a chess master had previously determined the quality of next moves that a player could make. The results indicated that the number of high quality first moves generated was much greater than if players had simply been selecting randomly from the population of all possible legal moves. It seems that expertise was used to generate a good move as the first one that was considered. Such data are suggestive but not critical (what theory would predict the opposite? – i.e., that people randomly generate options, see Lipshitz et al., 2001), however, if the general remit of NDM is decision analysis in 'messy' field settings does it matter that it is difficult to test specific predictions of the models?

This inability to test specific predictions is not necessarily a problem for NDM – after all, its entire goal, in a sense, is to *describe* how proficient decision makers make decisions in the field. But it is important that the techniques employed by NDM in collecting and analysing these qualitative data are rigorous and defensible. Failure to adopt such methods will impede the acceptance of NDM methods by other scientists (Klayman, 2001). Such rigour can be adopted. For example, Hoffman, Crandell, and Shadbolt (1998) demonstrated 82 per cent retest reliability in the reports of fire commanders across several months. Furthermore, extensive use of protocol analysis in cognitive science (e.g., Ericsson & Simon, 1984) is testament to their usefulness as sources of data. As Lipshitz et al. (2001) concluded, developing better understanding of and methods for rigorous observation and knowledge elicitation is a key challenge for the future of NDM.

Can NDM and more traditional lab-based methods for examining judgment and decision making, such as the cue-learning paradigm we have focused on in this and the previous chapter, be unified into a 'decision science' (see Cooksey, 2001)? Although NDM has taken a rather confrontational position against lab-based studies, as Klayman (2001) and Cooksey (2001) both suggest it would perhaps be more beneficial to the advancement of understanding to develop a synergy that uses both observation and experimentation to examine the behaviour of novices and experts in the lab and in the field.

Summary

Feedback is crucial for learning from our experience in decision problems. In many MCPL tasks the provision of outcome feedback alone is only effective if the environment is relatively simple. This may be because outcome feedback does not provide the decision maker with the information required to understand the cue–criterion relations. When cues and criterion are expressed as quantities of the same variable (as in the advice-taking task of Harries and Harvey, 2000) or when detailed information about task structure is provided (e.g., cognitive feedback) more substantial improvements are observed. Such improvements may be due to the interplay of trial-by-trial feedback, which accumulates throughout the course of experiencing a new environment, and feedforward information about the structure of an environment, which can be provided explicitly through instruction or through intuitions derived from knowledge of the world. Experiments using dynamic environments have revealed that people do a reasonable job of making decisions and allocating resources even if the decisions are not optimal in the classical sense. Studies of the way people use their experience to make decisions in field settings (naturalistic decision making) has provided important insights into how people generate options, and they seem to be 'primed' to know what to do often without explicitly making decisions.

This brings us to the end of our journey through the stages of judgment. In the next two chapters we shift our focus to examining some formal ways for appraising our probability judgments – we ask how good are our probability judgments and to what standards should they be compared?

5 Appraising probability judgments

Correspondence vs. coherence criteria

A health survey was conducted in a sample of adult males in British Columbia, Canada (of all ages and occupations). Mr F. was selected by chance from the sample. Which of the following statements is more probable?

(1) Mr F has had one or more heart attacks.
(2) Mr F has had one or more heart attacks and he is over 55 years old.

If you are like the majority of participants in psychological experiments (e.g., Tversky & Kahneman, 1983) you will have rated the second alternative as more probable than the first. This is the infamous 'conjunction error', because the probability of a conjunction, P(heart attack & over 55), cannot be more probable than one of its conjuncts P(heart attack). This is illustrated in the Venn diagram in Figure 5.1. One circle (labelled H) represents the proportion of men in the sample who have had at least one heart attack, the other circle (labelled O) represents the proportion of men in the sample who are over 55 years of age. The overlap between these two circles represents the proportion of men who have had at least one heart attack AND are over 55 years old (labelled H & O). From the diagram it is clear that the proportion of men who have had at least one heart attack (alternative 1 above) cannot be less than the proportion who have at least one heart attack AND are over 55 years old (alternative 2 above). In short, alternative 2 is a subset of alternative 1, and so cannot be more probable.

The common mistake – rating alternative 2 as more probable than alternative 1 – is classified as a failure of *coherence*. It is made by many people (students, medical professionals, psychology lecturers, etc.) and has been replicated using a variety of different scenarios (see Gilovich, Griffin, & Kahneman, 2002 for a survey). The reason it is called a failure of coherence is because it violates a basic principle of probability theory. This principle states that if A is a subset of B, then B cannot be less probable than A. Such a principle applies irrespective of what A and B refer to; it depends just on the formal relations between these sets.

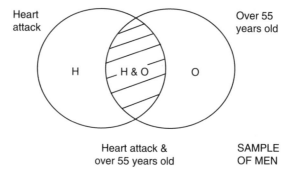

Figure 5.1 Venn diagram showing that the probability of a conjunction cannot be more than one of its conjuncts. The area of the left circle (H) corresponds to the proportion of men who have had at least one heart attack; the area of the right circle corresponds to the proportion of men over 55 years old (O). The shaded area (H & O) corresponds to the probability of both, and cannot be larger than either of the circles, because it is a subset of both of these sets.

Consider a related question: What is more likely, that an adult male in the USA dies from homicide or that he dies from suicide? If you share the responses of the majority (Lichtenstein, Slovic, Fischhoff, Layman, & Coombs, 1978), you will have rated homicide as more probable than suicide. This would also be an error, but of a different kind. It is classifiable as an error of *correspondence*, because in actual fact there are more deaths per year from suicide than from homicide. By overestimating the chances of homicide your probability judgment fails to correspond to the objective facts about homicide and suicide rates.

These two examples illustrate two different ways in which our probability judgments can go wrong. More generally, it is possible to distinguish two approaches to the analysis and appraisal of probability judgments, in terms of *coherence* and *correspondence* (Hammond, 1996). Coherence theories focus on structural relations between judgments or beliefs, and thus rely on formal models of appraisal such as logic or probability theory. In contrast, correspondence theories focus on the fit between judgments and the external environment. They tend to rely on the predictive accuracy of judgments, or their correspondence to properties in the environment.

Most of the models reviewed in this book are correspondence models (e.g., the lens model in chapter 3; associative or exemplar-based learning models in chapters 11 and 12). Learning or judgment is mediated by mechanisms that attune in some way to the statistical structure of the environment, and the central goal of these mechanisms is predictive accuracy. In contrast, the majority of research on judgmental biases concentrates on coherence criteria, and in particular the conformity of people's judgments with the laws of probability.

One of the claims to be advanced in this chapter and the next is that both approaches are critical to understanding human judgment, and that biases often arise when correspondence-based mechanisms are assessed in terms of coherence-based standards. This is not to exonerate the judgmental inconsistencies that people fall prey to, but to fit such behaviour into a wider cognitive framework.

The laws of probability as coherence criteria

Ever since their development in the seventeenth century, the laws of probability have been advocated as laws of sound reasoning (e.g., Laplace, 1812). This idea was formalized in the early twentieth century by Ramsey (1931) and de Finetti (1937). Essentially they showed that the laws of probability provide consistency constraints on judgments or beliefs. A set of probability judgments that violate the laws (termed *incoherent*) is defective because: (a) it would entail that your judgments depend on the precise form in which options are presented to you, and thus (b) if you bet in accordance with these judgments, you could be made to lose money irrespective of the outcomes of the events you bet on (in other words you would be vulnerable to a 'Dutch book').

To illustrate, let us return to the earlier question about the probability that a man suffers a heart attack (H) compared with the probability that a man suffers a heart attack and is over 55 (H & O). By the laws of probability a conjunction cannot be more probable than either of its conjuncts; that is, $P(H \& O) \leq P(H)$. However, suppose that you, along with the majority of respondents in the experimental studies, believe that $P(H \& O) > P(H)$, and that you are prepared to bet on these statements (don't feel guilty, insurance companies do it all the time). It can be shown that an unscrupulous person could place bets with you, on the basis of the odds implicit in your probability judgments, so that you will lose money regardless of the true outcomes (i.e., whether or not the man indeed suffers from a heart attack, and whether or not he is over 55 years old). For simplicity of exposition we will illustrate with exact figures, but the generality of the argument should be clear.

Suppose you estimate that there is a 25 per cent chance that a randomly selected man suffers a heart attack; that is, $P(H) = .25$, and a 50 per cent chance that he suffers a heart attack and is over 55 years old; $P(H \& O) = .5$. This means that you accept odds of 3 to 1 against H, and evens odds (1:1) on H & O. Given these odds, an unscrupulous opponent just needs to (a) bet $5 on H, and (b) bet $10 against H & O, to guarantee himself a sure gain. This is shown in Table 5.1. The columns correspond to the four possible outcomes: (i) heart attack and over 55 (H & O); (ii) heart attack and not over 55 (H & ¬O); (iii) no heart attack and over 55 (¬H & O); (iv) no heart attack and not over 55 (¬H & ¬O). For each outcome the first row shows how much money your opponent wins, the second row shows how much money your opponent loses, and the third row shows your opponent's net gain (and hence your net loss).

Table 5.1 An example of a Dutch book

	Possible outcomes			
	(i) H & O	(ii) H & ¬O	(iii) ¬H & O	(iv) ¬H & ¬O
Opponent wins	$15 on (a)	$25 on (a) & (b)	$10 on (b)	$10 on (b)
Opponent loses	$10 on (b)	$0	$5 on (a)	$5 on (a)
Opponent net gain	$5	$25	$5	$5

Notes: H = Man suffers heart attack; O = Man is over 55 years old. You offer odds of 3:1 against H, and even odds for H & O. Your opponent (a) bets $5 on H being true, and (b) bets $10 against H & O being true. There are four possible outcomes (i–iv), and your opponent has a net gain in each. Thus he wins regardless of what actually happens.

For example, if the man turns out to both have a heart attack and be over 55 (outcome 1), your opponent will win $15 from his bet on H, and lose $10 from his bet against H & O. This gives him a net gain of $5, and you a net loss of $5. However, if the man turns out to have a heart attack and not be over 55 (outcome 2), your opponent will win $15 from his bet on H, and win $10 from his bet against H & O. His net gain is $25, and your net loss is $25. The other two alternatives (outcomes 3 and 4) both result in a net gain for your opponent of $5. He loses $5 for his bet on H, but gains $10 for his bet against H & O.

Overall, then, whatever the outcome of the events, you will lose and your opponent will gain. So this is a compelling reason to avoid a Dutch book, and thus ensure that your probability estimates obey the laws of probability.

Are coherence criteria sufficient?

The demonstration that coherent beliefs must obey the laws of probability confirms the normative status of these laws, and serves as a basic premise in rational theories of decision making (e.g., Jeffrey, 1965; Savage, 1954). However, by itself the prescription to maintain a coherent set of probability judgments appears quite a weak constraint. So long as your judgments are coherent it seems that you can entertain any idiosyncratic probability assignment. For example, you can judge that the chance of intelligent life on Mars is .9, so long as you also judge that the chance of no intelligent life on Mars is .1.

This problem is typically dealt with in one of two ways, depending on one's theoretical persuasion. Some see it as a fundamental shortcoming of the coherentist approach, and argue that correspondence criteria are the appropriate means for appraising probability judgments (e.g., Gigerenzer, 2002). Others argue that the coherence constraint is sufficient, once we acknowledge the role played by Bayes' rule (see the section on Bayesian updating below) as a normative model of belief revision (for further discussion see Baron, 2000). A more moderate position, and the one that will be adopted in this chapter, is that these criteria are complementary rather than exclusive. The constraint of coherence serves to maintain the internal consistency of our probability judgments, whereas the requirement of correspondence (when available) serves to calibrate these judgments to the external world.

Correspondence criteria for probability judgments

Rather than concentrate on the internal coherence within a set of probability judgments, correspondence theories assess the fit between these judgments and some aspect or property of the external world. Thus frequentist theorists maintain that our judgments concern, and are assessable against, appropriate relative frequencies of events or instances. For example, responses to the question of whether a person is more likely to die through murder or suicide are assessed in the light of the actual death rates. On the face of it the claim that our probability judgments should correspond to the appropriate relative frequencies seems uncontroversial. However, under closer scrutiny the position is less clear. For one, how do we determine which is the appropriate relative frequency? In many real-world situations there are several different reference classes that may be relevant. For example, consider the task of estimating the probability that a particular individual X will die before 65. What is the relevant reference class here? People in general? What if X is a non-smoking female? Now the appropriate class is narrowed to deaths before 65 among female non-smokers. But successively refining the reference class seems to lead to a class made up of just the individual in question. Frequentists can sidestep this problem however. They can claim that in many cases there is a privileged level at which the reference class should be set, and that the context of the problem will make this clear. Thus when assessing a judgment about the probable death of an individual we use the reference class of people irrespective of gender. Presumably we also restrict ourselves to current death rates, and those in the geographical area for which the question is asked, and so on. This line of response reiterates the frequentist claim that there is no such thing as *the* probability of an event, but a range of probabilities (relative frequencies) depending on the chosen reference class.

A more pernicious problem for a strict frequentist is that in many situations there seems to be no appropriate reference class on which to base a probability judgment. For example, consider the sudden introduction of a congestion charge for vehicles entering central London. This was an event with no precedent, and yet everyone voiced an opinion as to its likely success. Indeed many commentators made quite specific predictions about the high chances of traffic chaos just outside the charge zone, the overcrowding of the public transport system, and so on. These predictions were certainly meaningful and open to assessment (indeed most proved incorrect), and yet it is difficult to generate one privileged reference class against which to assess such judgments. Similar examples surely pervade much of our everyday life – we are frequently faced with novel problem situations where we cannot appeal to a specific reference class, and yet are able to make probability judgments that are open to appraisal nonetheless. (This is not to argue that coherence criteria give us much guidance here – what will be argued later on is that other forms of appraisal become appropriate in such cases.)

Regardless of these problems, the laws of probability apply to relative frequencies as well as they apply to coherent degrees of belief. As long as your judgments are well calibrated to the appropriate relative frequencies, they will obey the laws of probability. For example, if you base your estimate of the probability that a man has a heart attack on the frequency of heart attacks in the male population, f(H), and your estimate of the probability that a man has a heart attack and is over 55 on the corresponding frequency in the same population, f(H & O), your are bound to obey the conjunction rule because f(H) ≥ f(H & O).

We have seen that probability judgments encompass at least two distinct forms of appraisal, coherence and correspondence, and that both can validly employ the axioms of probability as a normative model. One of the most useful theorems that can be derived from the axioms of probability is Bayes' rule.

Bayesian model of probability updating

Bayes' rule is a theorem derivable from the probability axioms, and is taken to provide a normative rule for updating one's probability judgments in the light of new evidence. Informally, Bayes' rule tells us how much to adjust our prior belief in a hypothesis on the basis of a new piece of evidence. To do this we must consider how likely the evidence would be if the hypothesis in question was true (and we didn't already know about the new evidence). This factor tells us how much to adjust our prior belief (our probability judgment before the new piece of evidence is known) to yield our posterior belief (our probability judgment after the new piece of evidence is known).

To illustrate the basic idea, imagine that you are a modern-day Robinson Crusoe, stranded on an isolated tropical island. You want to know whether there are any other inhabitants on the island. You have a prior degree of belief about this based on your background information (the location of the island, the absence of any buildings, etc.). Let's assume that you think it's pretty unlikely. As you walk along the beach you encounter a set of footprints (not your own). How much should this new piece of evidence alter your prior beliefs? Bayes' rule tells you to consider (1) how likely the footprints are if there are in fact other inhabitants, and (2) how likely the footprints are if there are in fact no other inhabitants. You then combine these two judgments with your prior belief to yield your posterior belief (see details below). In this case the appearance of footprints is very likely under the assumption that there are other inhabitants (and very unlikely under the assumption that there are no other inhabitants). Therefore you should adjust your prior belief upwards – the appearance of footprints greatly increases the chances of there being other inhabitants (how else could they have got there?).

More formally, for a set of mutually exclusive and exhaustive hypotheses $(H_1, H_2, \ldots, H_n)$, and an item of evidence E, Bayes' rule relates the *prior* probability of H_j (in the absence of any knowledge about E) to the posterior probability of H_j given that E is true:

$$P(H_j|E) = P(E|H_j) . P(H_j)/ \Sigma P(E|H_i) . P(H_i) \tag{5.1}$$

The focal idea is that once you learn E, your new estimate for the probability of H_j should be proportional to the product of your prior estimate for H_j and the probability of E if H_j is assumed true (known as the *likelihood*). The summation in the denominator of equation 5.1 serves to normalize this relative to all the other competing hypotheses. Intuitively, Bayes' rule tells us to compute $P(H_j|E)$ by considering all the different ways in which E can occur; that is, as a result of any one of the exclusive hypotheses $H_1 \ldots H_n$. For each of these hypotheses there is a particular prior probability that it is true, and a particular likelihood that if it is true, E will also be true.

We now present a more quantitative (and realistic) example. Imagine that you have a routine health check-up, and are tested for a rare disease. Suppose that the incidence of this disease among people with your profile (e.g., gender, age, race, etc.) is 1/1000. In the absence of any additional information this is the best estimate for the prior probability that you have the disease (note that this is a correspondence measure). The test for this disease (like most tests) is not perfect. In particular, the likelihood that you test positive, given that you have the disease, is 99 per cent. This is known as the sensitivity of the test. Not only does the test occasionally fail to detect the presence of the disease, however, sometimes it yields a positive result when the disease is not present. This is known as the false positive rate, and corresponds to the likelihood of a positive test given that the disease is not present. Suppose for this particular disease this likelihood is 5 per cent.

Now imagine that your test turns out to be positive. What is the probability that you have the disease? To calculate this posterior probability we can use Bayes' rule. Let H = you have the disease, ¬H = you do not have the disease, E = test is positive. From the figures given above we have: $P(E|H) = .99$, $P(E|\neg H) = .05$, $P(H) = .001$, $P(\neg H) = .999$. Because H and ¬H are exclusive and exhaustive, we can reformulate equation (5.1) as:

$$P(H|E) = P(E|H).P(H)/ [P(E|H).P(H) + P(E|\neg H).P(\neg H)] \tag{5.2}$$

Thus:

$$P(H|E) = .99 \times .001 / ((.99 \times .001) + (.05 \times .999)) = .019$$

So the positive test result has raised the probability that you have the disease from .001 to .019. Although this is a huge increase, the probability that you have the disease is still relatively low (1.9 per cent). As we shall see in the next chapter, many people find this kind of Bayesian reasoning difficult.

In short, if you have prior beliefs about a set of exclusive and exhaustive hypotheses (possibly just one hypothesis and its complement), and then encounter a new piece of evidence, Bayes' rule tells you how to update these beliefs given that you know, or can estimate, the likelihood that each of these hypotheses, if true, would have generated the evidence.

One reason why Bayes' rule has considerable practical application is that the likelihood of new data, given a specific hypothesis, is often an accessible and stable factor in an inference problem. This is because it is frequently determined by a stable causal mechanism – for example, the propensity that a disease causes certain symptoms; that a specific personality type leads to certain behaviours; that a particular DNA sequence appears in a specific population, and so on.

Note that by itself Bayes' rule only tells us how to pass from prior probability estimates to posterior estimates; it does not tell us how to set our priors in the first place. This fits with the idea that the laws of probability provide consistency relations between our beliefs – they tell us that if we hold certain probability judgments, then we ought, on pain of inconsistency, to hold certain others. It also fits with the claim that our probability estimates, in particular our priors, are sometimes appraisable in the light of their correspondence to features of the external environment, namely, observable frequencies.

Updating beliefs with uncertain evidence

In its canonical version Bayes' rule tells us how to update our probabilities when we find out something for *certain*, such as the result of a medical test. However, there will be occasions where we want to update our beliefs on the basis of *uncertain* evidence. This uncertainty may arise because we receive degraded or ambiguous evidence, or perhaps because the source of the evidence is itself open to question. For example, imagine you are a juror in a murder case. The key witness states that she saw the suspect running from the crime scene. There are two main sources of uncertainty here: the probability that the witness is reliable (she may be lying, or short-sighted, or trying to please the judge), and the probability that the suspect committed the crime, given that he was running away from the crime scene (perhaps he was an innocent bystander who came across the body and panicked). How should we reach an assessment of guilt based on the witness's testimony?

One formal approach in such cases is given by Jeffrey's rule (1965):

$$P(H|U) = P(H|E).P(E|U) + P(H|\neg E).P(\neg E|U)$$

In this equation uncertain evidence is denoted by U. It leads us to update our belief in the probability of E (and ¬E), and hence update our belief in the probability of H (given U). (It should be noted that Jeffrey's rule only holds given certain assumptions about the network structure of the related events. See Pearl, 1988, for details.)

To apply this rule to our crime example let us denote the witness statement 'Suspect was running from crime scene' by E*, the putative fact that the suspect was running from the crime scene by E, and the hypothesis that the suspect committed the crime by H.

The juror needs to compute the probability of H given E* – that is, the probability that the suspect did it, given the witness testimony. Suppose that the juror thinks the witness is reliable (e.g., unlikely to be biased, lying or shortsighted), and assigns $P(E|E^*) = .9$ and $P(\neg E|E^*) = .1$. In other words, the probability that the suspect was running from the crime scene, given that the witness said he was, is estimated at .9. From this it should follow (by axioms of probability) that the probability that he was not running away, given that the witness said he was, is .1 (i.e., $P(E|E^*) = 1 - P(\neg E|E^*)$).

The juror also needs to estimate $P(H|E)$ (the probability that the suspect did it, given that he was running from the crime scene) and $P(H|\neg E)$ (the probability that the suspect did it, given that he was *not* running from the crime scene). To keep things simple, let us assume that the juror can provide direct estimates of $P(H|E)$ and $P(H|\neg E)$. Suppose the juror estimates $P(H|E)$ as .7 (i.e., given that the suspect was running from the crime scene, it's likely he was guilty), and $P(H|\neg E)$ as .2 (i.e., given that he was not running from the crime scene, it's unlikely he was guilty). Plugging these figures into Jeffrey's rule we can work out the impact of the witness testimony on the belief in guilt:

$$P(H|E^*) = P(H|E).P(E|E^*) + P(H|\neg E).P(\neg E|E^*)$$

$$P(H|E^*) = (.7 \times .9) + (.2 \times .1) = .63 + .02 = .65$$

This final value makes sense given the juror's other estimates. The juror thought it likely (= .7) that the suspect was guilty if he was running from the crime scene, and the juror's slight uncertainty about the witness testimony has not reduced that estimate too much. There may be situations, however, in which uncertainty about the initial evidence is much higher, in which case one's estimates will be significantly reduced. We consider an example like this in chapter 7.

Despite the apparent obscurity of Jeffrey's rule, people are frequently engaged in making probabilistic inferences on the basis of uncertain information (e.g., doctors, lawyers, jurors, fortune tellers). It is unclear, however, whether people intuitively make computations in conformity with this rule. This is explored in subsequent sections in the next two chapters.

Although based on different conceptions of how to appraise judgments, both coherence and correspondence theories advocate that people's judgments ought to conform to the laws of probability. In the next chapter we present strong empirical evidence that people violate these laws.

Summary

This chapter introduces two ways of appraising probability judgments: coherence and correspondence. Coherence theories focus on structural relations between judgments or beliefs, and therefore rely on formal models of appraisal such as logic or probability theory. Correspondence theories focus on the fit between judgments and the external environment. They tend to rely on the predictive accuracy of judgments, or their correspondence to properties in the environment. The majority of research into judgmental biases has focused on coherence criteria. The chapter then explains the use of one particular benchmark against which judgments can be compared: Bayes' rule. This rule provides us with a normative model of belief updating. The final section of the chapter extends the use of Bayes' rule to cases with uncertain evidence (using Jeffrey's rule).

Now that you understand some of the formal rules for how people *should* update their beliefs and make judgments, it is time, in the next chapter, to examine how people *actually* make judgments under uncertainty.

6 Judgmental heuristics and biases

How do people actually make probability judgments? How do they process the information available to them to reach a singular estimate of what is likely to happen? The dominant approach to this question is provided by Kahneman and Tversky in their 'Heuristics and Biases' programme (e.g., Kahneman et al., 1982). They claim that rather than reason on the basis of the formal rules of probability, people often use simplifying or shortcut heuristics to reach a probability judgment. Moreover, while these heuristics are well adapted to specific information processing tasks, they can lead to systematic biases when used in inappropriate contexts.

Attribute substitution and natural assessments

At the heart of the heuristics and biases approach are the twin notions of attribute substitution and natural assessment (Kahneman & Frederick, 2002). The idea behind attribute substitution is very simple: when faced with a hard question about a particular quantity or attribute, people have a tendency to answer a different but easier question. Thus a difficult question about a target attribute (e.g., how probable is X?) is responded to by substitution of a more readily accessible heuristic attribute (e.g., how easily do instances of X come to mind?). What determines the accessibility of this heuristic attribute? Two factors – that it be related in some way to the target attribute, and that it be a natural assessment; that is, a relatively automatic and routinely used cognitive procedure.

In earlier expositions (Tversky & Kahneman, 1983) natural assessments were broadly characterized in terms of representativeness (the degree to which one thing resembles another) or availability (the ease with which examples come to mind). More recently, they have been couched in terms of more specific properties such as similarity, fluency (Jacoby & Dallas, 1981), causal propensity (Kahneman & Varey, 1990), and affective valence (Kahneman, Ritov, & Schkade, 1999).

The basic idea remains constant – the requirement to make a target judgment about an attribute activates other related attributes, and if the target attribute is unavailable, or is less accessible than a contending attribute, the agent is likely to respond with the substitute value. There is a wealth of empirical evidence in support of these claims (see the collection by Gilovich et al., 2002). This evidence is garnered through two main routes (often combined in the same experiment). First, and most dramatic, the demonstration of systematic biases, in particular the violation of basic laws of probability. Second, and more subtle, the demonstration that probability judgments correlate highly with the heuristic judgments that are alleged to replace them.

Errors of coherence

Judgmental heuristics can lead to errors of both coherence and correspondence. We start by reviewing some of the main violations of coherence.

Base rate neglect

Students and staff at Harvard Medical School were presented with the following problem (Casscells, Schoenberger, & Grayboys, 1978):

> If a test to detect a disease whose prevalence is 1/1000 has a false positive rate of 5 per cent, what is the chance that a person found to have a positive result actually has the disease, assuming you know nothing about the person's symptoms or signs?

As stated the problem was incomplete, because it did not mention the sensitivity of the test (the probability of a positive result given that the person has the disease). However, assuming this is very high (as is the case with most tests of this nature), the correct answer to this problem is around 2 per cent.

The striking finding in this experiment was that only 18 per cent of the participants (including staff) got the answer correct. The modal response was 95 per cent. How could medically educated people have got this so wrong?

One obvious explanation for the modal response of 95 per cent is that people assume that if the test is wrong 5 per cent of the time then it must be right 95 per cent of the time. This line of thought is appealing, but it is too simplistic. A false positive rate of 5 per cent does indeed imply a true positive rate of 95 per cent, but this latter rate corresponds to the probability that the test is positive given that the person has the disease, P(positive test|disease). But what we really want to know is the probability that the person has the disease given that they test positive, P(disease|positive test), and Bayes' rule tells us that to compute this we must take into account the prior probability of the disease (i.e., the base rate prevalence of the disease).

Why do respondents neglect the base rate information? A broad level explanation can be given in terms of attribute substitution (Kahneman & Frederick, 2002). People are faced with a difficult probability problem – they are asked for the probability of a disease given a positive test result, and this requires a relatively complex Bayesian computation. However, there is a closely related (but incorrect) answer that is readily accessible. This is the probability of the positive test given the disease, which is easily computed from the false positive value. Most respondents make do with this answer. Indeed this is an example of a more general bias known in psychology as the inverse fallacy (Dawes, 2001; Villejoubert & Mandel, 2002), or in legal cases as the 'prosecutor's fallacy' (see chapter 1 and Dawid, 2002).

Alert readers will notice that this diagnosis problem is very similar to the one solved in the last chapter using Bayes' rule. The false positive rate corresponds to the probability that the test is positive, given that the person does not have the disease, $P(E|\neg H)$. The sensitivity of the test is not mentioned in the problem, but it is instructive to compute the correct answers given a few different possible values (e.g., 100 per cent, 99 per cent, 95 per cent). The important point is that whatever the precise value for the sensitivity, the correct answer to the problem is very low (i.e., 2 per cent) rather than very high (i.e., 95 per cent).

As mentioned previously, the report of a positive test raises the probability of having the disease from 0.01 per cent to 2 per cent, which is a very significant rise. However, the final estimate is still relatively low. There is a chance that the test result is flawed, and this is in fact higher than the initial chance that the person has the disease. Bayes' rule tells us the normatively correct way to combine these two sources of uncertainty. People, however, seem to focus just on the positive test evidence, and ignore the prior information.

Base rate neglect has been demonstrated on innumerable occasions, and using different stimuli (Kahneman & Tversky, 1982b; Koehler, 1996; Villejoubert & Mandel, 2002). There have also been various experiments showing the conditions under which it can be alleviated (Cosmides & Tooby, 1996; Gigerenzer & Hoffrage, 1995; Girotto & Gonzalez, 2001; Sloman, Over, Slovak, & Stibel, 2003), and heated arguments as to its true reach (Gigerenzer, 1996: Kahneman & Tversky, 1996; Koehler, 1996). Some of these issues are discussed below.

Irrespective of these debates, one robust conclusion is that people do not automatically engage in full Bayesian reasoning when solving such problems. They tend to adopt shortcut solutions, and these can lead them to give erroneous answers. But the news is not all bad. These errors tell us something about the reasoning mechanisms people do in fact use. And, as we shall see, their reasoning can be improved when information is presented in an appropriate format.

However, the exact reason for why so many people ignore base rates in these problems is still the subject of controversy (perhaps there is no single reason, but a complex interaction of factors). In the next chapter we explore cases of base rate neglect in experienced rather than described settings, and advance an alternative explanation for it in terms of associative learning mechanisms.

The conjunction fallacy

One of the most basic rules of probability is the conjunction rule – that a conjunction cannot be more probable than either of its conjuncts. We met this rule in the previous chapter when we showed that it is incoherent to judge the probability of the statement 'A man suffers a heart attack' as less probable than the conjunctive statement 'A man suffers a heart attack and is over 55 years old'. We also noted that in experimental tests the majority of participants violated this rule. These 'conjunction fallacies' have been demonstrated with a wide range of different materials. The most famous example, now part of the psychology folklore, is the Linda problem. Suppose you are given the following personality sketch:

> Linda is 31 years old, single, outspoken and very bright. She majored in philosophy. As a student, she was deeply concerned with issues of discrimination and social justice, and also participated in anti-nuclear demonstrations.

Which of these statements is more probable?

(1) Linda is a bank teller.
(2) Linda is a bank teller and active in the feminist movement.

The majority response across a range of variations (e.g., embedding the statements in a longer list; asking for probability ratings for each statement rather than ranking) is to judge (2) as more probable than (1), in violation of the conjunction rule. Tversky and Kahneman (1983) accounted for this and various other examples of the conjunction fallacy in terms of the representativeness heuristic. The description of Linda is highly representative of an active feminist (F) and unrepresentative of a bank teller (B); the degree to which the description is representative of the conjunction (B & F) therefore lies somewhere in between these two extremes. This was the predominant ordering given by participants, for those asked to rank by probability and those ranking by representativeness.

In short, the close correlation between judgments of representativeness and judgments of probability, coupled with the violation of the conjunction rule for the latter, support the claim that people are making their probability judgments on the basis of representativeness rather than a formal probability model (another example of attribute substitution). This basic finding has been replicated on many occasions and with more refined 'similarity-based' models of the representativeness heuristic (Kahneman & Frederick, 2002).

As befits a famous example, there have been numerous objections to the Linda problem, with respect to both its interpretation and its methodology. One of the main challenges is mounted by frequentists such as Gigerenzer, who claim that when the conjunction problem is asked in terms of probabilities it does not have a unique normative answer. This is because the term 'probability' is polysemous – it encompasses multiple meanings – and not all of these possible meanings are bound by the laws of probability. For example, 'probability' can be interpreted non-mathematically, as referring to notions such as plausibility, credibility or typicality.

So when people give probability judgments that violate the laws of probability, they may be interpreting 'probability' in one of these non-mathematical senses. In that case, Gigerenzer and colleagues argue, they are not guilty of judgmental error. Moreover, when the mathematical reading of the term is clarified, by asking for a frequency judgment, people give judgments that conform better to the norms of probability.

We discuss the general frequentist argument in detail below. Here we focus on the argument that people interpret probability in a non-mathematical sense. The short answer is 'too bad for them'. The normativity of the conjunction rule holds regardless. People who violate it are being inconsistent, and lay themselves open to certain loss irrespective of how things turn out. And this is not just a remote possibility. In a recent set of studies using realistic conjunction problems (Sides, Osherson, Bonini, & Viale, 2002), people made sub-optimal monetary bets that violated the conjunction rule. Furthermore, the problems intentionally avoided the use of any terms such as 'probability', so people were not misled by semantic ambiguities.

The long answer is to agree that the notion of probability allows several possible interpretations (this is generally accepted in philosophical circles), and accept that people may be using a different sense to answer the conjunction problem. But this is just the first step. What is needed is a fuller account of what this concept may be, and why people systematically use it in such problems.

Are conjunction errors due to evidential support?

One of the most puzzling aspects of the conjunction error is how compelling it is, even to the initiated. Stephen Gould (1992, p. 469) expresses this succinctly:

> I know that the third statement [bank teller & feminist] is least probable, yet a little homunculus in my head continues to jump up and down, shouting at me – 'but she can't just be a bank teller; read the description'.

Is the mind really designed to make such a simple error? One way to avoid this damning conclusion is to argue that people are in fact answering a different question to that posed by the experimenter. This is not to rule out the laws of probability as the correct norms (as suggested by Gigerenzer, 2002), but to propose that people are giving answers that conform to a different set of norms. People have the right answer to the wrong question.

What might this 'wrong' question be? An obvious candidate is the degree to which the evidence (e.g., Linda's profile) *supports* the conclusion (e.g., Linda is a feminist bank teller). The notion of evidential support (or confirmation) is well established in statistics and probability theory. Informally, it corresponds to the degree to which a piece of evidence changes the probability of a hypothesis. Thus evidence E is positive support for hypothesis H if it increases the probability of the hypothesis, $P(H|E) > P(H)$, and it is negative support if it decreases the probability of the hypothesis, $P(H|E) < P(H)$. There are several different proposals for how degree of support is quantified and measured (see Fitelson, 1999; Tentori, Crupi, Bonini, & Osherson, 2007), but this does not matter for the current argument. The crucial thing about degrees of evidential support is that they need not conform to the axioms of probability. In particular, the degree of support that evidence E gives to hypothesis H_1 can be greater than the degree of support it gives to hypothesis H_2, even if H_1 is a subset of H_2 (and thus $P(H_1) < P(H_2)$).

This line of reasoning can be applied directly to the Linda problem (Lagnado & Shanks, 2002; see also Crupi, Fitelson, & Tentori, 2006). In this problem the evidence E is the short descriptive profile of Linda. There are three hypotheses: B = Linda is a bank teller; F = Linda is a feminist; B & F = Linda is a feminist bank teller. As shown above, according to the axioms of probability the probability that Linda is a feminist bank teller is less than the probability she is a bank teller, $P(B \& F) < P(B)$, because feminist bank tellers are a subset of bank tellers. However, the degree of support that the profile E gives to her being a feminist bank teller (B & F) can be greater than the degree of support it gives to her being a bank teller (B). This is because her profile raises the probability that she is a feminist bank teller ($P(B \& H|E) > P(B \& H)$), but it lowers the probability that she is a bank teller ($P(B|E) < P(B)$).

A crucial point to note is that even though the profile E raises the probability of Linda being a feminist bank teller, it can never raise it above the probability of Linda being a bank teller. However, if people are answering the original probability question with a judgment about support, they may fail to notice this, and thus violate the probability axioms. And the set-up of the problem encourages this kind of misreading. After all, it presents a strong piece of evidence (Linda's profile), and asks people to make a judgment on the basis of this profile. It is thus not surprising that many people respond by stating the degree to which that evidence supports the hypotheses in question, and therefore judge 'feminist bank teller' as more probable than 'bank teller'. They have given a sensible answer to the question, but unfortunately it is the wrong question.

This explanation of the conjunction error is not ad hoc – there is evidence from a range of studies suggesting that people are sensitive to relations of support (Briggs & Krantz, 1992; Tversky & Koehler, 1994; White & Koehler, 2006; see also the next section of this chapter). This account also fits well with the overarching framework of attribute substitution (Kahneman &

Frederick, 2002). People are asked a question about probability, but readily substitute this with a closely related question about degree of support. Both the context of the question, and the accessibility of the substitute judgment, conspire to elicit this incorrect response.

The disjunction problem

Bar-Hillel and Neter (1993) presented students with the following kind of question:

> Danielle is sensitive and introspective. In high school she wrote poetry secretly . . . Though beautiful, she has little social life, since she prefers to spend her time reading quietly at home rather than partying. What does she study?

Participants then ranked a list of subject categories according to one of several criteria: probability, predictability, suitability or willingness to bet. The lists included nested subordinate–superordinate pairs (e.g., in the case of Danielle both 'Literature' and 'Humanities') specifically designed so that the character profile fitted the subordinate category better than the superordinate.

There were two main findings. First, people consistently ranked the subordinate category as more probable than the superordinate, in violation of the extension law of probability (whereby a subordinate category cannot be more probable than a superordinate category that contains it). Bar-Hillel and Neter termed this a disjunction fallacy, because the superordinate category (e.g., Humanities) is a disjunction of subordinate categories (e.g., Literature, Art, etc.). Second, probability rankings were almost perfectly correlated with suitability, predictability and willingness-to-bet rankings (and in a subsequent experiment with actual betting behaviour). This suggests that participants in the different judgment conditions used the same underlying process to reach their estimates.

This study appears to show again that intuitive judgments of probability do not respect the laws of probability. After all, the probability of a subset (Danielle studies English literature) cannot be greater than the probability of its superset (Danielle studies one of the Humanities). What implications we draw from this depends on whether the people making the judgment are aware of the relevant subset relation. If they are unaware that English litera-ture is included as one of the Humanities, then they are not necessarily guilty of a violation of the disjunction rule. Perhaps they think the category of Humanities excludes the category of English literature (it does in the subject listings for certain British universities). Indeed the very fact that they have been asked both questions may encourage them to think English literature is not one of the Humanities. So it is possible that although the participants in the experiments violate the laws of probability according to the category structure assumed by the experimenters, they do not violate them according to their own category structures.

A clearer demonstration of a disjunction fallacy would require that people are aware of the relevant subset relations, and yet still persist in judging a subset as more probable than its superset. A set of experiments by Lagnado and Shanks (2002) comes closer to this, and is reported in the next chapter.

Support theory

In addition to identifying various heuristics that people use to reach probability judgments, Tversky and colleagues advanced a more general framework for understanding subjective probability judgments: support theory (Rottenstreich & Tversky, 1997; Tversky & Koehler, 1994). Support theory hinges on three central ideas: subjective judgments of probability are description-dependent, they derive from judgments of support, and they lead to subadditivity (see Brenner, Koehler, & Rottenstreich, 2002).

Description-dependence

Whereas standard theories of probability assign probabilities to events, support theory assigns probabilities to *descriptions* of events (termed hypotheses). This is motivated by the fact that people's intuitive probability judgments are sensitive to the way in which the events in question are described. Indeed, alternative descriptions of the same event can lead to very different probability estimates. For example, people's estimates of the probability that someone dies from *homicide* tend to be lower than their estimates of the probability that someone dies from *homicide by an acquaintance or stranger*, even though both refer to the same event (Rottenstreich & Tversky, 1997).

More generally, the idea is that people attach probabilities to representations of events, rather than to the events themselves. This means that probability assignments are not description-invariant (as would be expected on a normative theory), and hence can change according to the representation that is provided or invoked (see also chapter 9).

Support

How are subjective probabilities assigned to these hypotheses? According to support theory these assignments are derived from judgments of the strength of evidence (support, s) in favour of the hypotheses in question. In particular, the judged probability of hypothesis A is derived from the judged support for A relative to the judged support for alternative hypotheses. Thus the probability of A rather than B (where A and B are competing hypotheses) is computed via the formula:

$$P(A,B) = s(A) / (s(A) + s(B))$$

Subadditivity

One of the central claims of support theory is that the probability assigned to an hypothesis will typically increase if it is unpacked into a disjunction of components. This is supposed to occur both when the unpacking is implicit and when it is explicit. In the implicit case, the judged support for one hypothesis (A) is assumed to be less than (or equal to) the judged support for a disjunction formed by unpacking A into exclusive subcomponents (e.g., A_1 or A_2). Thus death through 'homicide' is judged to receive less support than death through 'homicide by an acquaintance or stranger'. More formally: $s(A) \leq s(A_1 \text{ or } A_2)$.

In the explicit case, the judged support for an unpacked hypothesis is assumed to be less than (or equal to) the sum of the supports for each of the subcomponents. That is, $s(A) \leq s(A_1) + (A_2)$. In this case death through 'homicide' is judged to receive less support than the sum of the separate supports given to 'homicide by an acquaintance' and 'homicide by a stranger'. Moreover, the latter sum is assumed to be greater than (or equal to) the support assigned to the implicit disjunction (A_1 or A_2).

This overall pattern is summarized in the equation:

$$s(A) \leq s(A_1 \text{ or } A_2) \leq s(A_1) + (A_2)$$

In short, the sum of two separate support assignments is assumed to be greater than the single support assigned to a disjunction (*explicit subadditivity*), which in turn is greater than the support assigned to the unpacked hypothesis (*implicit subadditivity*). These patterns are termed 'subadditive' (somewhat counter-intuitively), because the composite hypotheses are assigned less support, and hence less probability, than the sum of their parts.

Evidence for and against support theory

There is a wealth of empirical evidence for explicit subadditivity across a variety of domains (e.g., with medical doctors, Redelmeier, Koehler, Liberman, & Tversky, 1995; options traders, Fox, Rogers & Tversky, 1996; sports experts, Fox, 1999). The evidence for implicit subadditivity is more mixed (Fox & Tversky, 1998). Moreover, some recent studies have shown an opposite pattern of superadditivity (Sloman, Rottenstreich, Wisniewski, Hadjichristidis, & Fox, 2004).

Indeed Sloman and colleagues demonstrated that the question of whether an unpacked hypothesis garnered more or less support than its subcomponents depended on the typicality of these components. When the unpacked components were typical of the target hypothesis (e.g., the hypothesis 'disease' was unpacked into the most common subtypes such as heart disease, cancer, etc.) then judgments were additive (not subadditive). And when the unpacked components were atypical (e.g., 'disease' was unpacked into uncommon subtypes such as pneumonia, diabetes, etc.) then judgments were superadditive (i.e., the judged support for the disjunction was less than the judged support for the composite hypothesis).

These findings are difficult to reconcile with support theory's assumption that unpacking leads to greater probability judgments. However, they do not undermine the claim that subjective probabilities attach to descriptions not events, or the claim that they involve relations of evidential support. An important project for future research is to explore the psychological models that underlie judgments of evidential support. Our hunch is that they will be closely related to the mechanisms that allow us to learn about these relations (see chapter 11).

Errors of correspondence

In addition to assessing probability judgments by how well they fit together (coherence), they can also be assessed by how well they fit with features in the external environment (correspondence). How good are people's probability judgments when evaluated in terms of correspondence? There are two main ways of getting at this question.

First, one can compare people's judgments with the actual frequencies of events in the world. The results of such research are mixed. One early and influential set of studies looked at people's judgements about the frequencies of lethal events (Lichtenstein, Slovic, Fischhoff, Layman, & Coombs, 1978). In one study people judged the frequency of various causes of death (e.g., heart disease, homicide, diabetes, tornado); in another they rated which of two causes of death were more frequent (e.g., the comparison between homicide and suicide used at the beginning of chapter 5). These studies found that overall people's judgments corresponded moderately well with the actual frequencies (on average people could distinguish between the most frequent and least frequent causes of death). However, there were some notable and systematic deviations from the actual frequencies. There was a general tendency to overestimate rare causes of death (e.g., botulism, tornadoes) and underestimate common causes (e.g., heart disease, diabetes). In addition there was a more specific tendency to overestimate causes that were dramatic or sensational (see the discussion of availability below).

In contrast, there is also a rich stream of research that supports the opposite conclusion – that people's judgments of frequency correspond very well to the actual frequencies (for a review, see Sedlmeier & Betsch, 2002). Most of this research is conducted using trial-based paradigms, in which people are exposed to natural frequencies over the course of an experiment. One of the key claims is that people encode relative frequencies in an accurate and relatively effortless manner (Hasher & Zacks, 1979, 1984). This claim is tied in with specific theories about the cognitive mechanisms that people use to encode frequencies (Dougherty, Gettys, & Ogden, 1999; Hintzman, 1988). These kinds of learning models are explored in chapter 11.

It should be noted, however, that even if someone encodes relative frequencies accurately, this does not guarantee they will output a correspondent probability judgment. Lagnado and Shanks (2002) showed that people's relative frequency judgments corresponded more closely to the experienced frequencies than their probability judgments did. Indeed probability judgments were much more susceptible to systematic biases than frequency judgments were.

One way to reconcile the diverse findings is to argue that people are accurate encoders of frequency information, but they are sometimes exposed to biased samples (e.g., media coverage of dramatic deaths), or use biased search strategies (e.g., seeking information that favours one conclusion). Another is to accept that people sometimes encode probabilistic information in a biased fashion, and that this can depend on both the learning context and the mechanisms of learning (this alternative is elaborated on in chapters 7 and 11).

Another correspondence-based method for evaluating probability judgments is in terms of calibration (Brier, 1950; Lichtenstein, Fischhoff, & Phillips, 1982; Murphy & Winkler, 1977; Yates, 1990). Calibration applies to a series of single-case probability judgments. A person is well calibrated if, for each set of events to which they assign a specific probability p, the relative frequency of that event is equal to p. For example, imagine you are a weather forecaster. Each day you make a forecast about the probability of rain. Consider those days on which you assign a probability of .7 to rain. If the actual proportion of rainy days is 70 per cent, then you are perfectly calibrated. Note that although such measures of calibration depend on there being repeatable events and judgments, the judgments themselves are single-case probabilities (i.e., what is the probability of rain today?).

The appraisal of probability judgments via calibration was developed to assess weather forecasters (Murphy & Winkler, 1974, 1977). A striking finding from this research is that expert weather forecasters are almost perfectly calibrated (at least in Midwest America). On those occasions when they state that there is a 75 per cent chance of rain, rain indeed occurs 75 per cent of the time. And this holds through the range of probability values. Indeed there are several bodies of evidence showing that experts in specific domains tend to be well calibrated, including bridge players (Keren, 1987), air traffic controllers (Nunes & Kirlik, 2005) and economists (Dowie, 1976). This contrasts with the calibration performances of novices, which often exhibit overestimation (Brenner, Griffin, & Koehler, 2005; Lichtenstein & Fischhoff, 1977). Perhaps this is not too surprising. Becoming an expert requires learning about the probabilistic structure of one's domain, and also knowing how to make judgments that reflect this uncertain structure.

One important extension of the notion of calibration is to the study of confidence judgments. Here, rather than making probability judgments about events in the external world (such as rainfall or aeroplane collisions), people make judgments about the accuracy of their own judgments. The main research question is whether people are well calibrated when they express their subjective confidence in categorical judgments that can be either true or false. These experiments often involve laypeople's answers to general knowledge questions (but have also been extended to more real-world situations such as medical and financial forecasting). We will not explore the large literature on this subject (for reviews see Griffin & Brenner, 2004; Harvey, 1997; Juslin, Winman, & Olsson, 2000; Lichtenstein et al., 1982), but just note a few of the salient findings.

Overall people exhibit overconfidence in their responses, but this is modulated by contextual factors such as the difficulty of the test items, the nature of the response scale, the race and gender of the participants, and so on. There have been a variety of explanations offered for these effects, but no single comprehensive theory that does justice to all the empirical data.

A partial explanation for the overconfidence effect is given by Juslin and colleagues (Juslin et al., 2000; see also Gigerenzer et al., 1991). They argue that many of the experimental tests of confidence in general knowledge have a disproportionately large number of misleading or difficult questions. So although people might be well calibrated with respect to their normal performance on general knowledge questions, this can lead to overconfidence when the tests are artificially constructed by the experimenter to be difficult. Thus the crucial fault is not with their calibration per se, but with their inability to recalibrate according to the difficulty of the items. The explanation is only partial because some overconfidence remains even when task difficulty is controlled for (Klayman, Soll, Juslin, & Winman, 2006).

Nevertheless, this focus on the environment that an individual samples from (and the possible biases introduced by non-representative samples) coheres with one central theme in this book – that we need to look at the learning environment to properly understand the judgments people make.

Availability

In the introduction to chapter 5 we asked which was more likely, death by homicide or death by suicide. We noted that people often judged homicide more probable than suicide, despite the fact that the latter is more prevalent (see also the sharks versus aeroplane parts example in the opening paragraphs of the book). Why do people make such estimation errors? Answers to this question often appeal to the *availability heuristic*.

Tversky and Kahneman (1973) introduced availability as a heuristic method for estimating frequencies or probabilities. People use the availability heuristic whenever they base their estimates on the ease with which instances or occurrences come to mind. Despite the simplicity of its formulation, the heuristic covers a range of cases. For one, it applies both to the recall of previous occurrences (e.g., how often you remember team X beating team Y) and to the generation of possible occurrences (e.g., how many ways you can imagine a novel plan going wrong). Second, it need not involve *actual* recall or generation, but only an assessment of the ease with which these operations *could* be performed.

Availability is an ecologically valid cue to frequency estimates because in general frequent events are easier to recall than infrequent ones. However, the main evidence that people use the availability heuristic comes from studies where it leads to biased estimates. For example, under timed conditions people generate far more words of the form _ _ _ _ *ing* than of the form _ _ _ _ _*n*_, even though the first class is a subset of the second. This shows that the first form is more available in memory than the second. Further, when one group estimates how many words in a four page novel have the form _ _ _ _ *ing*, and another answers the same question for the form _ _ _ _ _ *n*_, estimates are much higher for the first. This suggests that in making their frequency estimates people relied on the ease with which they could retrieve instances (Tversky & Kahneman, 1983).

The availability heuristic furnishes one method for constructing a sample of events or instances. A more general account of sampling (and possible biases) is advanced by Fiedler (2000). This extends the analysis from memory-based search to environmental search. Both kinds of search can lead to biases in the resulting set of instances. On the one hand, the environment might be sampled in a biased way. Fiedler cites an example concerning the assessment of lie detectors. Many validity studies of such devices incorporate a pernicious sampling bias: of all the people who fail the test, validity assessments only include those who subsequently confess. Those who fail the test but are telling the truth are not counted (see positive test strategies; Klayman & Ha, 1987). Another common route to error is when people sample from a biased environment, such as the media, which over-represent sensational and newsworthy events (Fischhoff, 2002; Slovic, Fischhoff, & Lichtenstein, 1980).

Systematic biases can also arise when one generates a sample from one's own memory. This can occur because of the intrusion of associative memory processes (Kelley & Jacoby, 2000). Alternatively, it can result from the biased generation of possibilities or scenarios. For example, people tend to recruit reasons to support their own views, and neglect counter-arguments or reasons that support opposing conclusions (Koriat, Lichtenstein, & Fischhoff, 1980; Kunda, 1990). Fiedler (2000) argues that many judgmental biases arise because – rather than in spite – of our ability to process sample information accurately. Samples are often biased, and we lack the metacognitive abilities to correct for such biases.

The availability heuristic involves the generation of a set of instances, but it does not specify how people go from this set to a probability judgment. In certain cases this will be relatively transparent, such as when more instances of horse A winning a race rather than horse B are recalled and thus A is predicted to beat B. However, many situations will be more complicated. Suppose A and B have never raced against each other, and A has only raced in easy races, B in hard ones. In this case you may need to weight their number of wins differentially, and for this availability offers little guide.

Cascaded inference

Cascaded inference occurs when one makes a sequence of connected inferences. It is a pervasive feature of our thinking, allowing us to pursue extended paths of probabilistic reasoning. In a two-step cascaded inference you make an initial probabilistic inference on the basis of a known premise, and then make a second inference based on the output of this first stage. For example, suppose you are preparing to bet on a horse in the Grand National, and you know that rain will favour 'Silver Surfer'. You see dark clouds gathering by the race track (this is your known premise). From this you estimate the probability of rain (this is your first stage inference). Finally you estimate the probability that 'Silver Surfer' wins given this inference (this is the second stage).

In the previous chapter we saw how to conduct such inferences in a normative fashion using Jeffrey's rule. We also hinted that people may find this kind of computation too demanding. Early research in cascaded inference confirms this. Several researchers (e.g., Gettys, Michel, Steiger, Kelly, & Peterson, 1973; Steiger & Gettys, 1972) have shown that rather than employ Jeffrey's rule people adopt a 'best guess' or 'as-if' strategy: they make their second inference *as if* the most probable outcome at the first step is true rather than probable. In our example this would involve inferring from the dark clouds that it is likely to rain (a best guess), and then basing your probability estimate that 'Silver Surfer' wins on the tacit assumption that it does rain (an as-if inference).

An independent but very similar argument has been developed in the study of how people make category inferences. Most work in this field has concentrated on the categorizations that people make when they are presented with definite information. Anderson (1991), however, proposed a rational model of categorization where people are assumed to make multiple uncertain categorizations in the service of a prediction about an object or event. More specifically, he claimed that when people make a prediction on the basis of an uncertain categorization they follow a Bayesian rule that computes a weighted average over all potential categories.

In contrast to this *multiple category* view, Murphy and Ross (1994) have argued for a *single category* view, where just the most probable category is used to make a prediction. For example, consider the task of predicting whether the insect flying towards you on a dark night is likely to sting you. Let the potential categories in this situation be *Fly*, *Wasp* or *Bee*. According to the multiple category view you compute a weighted average across all three categories in order to determine the probability of being stung. In contrast, on the single category view you base your prediction only on the most probable category (e.g., just one of *Fly*, *Wasp* or *Bee*) and ignore alternative categories.

Murphy and Ross (1994) demonstrate that people's default strategy is to use just the most probable category for their predictions. This is consistent with the earlier research in cascaded inference, and suggests that in the face of uncertain premises people adopt strategies that simplify the computation problem. In the next chapter we propose associative mechanisms that may underlie these strategies.

Section summary

Biases in probability judgment appear to be systematic and robust, and imply that in many contexts people do not follow the laws of probability. However, it is unclear exactly what processes *are* involved. Sometimes judgments of similarity, availability or evidential support do seem to drive judgment, but a unifying framework for understanding these biases is lacking.

The frequency effect

The conclusion that people fail to reason in accordance with the laws of probability has not gone uncontested. The most vocal challenge is provided by Gigerenzer and colleagues (e.g., Gigerenzer, 1994; Gigerenzer & Hoffrage, 1995). They maintain that the classic demonstrations of judgmental biases are flawed because the problems are couched in terms of probabilities rather than *natural frequencies*. In support of this claim they show that re-casting the problems in terms of frequencies leads to a marked reduction in biased responses. For example, when people are asked to think of 100 women like Linda, and asked for the frequencies of both bank tellers and feminist bank tellers, they are much less likely to commit a conjunction error (Fiedler, 1988; Hertwig & Gigerenzer, 1999). Similar facilitation effects have been demonstrated in the case of base rate neglect (Cosmides & Tooby, 1996; Gigerenzer & Hoffrage, 1995; Sloman et al., 2003).

The so-called 'frequency effect', that presenting probability problems in a frequency format often reduces judgmental biases, is now well established (we met one example in the judgment made about the guilt of a defendant by mock jurors in chapter 1 – 'Is this person guilty?'). There are questions about the extent of this reduction, and situations where biases persist even with frequency judgments, but it is generally agreed that appropriate frequency representations facilitate human judgment. What remains controversial are the factors that drive this facilitation.

Let us present the frequentist explanation first. There are several strands to their argument. First, they maintain that single-case probabilities are ambiguous and incomplete. They are ambiguous because there are numerous senses of the term 'probability', some of which are non-mathematical. They are incomplete because they do not specify a reference class. Both of these problems are avoided if uncertainty is framed in terms of frequencies. These are clearly mathematical, and they always refer to some reference class.

Second, Gigerenzer and colleagues distinguish *natural* frequencies from frequencies per se. Natural frequencies are frequencies that have not had base rate information filtered out. They typically result from the process of natural sampling, where event frequencies are updated in a sequential fashion. In contrast, non-natural frequencies result from systematic sampling of the environment, or when frequency tallies are normalized.

Representing information in terms of natural frequencies can simplify Bayesian computations, because base rates are implicit in these counts, and do not need to be recalculated afresh. Gigerenzer illustrates this with the example of a preliterate doctor who must assess the probability of a new disease given a fallible symptom. She simply needs to keep track of two (natural) frequencies: the number of cases where the symptom and disease co-occur, f(S & D), and the number of cases where the symptom occurs without the disease, f(S & ¬D). To reach an estimate for the probability of disease given the symptom she can then apply a simplified version of Bayes' rule:

$$P(D|S) = f(S \ \& \ D) / [f(S \ \& \ D) + f(S \ \& \ \neg D)]$$

This is considerably simpler than the full Bayesian computation using probabilities or relative frequencies.

The third thread is an evolutionary argument. The idea here is that our cognitive mechanisms evolved in environments where uncertain information was experienced in terms of natural frequencies (Cosmides & Tooby, 1996). In short, the mind is adapted to process frequencies via natural sampling, and thus contains cognitive algorithms that operate over natural frequencies rather than probabilities.

The nested-sets hypothesis

In contrast to the frequentists, proponents of the nested-sets hypothesis uphold the validity of the original demonstrations of judgmental biases. They maintain that when making intuitive probability judgments people prefer to use representative or associative thinking, and are hence susceptible to judgmental biases. What facilitates judgments when problems are framed in terms of frequencies is that the critical nested-set relations are made more transparent (e.g., by using Venn diagrams, see Figure 5.1 in chapter 5). For example, when instructed to think of 100 women just like Linda, and asked for the frequencies of both bank tellers and feminist bank tellers, people are alerted to the structural fact that the set of feminist bank tellers is included within the set of bank tellers.

On the nested-sets hypothesis, then, judgments typically improve in a frequency format because the problem structure is clarified. This is not as a result of the frequency representation per se, but because such a representation makes the relevant set relations transparent.

Indeed Tversky and Kahneman (1983) were the first to demonstrate the frequency effect. They attributed it to a shift from a singular 'inside' view, where people focus on properties of the individual case, to an 'outside' view, where people are sensitive to distributional features of the set to which that case belongs. It is only by taking an outside view that people can perceive the relevant structural features of a probability problem (see Lagnado & Sloman, 2004b).

In support of the nested-sets hypothesis there is empirical data showing that the frequency format is neither necessary nor sufficient for facilitation. Thus numerous studies show that biases remain with frequency formats, and that biases can be reduced even with probability formats (Evans, Handley, Perham, Over, & Thompson, 2000; Girotto & Gonzalez, 2001; Sloman et al., 2003). For example, Sloman et al. (2003) showed that responses to both the conjunction and medical diagnosis problems improved in probability versions that provided cues to the relevant set structure, and declined in frequency versions that concealed this structure. There are also experiments that show a similar improvement when diagrammatic cues are given to set structure (Agnoli & Krantz, 1989; Sloman et al., 2003).

Finally, proponents of the nested-sets hypothesis question the appeal to evolutionary arguments. They argue that equally valid evolutionary stories can be spun for the primacy of single-case rather than frequency-based probabilities (see Sloman & Over, 2003, for details). After all, our ancestors back on the savannah were often required to make judgments and decisions about unique events. There would have been considerable evolutionary advantage in the ability to anticipate what might happen in novel and potentially one-off situations. (How many times can you stroll into a lion's den in order to compute the relative frequency of being eaten?) Another problem with the frequentists' evolutionary argument is that it neglects the possibility that the cognitive mechanisms that deal with uncertainty have *developed* from more primitive mechanisms (see Heyes, 2003).

Reconciliation

The two positions can be reconciled to some extent by noting an ambiguity in the claim that frequency formats facilitate probability judgment. There are two distinct ways in which frequency processing might aid judgment. First, it can serve as a form of natural assessment (see Kahneman & Frederick, 2002). That is, when asked for a probability judgment you might base your response on a frequency estimate because it is readily accessible. And if your frequency judgments are relatively accurate then coherence comes free, because frequencies automatically obey the laws of probability. For example, if you have an accurate memory for the number of bank tellers you have encountered, and (separately) for the number of feminist bank tellers, then the former will not be lower than the latter. Thus conformity to the probability laws is achieved without any appreciation of the necessary set relations.

The second way that frequency formats might facilitate judgment, and the focus of most of the debate, is through simplifying the computations necessary to solve a probability problem. On the nested-sets hypothesis this usually involves the clarification of the relevant set-inclusion relations. On the frequentist view this consists in the applicability of a simplified version of Bayes' rule (Gigerenzer & Hoffrage, 1995).

Cast in these terms the debate seems less pointed. Both parties can agree that frequency formulations are just one (albeit very significant) route to simplifying probabilistic computations. While this deals with the frequency effect itself, there are several general problems with the frequentist approach.

Theoretical confusion

Frequentists appear to confuse the judgments people make with the means we have of appraising them. It seems undeniable that people make single-case probability judgments. After all these are the judgments most germane to our short-term decision making. You want the doctor to tell you *your* chances of surviving *this* operation; a hunter needs to act on the probability that *this* antelope is tiring; a child wants to know the probability that *he* will receive a bicycle *this* Christmas.

Frequentists maintain that such statements are incomplete, or at worst meaningless. Their main argument for this is that we have no means of appraising these singular judgments – that the event in question either happens or it does not. In contrast, they argue, a frequency judgment can be assessed in terms of its correspondence with a relative frequency in a suitably chosen reference class.

One shortcoming with this argument is that single-case probability judgments *do* encompass various means of appraisal. Aside from the coherence-based methods discussed earlier, there are correspondence-based methods such as calibration (where repeated single-case probability judgments are assessed against the relative frequencies, see above). This highlights a second shortcoming with the frequentist argument. It assumes that if a probability judgment is to be appraised in terms of frequencies it must itself be a frequency-based judgment. But this does not follow. There is no reason why we cannot make singular probability judgments that are best appraised in terms of their correspondence to appropriate relative frequencies.

The importance of conditional probabilities and systematic sampling

Frequentists make much of the fact that natural frequencies arise from the process of natural sampling (indeed the evolutionary argument hinges on this fact). A tacit assumption here is that it is always best to retain base rate information in one's representation of uncertainty. But this seems to ignore the fact that (1) it may be computationally expensive to always maintain base rate information (see the discussion in chapter 11 about learning models), and (2) in certain circumstances base rate information is unnecessary. For example, in the case of our own actions we are primarily concerned with the likelihood of an effect occurring given that we do something. We may be quite unconcerned with how often we in fact carry out this action. Similarly, experimentation (by scientists or laypeople) seeks to establish the stable causal relations that hold between things, regardless of the base rate occurrence of these things. Of course the latter information is often used to estimate these causal relations, but the main focus of systematic testing is on conditional relations rather than base rate information.

This is not to deny the importance of base rate information, but just to point out that other forms of information, such as that concerning the relations between events, is also critical to our mastery of the environment (a fact recognized by Brunswik). Sometimes the frequentist rhetoric about natural frequencies obscures this fact. We aim to redress the balance in the next chapter.

Frequentists offer no account for probability biases

Another problem specific to the frequentist account is that it offers no explanation for the systematic judgmental biases that persist when problems are framed in a probability format. The nested-sets hypothesis is a development of Kahneman and Tversky's original position, and so can avail itself of the various heuristics they proposed to explain the biases. But, at best, the frequentist school shows us how to reduce these biases. It gives no principled explanation of why they arise.

Summary of debate about frequency effect

The evidence marshalled in favour of the nested-sets hypothesis undermines the claim that frequency processing provides a panacea to judgmental bias. Nevertheless the frequency effect is an established phenomenon, and has triggered important applications in the communication and teaching of uncertainty (Sedlmeier, 1999). Also, the frequentists' emphasis on the fit between cognitive mechanisms and the natural environments in which they operate is well taken. Despite this, most demonstrations of the frequency effect have been with word problems using summary numerical descriptions. This is clearly not the natural environment in which frequency processing algorithms would have evolved. A more appropriate test of their claims would be to locate people in a naturalistic environment where they are exposed to sequential information. Approaches that integrate judgment and learning into a unifying framework are be discussed in the next chapter.

Summary

This chapter outlines the systematic mistakes that people make when they reason probabilistically, and discusses attempts to explain and alleviate these biases. In particular, it surveys many of the problems identified by the heuristics and biases tradition, including base rate neglect, conjunction and disjunction problems, and misestimation of relative frequencies. The frequency effect – where judgments improve if the problems are formulated in terms of frequencies – is discussed, and alternative interpretations of this effect are critically evaluated.

In the next chapter we continue our examination of probability judgment. We propose a framework for thinking about the mechanisms that produce judgments that are usually correct but sometimes incoherent. The framework is based on the idea of 'associative thinking'.

7   Associative thinking

Judgments of probability or frequency are not conjured from thin air. They are usually made after some exposure to the domain in question. In particular, we often make judgments after learning something about the structure of the environment. It is natural to expect that the nature of this prior learning shapes the judgments we make; not just in the trivial sense that prior exposure provides us with data on which to base our judgments, but also in the deeper sense that the mechanisms that operate during learning are active in the judgment process itself.

This leads to a more general conception of a correspondence model of judgment – one that attunes in some way to statistical features of the environment. In the case of a frequentist theory the primitives are frequencies. Judgments are based on, and appraised in terms of, their match with appropriate real-world frequencies. But this is only one possibility. In this chapter we introduce an alternative correspondence model, one where people attune to statistical relations *between* events. In particular, we argue that our learning mechanisms encode the degree of contingency or association between events, and this is often used as a basis for judgment. While this measure usually provides a good proxy for probability judgments, there are situations where it can lead to probabilistic incoherence.

Central to this approach is the idea that probability judgments are best understood in the context of the learning that precedes them. This involves both the structure of the learning environment, and the learning mechanisms that operate within it. We discuss various learning models in chapter 11. Here we focus on an associative learning framework, because it seems to characterize human behaviour in a wide range of learning contexts.

Associative theories of probability judgment

Associative models of probability judgment (Gluck & Bower, 1988; Shanks, 1991) are usually applied to situations where people experience sequentially presented events. During this exposure people learn to associate cues (properties or features) with outcomes (typically another property or a category prediction), and these learned associations are supposed to form the basis for subsequent probability judgments. Analogues of several of the classic probability biases have been demonstrated within this paradigm. For example, Gluck and Bower (1988) demonstrated an analogue of base rate neglect. In their task people learned to diagnose two fictitious diseases on the basis of symptom patterns, and then rated the probability of each of these diseases given a target symptom. The learning environment was arranged so that the conditional probability of each disease was equal, but the overall probability (base rate) of one was high and of the other low. Given this structure, the target symptom was a better predictor of the rare disease than the common one, and in line with the associative model people gave higher ratings for the conditional probability of the rare disease (see chapter 11 for more details).

Within the same associative paradigm, Cobos, Almaraz, and Garcia-Madruga (2003) replicated this base rate effect. They also demonstrated a conjunction effect, in which people rated the probability of a conjunction of symptoms higher than one of its conjuncts, and a conversion effect, where people confused the conditional probability of symptoms given a disease with that of a disease given symptoms (analogous to the inverse fallacy, see chapter 6).

Lagnado and Shanks (2002) argued that these judgment biases arise because people attune to predictive relations between variables, and use these as a basis for their subsequent probability judgments. This can lead to error when there is a conflict between the degree to which one variable predicts another, and the conditional probability of one variable given the other. More specifically, on an associative model the degree to which one variable predicts another is measured by the contingency between these variables (known as ΔP). The contingency between outcome (O) and cue (C) is determined by the following equation:

$$\Delta P = P(O|C) - P(O|\neg C)$$

That is, the contingency between outcome O and cue C depends on the degree to which the presence of the cue raises the probability of the outcome. (Note that this is one possible measure of the degree of evidential support; see chapter 6.)

The key point here is that the contingency between an outcome and a cue is not equivalent to the probability of an outcome given that cue. They will have the same value when $P(O|\neg C) = 0$, but they will often differ. For instance, the probability that the next prime minister of Britain is a male, given that you say 'abracadabra' before the next election, is very high. But, of course, this probability is just as high if you fail to say 'abracadabra'. Thus the contingency between the next prime minister being male and you saying 'abracadabra' is zero, but the probability of the next prime minister being male given that you say 'abracadabra' is high. (And this will hold true until there are more female candidates for the post.)

The learning analogues of base rate neglect can thus be explained by the confusion between predictiveness (contingency) and probability. In these experiments people correctly learn that the contingency between the rare disease and the critical cue pattern is higher than that between the common disease and that cue pattern. Their mistake is to use this judgment to answer the question of which disease is most probable given the cue pattern.

Lagnado and Shanks (2002) extended this approach to the case of disjunction errors. They reasoned that if people use contingencies rather than conditional probability estimates, it should be possible to arrange the learning environment so they judge a subordinate category as more probable than its superordinate category, even though this violates a basic rule of probability. This is an extreme version of the conjunction error, because a subordinate category is by definition fully contained in the superordinate category (see chapter 6 for illustration of this point). It also mirrors the disjunction errors displayed by Bar-Hillel and Neter (1993) in one-shot verbal problems.

In Lagnado and Shanks' experiments people learned to diagnose diseases at two levels of a hierarchy, and were then asked to rate the conditional probabilities of subordinate categories (e.g., Asian flu) and superordinate categories (e.g., flu). The learning environment was arranged so that a target symptom (e.g., stomach cramps) was a better predictor of a subordinate disease than it was of that disease's superordinate category. In line with the associative account, people rated the conditional probability of the subordinate higher than its superordinate, in violation of the probability axioms. This suggests that people ignored the subset relation between the diseases, and based their conditional probability judgments on the degree of association between symptom and disease categories.

Extending the associative model

So far we have argued that probability judgments are sometimes based on learned associations, and that this can lead to judgmental biases. But probabilistic reasoning often involves more than the output of a numerical or qualitative estimate. People often reach their judgments through an extended path of reasoning, or through imagining possible scenarios.

An associative account of cascaded inference

The associative account readily extends to multistep or cascaded inferences. For example, the presence of a cue (item of evidence) can activate an associated outcome (step 1), and this in turn can serve as the input into another inference (step 2). Indeed 'as-if' reasoning is a natural consequence of associative inference, because nodes need just to be activated above a threshold to count as 'assumed true'. For example, recall the deliberations from chapter 6 about whether 'Silver Surfer' will win the horse race, given that there are dark clouds on the horizon. Presumably one has learned a strong association between dark clouds and rain. The presence of dark clouds thus activates an expectation of rain. One has also learned to associate rain on the race track with the sight of 'Silver Surfer' charging to the winning post. In short, the initial piece of evidence (dark clouds ahead) triggers a chain of association that results in a strong belief that 'Silver Surfer' will win the race.

As with the judgmental heuristics discussed in the previous chapter, this brand of 'as-if' reasoning has both a positive and a negative side. On the positive side it can greatly simplify inference, allowing reasoners to focus on just the most probable inference path, and to ignore unlikely alternatives. If the weather is most likely to be rainy, why bother considering how well the horses are likely to perform in the sunshine? On the negative side, the neglect of alternative possibilities can sometimes lead to anomalous judgments and choices.

The influence of hierarchy on judgment and choice

The potential dangers of 'as-if' reasoning are demonstrated in a set of studies by Lagnado and Shanks (2003). They focus on situations in which information is hierarchically organized, such that objects or individuals can be categorized at different levels of a category hierarchy. For example, different treatments for cancer might be grouped in terms of either drug therapy or surgery (Ubel, 2002). Or different newspapers might be grouped as either tabloids or broadsheets. (For non-British readers: tabloids are the kind of newspaper that have naked women and extensive sports coverage.)

Lagnado and Shanks (2003) argue that when reasoners are confronted with such hierarchies they naturally assume that the most likely category at the superordinate level includes the most likely subordinate category, and vice versa, that the most likely subordinate is contained in the most likely superordinate. For example, consider the simplified newspaper hierarchy illustrated in Figure 7.1. Suppose that tabloids are the most popular kind of paper, so if we pick someone at random they are more likely to read a tabloid than a broadsheet. It is natural to assume that the most popular paper will also be one of the tabloids (e.g., either the *Sun* or the *Mirror*). Furthermore, suppose that most tabloid readers vote for Party A, whereas most broadsheet readers vote for Party B. These two pieces of probabilistic information can be combined into a cascaded inference – someone picked at random is most likely to read a tabloid, and therefore is most likely to vote for party A.

How good are such inferences? In many situations they will be very effective, and reduce the computational load. However, there will be situations in which they may prove problematic. Consider a sample of 100 people, each of whom reads just one paper (see Figure 7.1). Among this sample tabloids are the most popular kind of paper, but the *Guardian* is the most popular paper. We term this a 'non-aligned' hierarchy, because the most probable superordinate does not align with the most probable subordinate.

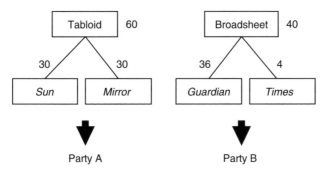

Figure 7.1 Simplified newspaper hierarchy and associated voting preferences. The numbers denote the frequencies of people (in a sample of 100) reading each paper. The frequencies are 'non-aligned', because although Tabloids are more popular than Broadsheets (60 > 40), the *Guardian* is the most popular newspaper (36 readers). (The structure used in Lagnado & Shanks, 2003.)

Such a structure raises two problems. First, it undermines the inference from superordinate to subordinate. The most popular superordinate (tabloid) does not include the most popular subordinate (*Guardian*). Second, it undermines the cascaded inference from newspaper readership (tabloid) to voting preferences (Party A). This is because there is an equally good (or bad) cascaded inference to the conclusion that someone picked at random is most likely to read the *Guardian*, and therefore to vote for Party B.

This highlights the possible perils of as-if reasoning. In an environment that is non-aligned, reasoning as if a probable categorization is true can lead to contradictory conclusions. When categorizing an individual X at the general level, one reasons as if X is a tabloid reader, and thus concludes that X votes for Party A. In contrast, when categorizing the same individual X at the specific level one reasons as if X is a *Guardian* reader, and thus concludes that X votes for Party B. But clearly the same body of information cannot support two contradictory conclusions about X.

In their experiments Lagnado and Shanks used this kind of non-aligned situation to show that as-if reasoning can lead to judgmental inconsistencies. They gave participants a training phase in which they learned to predict voting preferences on the basis of newspaper readership, using a learning environment similar to that shown in Figure 7.1. They then asked them probability questions in three different conditions (see Figure 7.2). In the *baseline* condition participants were simply asked for the likelihood that a randomly chosen individual would vote for Party A. In the *general level* condition participants were first asked which kind of paper (tabloid or broadsheet) a randomly chosen individual was most likely to read. They were then asked for the likelihood that this individual voted for Party A. In the *specific level* condition participants were first asked which specific paper (*Sun*, *Mirror*,

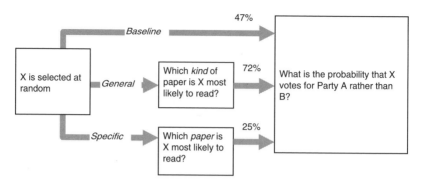

Figure 7.2 Test phase and mean probability judgments in each condition in Lagnado and Shanks (2003).

Guardian or *Times*) a randomly chosen individual was most likely to read. They were then also asked for the likelihood that this individual voted for Party A.

The judgments in all three conditions were based on the same statistical information. The learning environment was arranged so that overall half the people voted for Party A and half for Party B. In line with these frequencies most participants reported a probability of around 50 per cent in the *baseline* condition. However, in the other two conditions participants shifted their likelihood judgments depending on their answer to the question about newspaper readership. When they chose a tabloid as the most likely kind of paper, their mean judgments for Party A were raised to around 70 per cent. When they chose the *Guardian* as the most likely paper, their mean judgments for Party A dropped to around 25 per cent.

In sum, participants made very different probability judgments depending on whether they first categorized an individual at the general or the specific level. And this pattern was not alleviated by asking participants to make frequency rather than probability judgments. These results can be explained by participants' reliance on as-if reasoning. In the *general* condition they tend to reason as if the randomly selected individual reads a tabloid (neglecting the probabilistic nature of their evidence), and therefore judge them most likely to vote for Party A. In the *specific* condition they tend to reason as if the individual reads the *Guardian* (again neglecting the probabilistic nature of their evidence), and therefore judge them most likely to vote for Party B.

Furthermore, this use of as-if reasoning is readily explained by an associative account of probabilistic inference. During the learning phase participants build up associations between the newspapers (both at the general and the specific level) and the two parties (e.g., tabloid → Party A; broadsheet → Party B; *Guardian* → Party B, etc.). These learned associations are then used as a basis for their responses to the probability questions. In the *baseline* condition the balance of the learned associations does not favour one party over the other, so participants judge them equally likely. In the *general* condition the initial judgment that tabloids are more probable than broadsheets leads to an increased activation of the representation of tabloid. This raises their subsequent judgment about the likelihood of the individual voting for Party A, because tabloids were strongly associated with Party A. In contrast, in the *specific* condition an initial judgment that the *Guardian* is most probable leads to an increased activation of the representation of *Guardian* and this lowers their subsequent judgments about Party A (because the *Guardian* was strongly associated with Party B).

Medical choices

These experiments show that people modulate their judgments according to their initial uncertain categorizations; but what about their choices? Faced with a choice between various alternatives, do people allow the grouping of these options to influence their decisions? This is particularly pertinent when people are faced with a variety of options, all with an attendant degree of uncertainty. For instance, when faced with medical decisions people often have to choose between a variety of treatment options, each with a specific set of pros and cons. In order to help patients make better decisions in such situations some theorists recommend that similar options should be grouped together, thus reducing the complexities of the decision. For example, Ubel (2002) suggests that when presenting patients with information about different treatments for cancer, doctors should group like treatments together (i.e., forming superordinate groupings such as drug therapy and surgical therapy).

While the grouping of options into hierarchies is an important step in facilitating decision making, it also opens the door to the kind of flawed as-if reasoning discussed above. In particular, when grouping different medical treatments in the manner suggested by Ubel (2002) it is possible that information presented at the superordinate level has a distorting effect on judgments and choices made at the subordinate level. For example, if you tell patients that overall (at the group level) surgical therapy is better than drug therapy, this may lead them to pass over a particular drug treatment that is in fact the best option for them.

Lagnado, Moss, and Shanks (2006a) explored this possibility by presenting participants with either grouped or ungrouped information about the success rates of different treatments. In the *grouped* condition four specific treatments were grouped into two superordinate categories (surgical or drug therapy). The success rates for the different treatments were arranged in a non-aligned structure (see Figure 7.3) – the most effective particular treatment (e.g., drug 1) was not a subset of the most effective group level treatment (e.g., surgery).

In the *non-grouped* condition the four treatment options were presented without any superordinate grouping, but each treatment had the same success

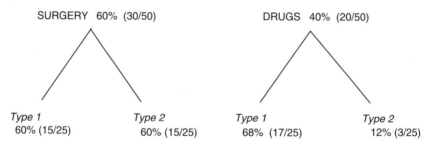

SURGERY 60% (30/50)   DRUGS 40% (20/50)

Type 1   *Type 2*   *Type 1*   *Type 2*
60% (15/25)   60% (15/25)   68% (17/25)   12% (3/25)

Figure 7.3 Success rates for treatments in Lagnado et al. (2006a).

rate as the corresponding treatment in the grouped condition. So the only difference between the conditions lay in the superordinate grouping.

All participants learned about the success rates of the different treatments by making predictions for 100 patients on a trial-by-trial basis. For each patient they were told which treatment the patient had been given, and then predicted whether the treatment would succeed or fail. After each prediction they received feedback as to the actual success or failure.

At the end of this training phase participants in both conditions were asked to make various choices. Those in the non-grouped condition simply had to choose the treatment they considered most effective. In line with the success rates they had just experienced, 75 per cent of participants chose the most effective treatment (drug type 1). In the grouped condition participants were first asked to choose the most effective treatment at the superordinate level, and were then asked to choose the best specific treatment. In response to the first question most correctly chose the most effective superordinate category (surgical therapy). However, in response to the second question only 25 per cent chose the most effective treatment.

These results fit with the idea that people engage in as-if reasoning. In this case they expect the best treatment at the general level to include the best specific treatment. Having selected surgical therapy as the best superordinate category they are less likely to choose drug type 1 as the best specific treatment. This contrasts with participants in the non-grouped condition, whose choices are not distorted by the superordinate grouping.

Once again it is important to reiterate that we do not want to conclude from this study that grouping is a bad thing, or that the strategies people adopt are maladaptive. We have used a non-aligned structure to expose the operation of as-if reasoning, but we hypothesize that non-aligned structures are unlikely to be commonplace. In most situations as-if reasoning serves us fine; indeed it is likely that we construct hierarchies that observe alignment, and thus permit such simplifying strategies. However, these findings do suggest that probabilistic reasoning is underlain by heuristic processes rather than Bayesian computations over veridical probability representations.

Associative thinking and mental simulation

The idea that people use associative processes to make inferences and reason about probabilities is not new (Dawes, 2001, Hastie & Dawes, 2001; Sloman, 1996). Indeed Hume (1748) is probably the grandfather of this claim. However, the link between associative thinking in *judgment* and associative *learning* is seldom made explicit. We have tried to build a bridge in this chapter, arguing that the associative mechanisms that learn predictive relations in the environment also direct subsequent judgments and choices. This fits with the overall aim of this book to argue for a reorientation of research on judgment and decision making to focus more on reasoners' behaviour when they can learn from feedback and less on what they do on one-shot, verbally described and often ambiguous, judgment problems.

This link between mechanisms of learning and judgments also bears on the question of *mental simulation*. This is another cognitive heuristic proposed by Kahneman and Tversky (1982a) to explain how people reach probability judgments. They argue that people construct a suitable causal model of the situation under question, and then 'run' a mental simulation of this model using certain parameter settings. The success or ease of achieving the target outcome is then used as a proxy for the probability of that outcome, conditional on the initial parameter settings. (We met this heuristic in chapter 4 in the discussion on how fire chiefs simulate strategies in dynamic environments.)

The simulation heuristic is particularly applicable to situations where people make plans or predictions about the future (Kahneman & Lovallo, 1993; Ross & Buehler, 2001). A robust empirical finding, termed the *planning fallacy*, is that people tend to underestimate the amount of time it will take to complete a task or project (Buehler, Griffin, & Ross, 1994, 2002; Kahneman & Tversky, 1979b), even when they have knowledge about the frequency of past failures. An example is the tendency of students to underestimate how long it will take them to finish an academic assignment. Buehler et al. (1994) found that students nearing the end of a one year honours thesis underestimated their completion time by an average of 22 days.

The standard explanation for the planning fallacy is that people focus on their mental simulations of the project or task, generating a plausible set of steps from initiation to completion (Kahneman & Tversky, 1979b; Buehler et al., 2002). This focus on plausible scenarios overrides the consideration of other factors, such as the past frequencies with which completion was delayed.

Simulating an associative model

Discussions of mental simulation often neglect the influence of prior learning on how people 'run' these simulations. But just as learned associations can fuel our predictions about future states of the world, so can they drive our mental simulations. In predictive or associative learning, learning is driven by the error correction of predictions or expectations about the environment (see chapter 11 for details). On the basis of a set of cues, and their associations with possible outcomes, a predicted state of the world is generated. This is then compared against reality (i.e., the actual outcomes), and the cue–outcome associations are updated.

Thus a mental simulation can be construed as the generation of a prediction or expectation about the world, but one that does not receive immediate corrective feedback. And the previously learned associative links between concepts (cues and outcomes) serve as the tramlines along which these simulations are run.

This can be illustrated with the Linda problem discussed in chapter 6. Recall that people were asked to read a short profile of Linda, and then separately judge the probability that she is a bank teller, and the probability that she is a feminist bank teller. On an associative account of this problem the profile of Linda activates specific cues and concepts in the mind of the participant (e.g., female, philosophy student, cares about discrimination and social justice, etc.). These serve as the initial settings on which mental simulations can be run. As the simulations are run, they are directed by previously learned associations (e.g., women concerned with discrimination tend to be feminists; philosophy students tend not to care about money, etc.). The ease with which these simulations arrive at the target category (i.e., bank teller, feminist or feminist bank teller) is then used as a proxy for the probability of that category (given the initial profile).

In the case of Linda's profile (and the associations it is likely to prime) it is not surprising that people rate a feminist as the most probable category, and feminist bank teller as more probable than bank teller. It would be very easy to move from Linda's profile (via the implied associations) to the category feminist, and very hard to move from Linda's profile to the bank teller category. The activation of the feminist bank teller would be intermediate between these two extremes. The information in the profile activates the feminist part, but inhibits the bank teller part.

This associative account can be combined with the higher level analysis of the Linda problem given in chapter 6. In that chapter we suggested that instead of judging the probability of the various categories (bank teller, feminist, etc.), people judge the evidential support that Linda's profile gives to those categories. And they rate 'feminist bank teller' as more probable than 'bank teller' because Linda's profile supports 'feminist bank teller' more than it supports 'bank teller'. It seems plausible to see the associative account offered in this chapter as an implementation of such inductive reasoning. On this view, associative links between variables represent relations of evidential support in a complex network. Thus the overall effect of Linda's profile (and the implied associative links) is to raise the activation of 'feminist bank teller' but to lower the activation of 'bank teller'.

As mentioned previously, this associative account naturally extends to cascaded inference. Indeed in the Linda problem people are likely to engage in various cascaded inferences. From the information that Linda is a philosophy student they might infer that she is not interested in money, and from this infer that she is unlikely to work in a bank. And so on.

One special feature of cascaded inference is that it can be iterated without intermediate feedback from the environment (see Figure 7.4). A sequence of these mental simulations can then be constructed, corresponding to the pursuance of a path of inference. And the longer these inferences are spun out without external correction, the more they might deviate from reality.

This is just a sketch of how mental simulation and associative thinking might tie together. Much more needs to be said about the representations and mechanisms involved. For example, the role of causal models over and above associative models might prove crucial, especially when dealing with the simulation of possible actions (Pearl, 2000; Sloman, 2005; Sloman & Lagnado, 2004, 2005). But whatever the computational machinery that underlies our learning, it is also likely to subserve our mental simulations, and hence our probability judgments too.

Summary

It is argued that the way in which people learn about the statistical structure of their environment determines how they arrive at probability judgments,

Predictive learning

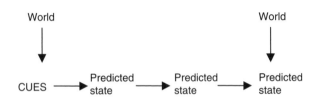

Multiple path inference

Figure 7.4 Associative paths of inference and mental simulation.

whether accurate or biased. Building on this idea we propose a unified account of probabilistic learning and judgment based on associative thinking. In particular, we argue that our learning mechanisms encode the degree of contingency or association between events, and this is often used as a basis for judgment. In situations where contingency and probability conflict, people will make systematic errors because they attune to the contingencies rather than the conditional probabilities. Many of these errors have direct analogues in the one-shot verbal problems studied in the heuristics and biases programme. We extend this model to the more complex case of multistep inference, where people pursue chains of probabilistic reasoning. We also highlight a new type of judgment and choice anomaly that arises when people confront 'non-aligned' environments. Finally, we propose a sketch of how associative models might underpin mental simulation.

The last three chapters have covered various aspects of probability judgment from basic appraisal methods, to the characteristic biases and errors people make in their judgments, to finally a sketched proposal for a unified account of probabilistic learning and judgment. In the following three chapters we move away from the world of probability judgment to the world of choices and decisions. First we present a framework for analysing decisions, then we ask how decisions are actually made and finally we examine the influence of time on our decision making.

8 Analysing decisions I: A general framework

Every day we are faced with decisions. Some small – should you take your umbrella to work? Should you have salmon or steak for dinner? Some larger – should you take out travel insurance? Should you buy a laptop or a desktop computer? And some monumental – should you believe in God? Which football team should you support? Despite their diversity these decisions all share a common structure. They involve choices between several options, they concern future states of the world that are uncertain or unknown, and they have varying degrees of importance or value to you.

One of the major achievements in the twentieth century was the development of a general decision-theoretic framework to address such questions (Ramsey, 1931; Savage, 1954; von Neumann & Morgenstern, 1947). This work itself built on pioneering work by mathematicians through the centuries (Bernoulli, 1954; Pascal, 1670). In this chapter we present a simplified version of this framework, and several of its key assumptions. In the subsequent chapter we see how well people conform to these axioms, and outline a model of actual human choice behaviour.

A framework for analysing decisions

Acts, states and outcomes

The core ingredients for any decision problem are acts, states and outcomes. The set of acts $\{A_i\}$ are the options that the decision maker must choose between; the set of states $\{S_j\}$ correspond to various possible ways in which the world might turn out; the set of outcomes $\{O_{ij}\}$ are the different possible consequences of each act given each possible state.

To illustrate, consider a decision problem faced by many inhabitants of the UK when summer finally arrives. Should they have a barbecue? In this case they must choose between two acts: to have a barbecue (A_1) or to eat indoors (A_2). There are two possible states of nature relevant to the outcomes: sun (S_1) or rain (S_2). And there are four possible outcomes, depending on the action taken and the state of nature that obtains: a sunny barbecue (O_{11}), a wet barbecue (O_{12}), a meal indoors while it is sunny (O_{21}), and a meal indoors while it rains (O_{22}). A decision matrix for this problem is shown in Table 8.1.

Utilities

The next step in the decision problem is to assign utilities to the different outcomes. Ignoring various complications and subtleties (to be discussed later) the utility of an outcome corresponds to how much the decision maker values that outcome. Although it is convenient to work with exact figures here, it is not essential to the decision-theoretic approach that people themselves can assign precise numerical values to each outcome. What is crucial is that people can order the outcomes in terms of which they prefer (with ties being allowed), and can express preferences (or indifference) between gambles involving these outcomes.

One method to infer a person's utility scale from their preferences is as follows: Assign 100 to the most preferred outcome (O1), 0 to the least preferred outcome (O2), then find the probability P such that the decision maker is indifferent between outcome O3 for certain or a gamble with probability P of O1 (gain 100) and probability $1 - P$ of O2 (gain 0). The utility for O3, U(O3), is then equal to p. U(O1) $= 100p$. For example, if the decision maker is indifferent when $P = .5$, then their utility for O3 is $= 50$. This process can be repeated for all outcomes in the decision problem. (Note that this method requires establishing a prior subjective probability scale. See Ramsey, 1931, and Savage, 1954, for a method that allows both to be established simultaneously.)

Returning to our barbecue example, suppose that the decision maker values the four outcomes using a scale from 100 (most satisfactory) to 0 (least satisfactory). He values a sunny barbecue highest, and assigns this outcome a value of 100. He values a wet barbecue lowest (O_{12}), and assigns this a value of 0. He also prefers a meal indoors listening to the rain (O_{22}) to a meal indoors looking at the sun (O_{21}), and values these outcomes 50 and 30 respectively. These assignments are shown in the decision matrix in Table 8.1.

Probabilities

To complete the decision matrix the decision maker needs to assign probabilities to the possible states of the world. Sometimes objectively agreed estimates for these probabilities might be available, otherwise the decision

Table 8.1 Decision matrix for a barbecue

	Sunny		Rainy	
Barbecue outside	100	O_{11}	0	O_{12}
Meal indoors	30	O_{21}	50	O_{22}

maker must use his or her own subjective estimates. The literature on subjective probability estimates is vast and divisive, and was explored in detail in chapters 5 and 6. What is generally agreed is that the decision maker should assign probabilities bounded by zero (= definitely will not happen) and one (= definitely will happen), with the value of ½ reserved for a state that is equally likely to happen as not. In addition, the probabilities assigned to mutually exclusive and exhaustive sets of states should sum to one (see chapter 5 for more details about constraints on probability estimates).

For the purposes of the barbecue example we will assume that the probability of rain is .5. Note that in this situation the probability of rain remains the same regardless of which act we actually take. This will not always be the case: sometimes one's actions themselves influence the probability of the relevant states of nature. And indeed, as far as those living in England are concerned, it often appears as if the probability of rain jumps as soon as a barbecue is decided on.

Maximizing expected utility

At this point we have a representation of the decision problem faced by the decision maker, including the assignments of probabilities and utilities. The elements that make up this specification are subjective, and may differ from individual to individual. However, the rules that take us from this specification to the 'correct' decision are generally considered to be 'objective', and thus not subject to the whims of the decision maker. Indeed there is only one central rule – the principle of maximizing expected utility (MEU).

This principle requires the computation of the *expected utility* of each act. The notion of expected utility has a long pedigree in mathematics and economics (Bernoulli, 1954; Pascal, 1670). The basic idea is that when deciding between options, the value of each possible outcome should be weighted by the probability of it occurring. This can be justified in several ways: in terms of what one can expect to win or lose if a gamble is repeated many times, or through constraints of coherence (Baron, 2000; Lindley, 1985; see also chapter 5).

Applied to the general decision problem the expected utility of each act is computed by the weighted sum of the utilities of all possible outcomes of that act. Thus the utility of each outcome, $U(O_{ij})$, is multiplied by the probability of the corresponding state of nature $P(S_j)$, and the sum of all these products gives the expected utility:

$$EU(A_i) = \Sigma \ U(O_{ij}). \ P(S_j)$$

Once the expected utility of each possible act is computed, the principle of MEU recommends that the act with the highest value is chosen.

In our example the expected utility of having a barbecue is a weighted sum over the two possible states of nature (rain or sun):

$$EU(A_1) = U(O_{11}).\ P(S_1) + U(O_{12}).\ P(S_2)$$
$$= 100 \times .5 + 0 \times .5 = 50$$

The expected utility of not having a barbecue (A_2) is:

$$EU(A_2) = U(O_{21}).\ P(S_1) + U(O_{22}).\ P(S_2)$$
$$= 30 \times .5 + 50 \times .5 = 40$$

Finally, the principle of MEU recommends that we select the act with the highest expected utility, in this case to have a barbecue.

Why maximize?

So far we have simply presented the decision framework, and shown how to compute the expected utility of acts. We have not said why the principle of MEU is the appropriate rule to follow (although the fact that it would give us the best return in the long run is not too bad a reason to adopt it). One of the major achievements in the theory of decision is that this principle can be shown to follow from a few basic postulates, each of which seems intuitively plausible. What theorists have shown is that if you accept these postulates then you accept (on pain of inconsistency) the principle of MEU. We discuss these axioms in later sections.

Status of decision framework

The framework presented above is standard in most analyses of decision making. However, the status of this framework and its relevance to human decision making can be construed in several different ways. First, there is the distinction between *normative* and *descriptive* models. A normative model of decision making tells us how people ought to make decisions; a descriptive model tells us how people actually do make decisions.

Second, there is the distinction between 'as-if' and 'process' models. An 'as-if' model states that the choice behaviour of an agent can be represented 'as if' they have certain utility and probability functions, and maximize expected utility, but does not claim that they actually do this. Essentially as-if models predict the outputs of an agent in terms of the inputs it receives, but don't specify exactly how this is achieved. In contrast, a process model tells us how the agent actually carries out these computations. A process model of decision making claims that the agent does have actual utility and probability functions (prior to making a choice), and makes expected utility computations in order to decide what actions to take.

Note that this distinction applies to both normative and descriptive models. In the case of normative models the classic position is that the principle of MEU is an 'as-if' model (e.g., Luce & Raiffa, 1957; Raiffa, 1968).

That is, if agents' choices are consistent with some basic axioms (see below), then their behaviour can be represented as if they are maximizing expected utility. But on this view it is the preferences that are primary, not the utilities. We should not say that someone prefers A to B because they assign A higher expected value; rather, we assign them a higher expected utility to A because they prefer A to B. So the validity of the model reduces to the validity of some basic axioms about preferences.

In contrast, it is also possible to construe the standard decision framework as a process model (for ideal agents). In order to make a good choice the decision maker should assign utilities and probabilities to the alternatives, and then select the option that maximizes expected utility. This approach is explicitly advanced in numerous texts on decision analysis (e.g., Hammond, Keeney, & Raiffa, 1999), and is implicit in most presentations of the decision-theoretic framework.

In cognitive psychology as-if models are often referred to as computational or rational models (Anderson, 1991; Marr, 1982). They seek to establish what an agent is trying to compute, rather than how the agent is actually computing it. In the case of decision making, then, an 'as-if' model succeeds in modelling human behaviour to the extent that it captures the macro-level choice behaviour.

On the other hand, process models strive to describe the actual cognitive mechanisms that underpin this behaviour. In the case of decision making, proponents of MEU as a process model must not only show that people's choice behaviour conforms to this principle, but also that people's assessments of probability and utility *cause* their choices via this principle.

In the rest of this chapter we look at the descriptive adequacy of both as-if and process models. Note that if the principle of MEU fails as an 'as-if' model then it seems to automatically fail as a process model (indeed most empirical critiques of MEU proceed in this way). However, it is important not to move too quickly here. A principle such as MEU may fail to apply to some cases of choice behaviour (especially those specifically devised to refute it), and yet still serve as an appropriate framework within which to develop good process models (see Busemeyer & Johnson, 2004; Usher & McClelland, 2001).

The axioms of expected utility theory

As noted above, a fundamental insight of decision theory is that the question of whether an agent's choice behaviour can be represented in terms of the principle of MEU is reducible to the question of whether the agent obeys certain basic choice axioms. There are several different axiomatic systems, but it is possible to extract a core set of substantive principles: cancellation, transitivity, dominance and invariance. (For notational convenience we will refer to the general overarching framework of expected utility theory as EUT.)

The first of these postulates, *cancellation* or the *sure-thing principle*, holds that states of the world that give the same outcome regardless of one's choice can be eliminated (cancelled) from the choice problem. This principle is fundamental to EUT, but has been questioned as both a normative and a descriptive rule. It is discussed in detail in the next section. The second principle, *transitivity*, states that if option A is preferred to option B, and option B preferred to option C, then option A is preferred to option C. Although generally accepted as a normative rule, people sometimes violate this principle (remember Barry and his lollipops in chapter 2). However, violations of transitivity seem to be the exception rather than the rule.

The principle of *dominance* states that if option A is better than option B in at least one respect, and at least as good as option B in all other respects, then option A should always be preferred to B. It has strong normative appeal – why prefer option B if it can never deliver more than option A, and will sometimes deliver less? However, people sometimes violate this axiom, especially in its weaker 'stochastic' version. This happens when people are presented with repeated choices between two options, one of which delivers a prize (e.g., money) with a higher probability than the other. People often 'probability match' in these circumstances; that is, they distribute their choices between the two options according to the probabilities that the options deliver the prize. For example, if option A gives a prize 70 per cent of the time, and option B gives the same prize 30 per cent of the time, then people choose option A 70 per cent of the time and option B 30 per cent of the time. This is a violation of stochastic dominance, because the person can expect to win the highest sum if they choose option A all the time (see chapter 11 for more details).

The principle of *invariance* states that someone's preferences should not depend on how the options are described or on how they are elicited. This also has strong normative appeal, but appears to be violated in many cases of actual choice behaviour (see sections on framing and preference reversals in the next chapter, and the medical treatment example in chapter 1).

The sure-thing principle

One of the central principles in Savage's (1954) decision model is the 'sure-thing' principle: if someone would prefer option A to option B if event X occurs, and would also prefer option A to option B if event X does not occur, then they should prefer A to be B when they are ignorant of whether or not X occurs.

Savage illustrates this principle with the following example:

> Imagine that a businessman is considering whether or not to buy a property. The businessman thinks that the attractiveness of this purchase will depend in part on the result of the upcoming presidential election. To clarify things he asks himself whether he would buy if he knew that the Republican candidate would win, and decides that he would. He

then asks himself whether he would buy if he knew that the Democratic candidate would win, and again decides that he would. Given that he would buy the property in either event, this is the appropriate action even though he does not know what the result of the election will be.

On the face of it this seems like a compelling principle. Why should your choice between options be affected by events that have no impact on the outcomes of interest? However, Allais (1953) and Ellsberg (1961) both presented situations in which people's intuitive choices appear to violate this principle.

The Allais paradox

Imagine that you are faced with two choice problems:

Problem 1
You must choose between:
(a) $500,000 for sure
(b) $2,500,000 with probability .1, $500,000 with probability .89, nothing with probability .01

Problem 2
You must choose between:
(c) $500,000 with probability .11, nothing with probability .89
(d) $2,500,000 with probability .1, nothing with probability .9

Most people choose (a) rather than (b) in problem 1, and (d) over (c) in problem 2. But this pattern of choices is inconsistent, and violates the sure-thing principle.

To show that it is inconsistent, let us denote $U(x)$ as the utility that you assign to x. Then a preference for (a) over (b) implies (according to the principle of MEU) that:

$$U(\$500,000) > .1\ U(\$2,500,000) + .89\ U(\$500,000) \tag{8.1}$$

In other words, you prefer a sure gain of $500,000 to the combination gamble with a .1 chance of $2,500,000 and a .89 chance of $500,000.

But equation (8.1) can be rearranged by subtracting .89 U ($500,000) from both sides, so that:

$$U(\$500,000) - .89\ U(\$500,000) > .1\ U(\$2,500,000)$$

Which reduces to:

$$.11\ U(\$500,000) > .1\ U(\$2,500,000) \tag{8.2}$$

Therefore your preference for (a) over (b) implies that you prefer a .11 chance of $500,000 to a .1 chance of $2,500,000.

However, in problem 2 you preferred (d) over (c). This implies (via MEU) that:

$$.1 \ U(\$2,500,000) > .11 \ U(\$500,000) \tag{8.3}$$

In other words, you prefer a .1 chance of $2,500,000 to a .11 chance of $500,000. Clearly (8.2) and (8.3) are inconsistent, and yet both are direct implications of your pattern of preferences according to the principle of MEU.

Why is this a violation of the sure-thing principle? This is best shown by re-representing the problem (Savage, 1954). The Allais problem can be represented as a 100 ticket lottery with payoffs as shown in Table 8.2. Presented in this manner the application of the sure-thing principle becomes clear. It states that if a ticket from 12 to 100 is drawn it should have no impact on one's pattern of preferences. This is because these tickets do not discriminate between either pair of gambles (they have the same values for each pair). According to the sure thing (or cancellation), this allows us to reduce the problem to the cases of tickets 1–11. And from inspection of the table it is clear that these are identical in both problems. This should persuade you (does it?) that if you prefer (a) to (b) you should also prefer (c) to (d), on pain of inconsistency.

Of course you may still persist in the 'inconsistent' pair of choices, and argue that it is the sure-thing principle (and cancellation) that is incorrect. In fact you would be in good company here, as many prominent thinkers, including the Nobel laureate Allais, maintain that the sure-thing principle is inadequate in such cases. In opposition to this, theorists such as Savage have argued that once the Allais problem is re-represented to make the sure-thing principle transparent (as in Table 8.2), it is your 'inconsistent' pattern of choices that should be abandoned, not the sure-thing principle. An interesting footnote to this debate is that when people are shown the re-represented Allais problem, they are indeed more likely to obey the sure-thing principle (Keller, 1985; for recent work on the effects of re-representing decision problems see Lan & Harvey, 2006).

Table 8.2 Savage's representation of the Allais paradox

		Ticket number		
		1	*2–11*	*12–100*
Problem 1	a	500 000	500 000	500 000
	b	0	2 500 000	500 000
Problem 2	c	500 000	500 000	0
	d	0	2 500 000	0

Let us return to the original formulation of the Allais problem. Why do people prefer (a) to (b) in problem 1, but prefer (d) to (c) in problem 2? Savage himself had a plausible psychological explanation for such findings. He argued that people prefer (a) to (b) because the extra chance of winning a very large amount in (b) does not compensate for the slight chance of winning nothing. In contrast, the same people might prefer (d) to (c) because while the chance of winning something is pretty much the same for both options, they prefer the option with the much larger prize. This explanation has been developed more fully by various psychologists, and will be explored in the next chapter.

Extensions of the Allais problem

Whatever your position on the normative status of the sure-thing principle, its status as a descriptive model does seem to be undermined by people's responses to the Allais problem. Indeed over the past decades numerous versions of this problem have been presented to people, and violations of the principle are regularly observed. Kahneman and Tversky (1979a) presented people with a range of Allais-like problems, and demonstrated systematic violations of the principle of MEU. For example, they gave participants the following pair of problems:

Problem 1
You must choose between:
(a) $4000 with probability .8
(b) $3000 for sure

Problem 2
You must choose between:
(c) $4000 with probability .2
(d) $3000 with probability .25

In this experiment 80 per cent of participants preferred (b) to (a), and 65 per cent preferred (c) to (d). But this pattern of preferences violates the principle of MEU because a preference for (b) over (a) implies:

$$U(\$3000) > .8\ U(\$4000) \tag{8.4}$$

Whereas a preference for (c) over (d) implies:

$$.2\ U(\$4000) > .25\ U(\$3000) \tag{8.5}$$

Which (if both sides are multiplied by 4) is equivalent to:

$$.8\ U(\$4000) > U(\$3000)$$

So (8.4) and (8.5) are inconsistent.

Kahneman and Tversky also demonstrated violations of the principle of MEU with non-monetary gambles. For example, they presented participants with the following two problems:

Problem 3
(a) A 50 per cent chance to win a 3-week tour of England, France and Italy
(b) A 1-week tour of England for sure

Problem 4
(c) A 5 per cent chance to win a 3-week tour of England, France and Italy
(d) A 10 per cent chance to win a 1-week tour of England

Most participants preferred (b) to (a) (demonstrating questionable taste), but also preferred (c) to (d). Here again this pattern violates the principle of MEU.

Ellsberg's problems

Another choice paradox, devised by Ellsberg (1961), also challenges the status of the sure-thing principle. Imagine you are presented with two urns each containing 100 balls. Urn 1 contains an unknown number of red and black balls – there could be any number of red balls from zero to 100. Urn 2 contains exactly 50 red balls and 50 black balls. You are asked four questions, in each of which you must stake $100 on one of two bets (with the option of expressing indifference):

(1) Given a draw from Urn 1, would you rather bet on Red or Black?
(2) Given a draw from Urn 2, would you rather bet on Red or Black?
(3) If you have to bet on Red, would you rather it be on a draw from Urn 1 or Urn 2?
(4) If you have to bet on Black, would you rather it be on a draw from Urn 1 or Urn 2?

How did you choose? Overall people tend to be indifferent between red and black in questions 1 and 2, but prefer to bet on a draw from Urn 2 in both questions 3 and 4. But this is problematic for the principle of MEU, because it appears to demonstrate an inconsistent pair of probability judgments. On the one hand, your preference for Urn 2 in question 3 suggests that you think that a red ball from Urn 2 is more probable than a red ball from Urn 1. On the other hand, your preference for Urn 2 in question 4 suggests that you think that a black ball from Urn 2 is more probable than a black ball from Urn 1.

According to Ellsberg (1961) this example shows that people reason differently when they know the exact probabilities (Urn 2) than when they are ignorant of the exact probabilities (Urn 1), and this difference is not captured given the standard MEU principle.

Ellsberg presented another case (which has become the standard example in the literature). Imagine an urn that contains 30 red balls, and 60 black or yellow balls in an unknown proportion. One ball is to be drawn at random. Would you bet on red or black? The payoff matrix is shown in Table 8.3.

Most people prefer to bet on red in this case (option 1). However, now consider a choice problem with a different payoff matrix (see Table 8.4.) Here the choice is between (3) betting on 'red or yellow', or (4) betting on 'black or yellow'. Which would you choose?

With this payoff matrix, most respondents prefer to bet on black or yellow (option 4). But this is a clear violation of the sure-thing principle (and thus MEU), because the two pairs of options differ only in their third column, and this is constant for either pair. If you prefer to bet on red in the first problem, why should you prefer to bet on 'black or yellow' in the second problem?

Ambiguity aversion

Ellsberg concluded that people prefer to bet on outcomes with known probabilities rather than on outcomes with unknown probabilities. This is problematic for most versions of EUT, because the theory assumes that there is no substantial difference between a definite (known) probability judgment and an uncertain probability judgment with the same numerical value. Ellsberg termed this 'ambiguity aversion': people are less willing to bet on

Table 8.3 Payoff matrix for Ellsberg's problem 1

Number of balls	30	60	
Colour of ball	Red	Black	Yellow
1 – bet on red	£100	£0	£0
2 – bet on black	£0	£100	£0

Table 8.4 Payoff matrix for Ellsberg's problem 2

Number of balls	30	60	
Colour of ball	Red	Black	Yellow
3 – bet on red or yellow	£100	£0	£100
4 – bet on black or yellow	£0	£100	£100

ambiguous outcomes than on unambiguous outcomes, even if they both have equivalent probabilities.

There have been numerous studies confirming people's preference for known over unknown probabilities (e.g., MacCrimmon & Larsson, 1979; Slovic & Tversky, 1974). As noted above, this finding does not fit with standard EUT; however, is it also not explained by the main model of human choice (prospect theory). We return to the issue of ambiguity aversion once we have presented this theory in the next chapter.

Summary

In this chapter we have introduced the dominant framework for modelling choices (EUT), and its central maxim of maximizing expected utility (MEU). The status of this framework has been discussed in terms of the distinction between normative and descriptive models, and the distinction between process and 'as-if' models. We have shown how representing someone's choices in terms of MEU depends on their preferences satisfying certain basic axioms, and discussed two of the classic demonstrations that people's intuitive preferences violate these axioms (Allais' and Ellsberg's problems). In the next chapter we turn to the issue of how people *actually* make choices and present one of the most successful models of human choice – prospect theory.

9 Analysing decisions II: Prospect theory and preference reversals

How do people actually make choices? The dominant account of human choice is prospect theory (Kahneman & Tversky, 1979a, 1984; Tversky & Kahneman, 1992). Prospect theory preserves the idea that our choices involve maximizing some kind of expectation. However, the utilities and probabilities of outcomes both undergo systematic cognitive distortions (non-linear transformations) when they are evaluated. Moreover, prior to this evaluation the decision maker must construct a mental representation of the choice problem. This invokes several cognitive operations not captured by the standard EUT, such as the framing of options relative to some reference point, and the editing of gambles to simplify the choice problem. In this chapter we outline the theoretical model that explains these cognitive operations and distortions, and the empirical evidence that supports it.

Reference-dependence

Before decision makers can evaluate their options they must represent the problem in a meaningful way. One of the key insights in prospect theory is that the mental representations people use in choice situations have features that reach beyond anything given in economic theory. This is exemplified by Kahneman and Tversky's claim that people usually perceive outcomes as gains or losses relative to a neutral reference point. This simple observation leads to a substantial reworking of the traditional notion of utility, and its role in choice behaviour.

The value function

A milestone in the development of classical EUT was the distinction between money and its utility, and the idea that in general money has diminishing marginal utility (see chapter 2). This is illustrated by the fact that the same amount of money, say $100, has more value for a pauper than a prince. Applied to a single individual, it amounts to the claim that one values the move from $100 to $200 more than the move from $1100 to $1200. In technical terms, the subjective value of money is a concave function of money (see Figure 2.1 for a graphical illustration). A direct consequence of this relation between utility and money is that people will in general be *risk-averse*. That is, they will prefer a sure amount $x to a gamble with the same expected value (e.g., a 50 per cent chance of winning $2x$).

Traditional theories of EUT also assumed that people evaluate gambles in terms of the overall states of wealth they lead to. So a pauper with $1 to his name evaluates a win of $10 as a transition from $1 to $11, whereas a prince with $1 million to his name evaluates the same win as a transition from $1 million to $1,000,010. And thus a potential gain of $10 means more (is more valuable) for the pauper than for the prince. The radical proposal made in prospect theory (and beforehand by Markowitz, 1952) is that people do not evaluate the outcomes of gambles in terms of the overall states of wealth to which they lead, but as gains (or losses) relative to a neutral reference point. So the pauper and prince, despite their different starting points, can show similar behaviour when faced with the same choices between gambles. (This explains why rich people can still be mean.)

Furthermore, this neutral reference point is malleable, and open to manipulation. This means that the same underlying choice problem can be given different reference points, and consequently lead to divergent choices (see framing effects below). So two princes (or the same prince at different times) might make very different choices (e.g., about who to marry) depending on their reference frame.

The flipside to risk aversion in the domain of gains is risk-seeking in the domain of losses. Just as the difference between a gain of $10 versus $20 appears greater than the difference between $110 and $120, so a loss of $20 versus $10 will appear greater than that between losses of $120 and $110. This diminishing function for losses (now reflected by a convex function) implies risk-seeking. One prefers a probable loss to a sure loss with the same expectation. For example, people typically prefer an 80 per cent chance of losing $1000 to a sure loss of $800.

This overall pattern of preferences is summarized by the S-shaped value function shown in Figure 9.1. It has a concave shape in the domain of gains (upper right quadrant) and a convex shape in the domain of losses (lower left quadrant). It captures several key claims of prospect theory: people tend to evaluate gambles in terms of gains or losses relative to a neutral point, and they are often risk-averse for gains but risk-seeking for losses.

As well as fitting a range of empirical studies (see below), the idea that people evaluate outcomes in terms of changes of wealth rather than final states of wealth has strong parallels in psychophysics. Our responses to sensory and perceptual stimuli often track relative rather than absolute changes, and exhibit a similar relation of diminishing sensitivity to such changes (e.g., habituation).

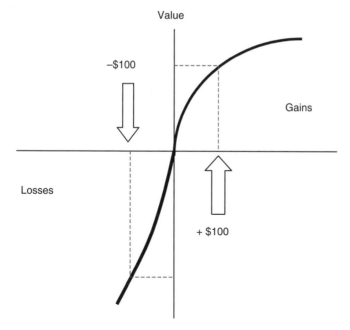

Figure 9.1 The value function of prospect theory.

The isolation effect

A vivid demonstration that people evaluate outcomes in terms of changes of wealth rather than final states of wealth is given in the *isolation effect* (Kahneman & Tversky, 1979a).

Consider problem 1:

> In addition to whatever you own, you have been given $1000. You are now asked to choose between:

> A: A 50 per cent chance of $1000; B: $500 for sure.

The majority of participants (84 per cent) in Kahneman and Tversky's experiment chose option B, demonstrating risk-aversion in the domain of gains.

Now consider problem 2:

> In addition to whatever you own, you have been given $2000. You are now asked to choose between:

> C: A 50 per cent chance of losing $1000; D: A sure loss of $500.

In this case the majority of participants (69 per cent) prefer C. This demonstrates risk-seeking in the domain of losses, and fits with the predictions of prospect theory noted above. However, these two choice problems are identical if construed in terms of final states of wealth:

A = $1000 + 50% chance of $1000 = $2,000 − 50% chance of $1000 = C

B = $1500 for sure = D

These choices conflict with the prescriptions of EUT, which requires that the same pattern of choices be made in both problems (e.g., either A and C, or B and D). Moreover, they also contradict the simple assumption of risk-aversion, because in problem 2 the risky option is preferred to the sure loss. At heart the observed choices reflect people's failure to integrate the initial bonus (either $1000 or $2000) into their evaluations of the gambles. They focus on the changes in wealth that the different options entail rather than their final states (which are equivalent).

Losses loom larger than gains

Another crucial feature of the value function is that it is much steeper in the domain of losses than in the domain of gains (see Figure 9.1). This implies that the displeasure caused by a loss of $100 is larger than the pleasure from a gain of $100, and hence that people are more averse to losses than they are attracted by corresponding gains. There is a wealth of empirical data in support of loss-aversion, and it has been extended to many real-world situations (see the collection by Kahneman & Tversky, 2000).

The simplest example of loss-aversion is the fact that people dislike gambles that offer an equal probability of winning or losing the same amount of money. That is, they tend to reject gambles that offer a 50 per cent chance of winning $X and a 50 per cent chance of losing $X (especially when X is a large amount). More realistic demonstrations of loss-aversion are given by the *endowment effect* and *status quo bias*.

The endowment effect was introduced by Thaler (1980). It hinges on a simple principle of behaviour that many of us learned in the school playground – once you acquire something, you are often reluctant to give it up, even if offered a price (or inducement) that you yourself would not have paid for the object in the first place. The sharing of different colour sweets among children comes to mind here.

The endowment effect has been demonstrated in numerous experiments. One of the best known was conducted by Kahneman, Knetsch, and Thaler (1990). They randomly distributed university mugs (worth about $5) to some of their students. All students were then given questionnaires. The students who had received mugs (the 'sellers') were effectively asked how much they would be prepared to sell their mugs for. The students who had not received mugs (the 'choosers') were asked about their preferences between receiving the mug or various amounts of money.

From a normative point of view both the sellers and the choosers face the same decision problem: mug versus money. However, if we factor in loss-aversion, then their situations are quite different. The sellers are contemplating how much money they would accept to *give up* their mug, while the choosers are contemplating how much they would pay to *acquire* the same mug. In other words, sellers are evaluating a potential loss (of a mug), while choosers are evaluating a potential gain.

In line with the predictions of loss-aversion, the median value of the mug for the sellers was about $7, while for the choosers it was about $3. Simply by endowing some students with the mug in the first place, their evaluations of its worth had shifted markedly relative to other non-endowed students. This effect has been replicated and extended in many studies (see several papers in the collection by Kahneman & Tversky, 2000).

Closely related to the endowment effect is the *status quo bias*. This amounts to the preference to remain in the same state (the status quo) rather than take a risk and move to another state, and is explained by the potential losses incurred by shifting from the status quo looming larger than the potential gains. Samuelson and Zeckhauser (1988) demonstrated this effect in the context of a hypothetical investment task. One group of participants were told they had inherited a sum of money, and had to choose from various investment options (moderate risk, high risk, etc.). The other group were told they had inherited a portfolio of investments, most of which were concentrated in one specific option (e.g., moderate risk). They then had to choose from the same array of investment options as the other group (and were told that transaction costs were minimal). Across a range of scenario manipulations participants in the latter condition showed a strong status quo bias. They preferred to stick with the previously invested option, and this tendency increased with the number of available options.

The phenomenon of loss-aversion, and its correlative effects of endowment and status quo biases, is firmly established in experimental studies and indeed the economic world beyond the laboratory. Although seemingly irrational in the context of business and market transactions, it has roots in lower-level psychological laws that seem adaptive to basic environmental demands. Thus the asymmetry of people's reactions to pain versus pleasure is eminently sensible in a world that punishes those who ignore danger signs more than it rewards those who pursue signs of pleasure.

The fourfold pattern

Prospect theory was constructed to fit a wide range of choice behaviour. Much of this is summarized by the 'fourfold' pattern shown in Table 9.1. The value function alone, however, only explains a 'twofold' pattern of

Table 9.1 The fourfold pattern of choice behaviour for simple gambles

	Gains	*Losses*
Small probabilities	Risk-seeking	Risk-aversion
Medium and large probabilities	Risk-aversion	Risk-seeking

risk-aversion for gains and risk-seeking for losses. It does not account for the opposite pattern observed when the probabilities involved are small. To capture the whole pattern Kahneman and Tversky introduced the notion of decision weights.

Decision weights

Just as decision makers transform the 'objective' utility of a gain or a loss into a subjective value (via the value function), so they transform the 'objective' probability of an outcome into a decision weight. The decision weight function (see Figure 9.2) is also non-linear. Its central features are the overweighting of small probabilities, the underweighting of moderate and large probabilities, and extreme behaviour close to zero or one.

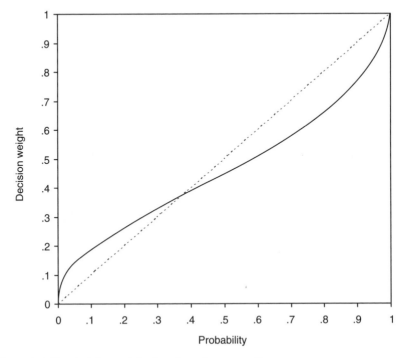

Figure 9.2 The decision weight function of prospect theory.

This function can explain risk-seeking with gambles that offer small probabilities of positive outcomes (e.g., the widespread purchase of lottery tickets), and risk-aversion with those that offer small probabilities of negative outcomes (e.g., the widespread purchase of insurance). This is demonstrated in the following two problems:

Problem 1
Choose between (i) a .001 chance of winning $5000; (ii) $5 for sure.

The majority of participants (72 per cent) chose option (i), indicating risk-seeking (and replicating the behaviour of thousands of lottery players worldwide).

Problem 2
Choose between (i) a .001 chance of losing $5000; (ii) losing $5 for sure.

In this case the majority (83 per cent) went for the sure loss (ii), exhibiting the risk-averse behaviour that insurers worldwide know and love.

It is important to distinguish the over- or under*weighting* of probabilities introduced by the decision weight function from the over- or under*estimation* of probabilities discussed in the previous chapters. The latter concerns how people estimate a probability on the basis of information such as its availability to memory, whereas the former concerns how people weight this estimate when they make a decision or choice. Someone can judge that an outcome has a specific probability (e.g., that their chance of winning the national lottery jackpot is 1 in 13 million), and yet overweight this probability when they choose to buy a ticket. More worryingly, people can both overestimate a probability (due to a cognitive bias), and overweight it when making a decision. For example, media scare stories might make us overestimate a very small probability (e.g., death by the flesh-eating Ebola virus), and then we might also overweight this estimate in our choice behaviour (e.g., whether to purchase travel insurance).

There are now numerous empirical studies showing how people's decision weights approximate the non-linear function in Figure 9.2, both when precise probabilities are given in the problem, and when they must be estimated by the decision maker. There are also several variations on the precise shape and parameters of the curve (e.g., Wu & Gonzalez, 1996). We will spare the reader the gory details. The important take-home message is that when people evaluate decision options they often seem to distort the stated or experienced probabilities. Thus far, however, we lack a deep psychological explanation for why people do so (but see Hogarth & Einhorn, 1990 for one suggestion).

The certainty effect

The non-linearity of decision weights, and their extreme behaviour near to zero and one, also accounts for the *certainty* effect. This is essentially a generalization of the findings in the Allais problems (discussed in chapter 8): people place special emphasis on outcomes that are guaranteed to occur (or guaranteed not to occur). For a striking illustration of this (not as yet empirically tested, because of difficulties getting ethical approval) consider a game of Russian roulette. Imagine it is your turn to place the gun to your temple. How much would you pay to reduce the number of bullets from 1 to zero? Presumably more than you would pay to reduce the number of bullets from 4 to 3. This suggests that a shift from uncertainty to certainty (e.g., increasing the chances of survival from 5/6 to 1) is weighted more than an equivalent shift from one uncertain state to another (e.g., an increase from 3/6 to 4/6).

This emphasis on certainty cuts two ways. When people are considering possible gains they often prefer a certain win to a probable win with greater expected monetary value. For example, they prefer a certain option of $3000 to an 80 per cent chance of $4000 (see problem 1, Table 9.2). In contrast, when considering possible losses people often prefer a probable loss of a greater amount to a definite loss of a smaller amount, even when the latter has less expected monetary value. For example, they prefer an 80 per cent chance of losing $4000 to a certain loss of $3000 (see problem 1′, Table 9.2).

This relationship between positive and negative gambles, along with the four-fold pattern noted above, is summarized in the *reflection effect* (Kahneman & Tversky, 1979a). This has effectively become an empirical law of choice behaviour, and states that the preference ordering for any pair of gambles in the domain of gains is reversed when the pair of gambles is transformed so that losses replace gains. This effect is displayed in Table 9.2, which shows the patterns of responses elicited in experimental studies (Kahneman & Tversky, 1979a). Note that the preference orderings for gambles with

Table 9.2 Preferences between positive and negative prospects

Positive prospects		Negative prospects	
1	(4000, .80) < (3000) 20% 80%	1′	(−4,000, .80) > (−3000) 92% 8%
2	(4000, .20) > (3000, .25) 65% 35%	2′	(−4000, .20) < (−3000, .25) 42% 58%
3	(3000, .90) > (6000, .45) 86% 14%	3′	(−3,000, .90) < (−6,000, .45) 8% 92%
4	(3000, .002) < (6000, .001) 27% 73%	4′	(−3,000, .002) > (−6,000, .001) 70% 30%

Source: Adapted from Kahneman and Tversky (1979a).

positive outcomes (first column) are reversed in the corresponding gambles with negative outcomes (second column).

Framing

As mentioned above, one of prospect theory's main insights is that the choices people make are determined by their mental representations of the decision problem, and that this often involves encoding the outcomes in terms of gains or losses relative to a specific reference point. The classic demonstration of this is the Asian disease problem (Tversky & Kahneman, 1981).

> *Problem 1*: Imagine the USA is preparing for the outbreak of an unusual Asian disease, which is expected to kill 600 people. Two alternative programmes to combat the disease have been proposed. Assume that the exact scientific estimates of the consequences of the programme are as follows:
>
> If Programme A is adopted, 200 people will be saved.
>
> If Programme B is adopted, there is a 1/3 probability that 600 people will be saved and a 2/3 probability that no people will be saved.
>
> Which of the two programmes would you favour?

When participants are presented with problem 1, the majority (72 per cent) prefer option A. This reflects risk-aversion – people prefer the sure gain of 200 lives to the 1/3 chance of saving 600 lives. Now consider a second version of this problem, identical except for the way in which the gambles involved in the two programmes are described.

> *Problem 2*: Same background scenario.
>
> If Programme C is adopted, 400 people will die.
>
> If Programme D is adopted, there is a 1/3 probability that nobody will die and a 2/3 probability that 600 people will die.
>
> Which of the two programmes would you favour?

When presented with problem 2 the majority of people (78 per cent) select option D (even if they have already answered problem 1). This reflects risk-seeking – they prefer the gamble over the sure loss.

Of course the two problems are identical except for the framing of the outcomes. In problem 1 outcomes are framed as possible gains relative to a reference point of 600 people dying. In problem 2 they are framed as possible losses relative to a reference point of no one dying. As predicted by prospect theory, respondents shift their choices according to the reference frame they adopt. When the reference state is 600 deaths, they evaluate the outcomes as gains, and are risk-averse; when it is zero deaths, they evaluate the outcomes as losses, and are risk-averse.

This demonstration is compelling for various reasons. It simultaneously highlights people's susceptibility to reference frames, and their risk-aversion in the domain of gains but risk-seeking in the domain of losses. It also shows a clear violation of the principle of invariance, which lies at the heart of the standard EUT.

The Asian flu problem has proved robust across a wide variety of domains, including politics, business, finance, management and medicine (you might recall we met a version of the problem back in chapter 1 in the discussion of which medical treatment to adopt – for a review of all these domains see Maule & Villejoubert, 2007). The framing effect is also demonstrated in the real world by innumerable marketing and advertising ploys, for example, the preponderance of labels that inform us that products are 95 per cent fat free rather than 5 per cent fat (which confuses those of us who prefer our dairy products with lots of fat).

Ironically, the ease with which framing effects can be exhibited has deflected researchers from uncovering the psychological processes that underlie these effects. This seems to be an area ripe for future research, and one that could benefit from ongoing work in mainstream cognitive psychology (Rettinger & Hastie, 2001, 2003). In particular, although Kahneman and Tversky did introduce several editing operations in their original model (1979a), these have not been elaborated in subsequent developments (e.g., Tversky & Kahneman, 1992). Maule and Villejoubert (2007) have introduced a simple information-processing model that is a step in this direction. Their framework accentuates both the editing phase – how people construct internal representations of the decision problem, and the evaluation phase – how these internal representations generate actual choices.

Ambiguity aversion or ignorance aversion?

At the end of the last chapter we discussed Ellsberg's problem, and noted his proposal that decision makers have a basic aversion to uncertainty or ambiguity. This is not captured by standard EUT, but neither is it accommodated within the standard formulations of prospect theory. However, the claim that people are averse to uncertainty is not borne out by their choice behaviour in the domain of losses, where they often prefer the uncertain gamble over the sure loss (e.g., see problem 1' in Table 9.2).

An alternative to ambiguity aversion is the idea that people are reluctant to choose options that they are ignorant about (Heath & Tversky, 1991). This can explain the patterns of choices in Ellsberg's problems, but also has the potential to generalize to a wider range of situations. Indeed this position argues that ignorance and uncertainty are often confounded, but if they can be teased apart people will show an aversion to ignorance rather than uncertainty per se.

To demonstrate this 'ignorance aversion' Heath and Tversky asked participants for their willingness to bet on uncertain events in various situations, including those in which they thought they had good knowledge, those in which they thought they had poor knowledge, and chance events. For example, participants gave their preferences between gambles on sporting events, results of political elections, and random games of chance. The main finding was that people preferred to bet in situations where they thought they had some competence rather than on chance events that were matched in terms of probabilities. Conversely, they preferred to bet on chance events rather than on probability matched events in situations where they thought they had little competence.

In short, people prefer to bet on uncertain events that they are knowledgeable about (or think they are) rather than on matched uncertain events of which they are ignorant. This may explain why betting shops are very happy to provide their punters with information about the events on which they can bet, and why gambling houses encourage those who think they have a special system to beat the roulette wheel. This notion of ignorance aversion has been tested in various domains, and extended in several directions (Fox & Tversky, 1995; Tversky & Fox, 1995). It has also been incorporated into an extended version of prospect theory (the two stage model, see Fox & See, 2003 for an overview).

How good a descriptive model is prospect theory?

The empirical data reviewed through the course of this chapter are largely consistent with prospect theory, especially when it is extended in certain natural ways (Fox & See, 2003; Kahneman & Tversky, 2000). Of course this should not be too surprising, as prospect theory was conceived precisely to accommodate many of these findings. However, it has also done a good job of predicting a range of novel empirical data, in areas as diverse as medicine, sports and finance. There are, however, a few shortcomings that deserve mention.

First, even though prospect theory is a descriptive theory of actual choice behaviour, it does not give deep psychological explanations for many of the processes it proposes. For example, there are no detailed accounts of how people frame decision problems, select reference points, or edit their options. Neither is there a clear cognitive account of how people integrate decision weights and values to yield a final decision. In such areas the theory operates more at the as-if level than the process level.

Second, there are certain factors that prospect theory does not include, but that seem to have a strong influence on people's decision making. Some of these are discussed in a later chapter (13) on decisions and emotion (e.g. Rottenstreich & Hsee, 2001). One prominent factor that has received attention from decision theorists is the notion of regret (see Loomes & Sugden, 1982; also Baron, 2000, for discussion). If we make a decision that turns out badly (compared to other possible outcomes), we seem to suffer something over and above the disutility of the actual outcome. We regret our decision. Similarly, if our decision leads to a much better outcome than the other alternatives, we gain something over and above the actual gain. We 'rejoice' in our decision. Thus it is argued that when making a decision people take these possibilities of regret or rejoicing into account. They anticipate how much they might regret or rejoice in a particular decision (by comparing its outcome with other possibilities). But prospect theory does not incorporate these factors in the decision-making process.

However, it seems unlikely that a full account of choice behaviour can be built on the notion of regret (Baron, 2000; Starmer & Sugden, 1993, 1998). Discussion of these issues lies outside the scope of this book, but interested readers should refer to work by Loomes, Sugden and Starmer (e.g., Loomes, Starmer, & Sugden, 1992; Starmer, 2000). For now we conclude that while the notion of regret has a role to play in a psychological theory of decision making, the most fruitful direction might be to supplement prospect theory rather than replace it.

Interim summary

So far in this chapter we have introduced the main psychological theory of choice behaviour, prospect theory. On this theory people base their choices on their mental representations of the decision problem, and thus objectively given (or experienced) utilities and probabilities undergo cognitive distortions prior to choice. This leads to a variety of departures from EUT, including framing effects, loss-aversion, the endowment effect, the certainty effect, ambiguity aversion, and so on.

As discussed above, the principle of invariance (which is critical to EUT) states that people's preferences should not depend on the way in which the choice options are described or the way in which their actual preferences are elicited. We have already seen situations where the framing of a problem drastically alters their choices. In the next section we visit situations where the means of eliciting someone's preferences radically changes the preferences themselves.

Preference reversals

The idea that human choice might conform to rational principles was seriously shaken by the discovery in the 1970s of reversals of preference between a pair of choice alternatives as a result of changes in the method of eliciting the preference. How can it be rational to prefer option A to option B when one's preference is evaluated by one method and to prefer B to A with a different method? If someone prefers a burger to pasta at a particular moment, then surely this is a reflection of some underlying fact about their nervous system and bodily state. How can their preference suddenly switch in a seemingly random way, merely as a result of varying the method of ascertaining that preference?

The classic demonstration was reported by Lichtenstein and Slovic (1971) who asked their participants to choose between the following pair of gambles:

A: Win $2.50 with probability .95, lose $0.75 with probability .05
B: Win $8.50 with probability .40, lose $1.50 with probability .60

Gamble A gives a high probability (.95) of winning a small amount ($2.50) and a very small probability (.05) of losing an even smaller amount ($0.75), while gamble B gives a medium probability of winning a large amount and a slightly larger probability of losing a modest amount. The expected value of gamble A is $2.34 and that of gamble B is $2.50 so a risk-neutral person (someone who neither seeks nor avoids risk per se) would choose B. Participants were asked either to pick the gamble they would prefer to play or to put a price on each gamble. In this latter case, they stated the monetary amount they would be prepared to accept to sell the gamble. The striking outcome was that Lichtenstein and Slovic's participants (and thousands of people tested in subsequent experiments) chose gamble A but put a higher price on gamble B. It thus seems that the ordering of preference between alternatives is not independent of the method of eliciting that preference, a clear violation of rational behaviour. Lichtenstein and Slovic (1973) showed, moreover, that gamblers in the more naturalistic setting of a Las Vegas casino were prone to the same tendency.

Another striking example of preference reversal can be observed when choice is compared to matching. Matching refers to generating a value for an attribute so as to make a pair of alternatives equally attractive. Consider this pair of candidates for an engineering job who differ (on a scale from 0 to 100) in their technical expertise and interpersonal skills (Tversky, Sattath, & Slovic, 1988):

	Technical knowledge	Human relations
C:	86	76
D:	78	91

When participants had to choose between the candidates they tended to opt for candidate C who had better technical knowledge. Participants in the matching condition were given a missing value for one of the four pieces of data and asked to fill in the value that would make the candidates equally attractive. Suppose the missing datum was the human relations score of candidate D. If people's preferences are stable and in the order elicited in the choice test, then they should suggest a value greater than 91, as such a value would be needed to make candidate D as attractive as candidate C. However, they tended to do the opposite, suggesting that in the matching test they preferred candidate D. Again their preferences seem to be reversed by a simple change in the elicitation method.

Compatibility and evaluability

Why might such reversals occur? Although several hypotheses have been proposed, there seems to be good support for the idea that different forms of elicitation draw emphasis to different features or dimensions of the problem (the so-called *compatibility* hypothesis). Applied to the original version (choice between gambles A and B), the idea is that more weight is put on the monetary values associated with the gambles in the pricing than in the choice condition. Since setting a price for something focuses attention on money values, these values receive more attention or become more salient in pricing. Conversely, in choice the probabilities become relatively more salient. These proposals are supported by evidence from Wedell and Böckenholt (1990) whose participants reported relying more on monetary values in pricing and more on probabilities in choice. An extension of the compatibility hypothesis to the matching problem (as in the example with candidates C and D) has been proposed by Tversky et al. (1988).

With these examples (apart from the Las Vegas gamblers), one can of course argue that people's behaviour in hypothetical laboratory decisions may not tell us very much about how they behave in more realistic cases where significant amounts of their own money or utility are at stake. Economists have therefore expended considerable effort in looking for preference reversals in real markets. A study by List (2002) provides very clear evidence that this type of non-normative behaviour does indeed span both the laboratory and the 'real' world, and also demonstrated reversals in a third context in addition to the two varieties mentioned above (choice versus pricing and choice versus matching). List studied people buying sports cards at a specialist show. In one condition, collectors entered separate bids for two sets of 1982 baseball cards, worth about $4, which they viewed alongside each other. These are sought after by baseball fans. One set comprised 10 mint-condition cards, while the other bundle included these same 10 cards together with 3 additional cards in very poor condition. The collectors who were the participants in this study submitted higher bids, as one would expect, for the 13-card than for the 10-card bundle. In a second condition, collectors evaluated each bundle in isolation. That is to say, they made a bid either for the 10- or for the 13-card bundle. The striking finding was that in this second case, the collectors stated a higher value for the 10-card bundle. Hence a preference for the 13-card bundle in the condition where they were evaluated side by side (called joint evaluation) was reversed when participants evaluated the bundles individually (called separate evaluation). In some way, the presence of three poor quality cards led to a reduction in the perceived value of the set when that set was evaluated on its own, but when it was directly comparable with another set that did not contain these inferior cards, their influence on decision making was downplayed. Why should this be?

A plausible possibility suggested by Hsee (1996), called the evaluability hypothesis, is that some attributes of a choice option may be harder to evaluate in isolation than others. Whether a bundle of baseball cards containing 10 mint cards is good value or not is difficult to judge. Other attributes are easier to gauge: the quality of the cards, for instance. Collectors may have no difficulty appreciating that a bundle with 3 out of 13 inferior cards is a poor purchase. Hence when judged separately, the 10-item bundle is valued higher than the 13-item one as the latter suffers from having an easily evaluated attribute: low quality. In joint evaluation, by contrast, seeing the bundles side by side makes it easier to give appropriate weight to the quality dimension. As the 13-card bundle includes everything that's in the 10-card one, the collectors could see readily that the poor quality of the three additional cards was insignificant.

These reversals have very considerable policy implications as they imply that the method of eliciting the public's preferences for environmental, legal, healthcare, and other programmes may matter in ways that are often ignored. Examples abound of apparently incomprehensible judgments or decisions in these applied fields. People in a study by Desvousges, Johnson, Dunford, Boyle, Hudson, and Wilson (1992) were willing to pay $80, $78 and $88 towards a scheme described (to different groups) as saving 2000, 20,000 or 200,000 birds, respectively. The scale of outcomes was plainly extremely hard to place on any objective mental scale. Yet, if they had seen the options simultaneously, people would of course have realized that the amount contributed should be more closely related to the number of birds saved. Similarly, Jones-Lee, Loomes, and Philips (1995) found that the amount people were willing to pay for a programme designed to reduce road accidents increased by only about 30 per cent when the number of projected accidents avoided was increased by 200 per cent. Again, people would of course appropriately scale these amounts if shown their judgments side by side.

Other instances of preference reversal may require a rather different explanatory approach from that offered by the evaluability hypothesis. In a striking example, Redelmeier and Shafir (1995) asked family practitioners to consider the following problem:

> The patient is a 67-year-old farmer with chronic right hip pain. The diagnosis is osteoarthritis. You have tried several non-steroidal anti-inflammatory agents (e.g., aspirin, naproxen and ketoprofen) and have stopped them because of either adverse effects or lack of efficacy. You decide to refer him to an orthopaedic consultant for consideration for hip replacement surgery. The patient agrees to this plan. Before sending him away, however, you check the drug formulary and find that there is one non-steroidal medication that this patient has not tried (ibuprofen). What do you do?

The family practitioners' task was to choose between:

> E: refer to orthopaedics and also start ibuprofen, and
> F: refer to orthopaedics and do not start any new medication.

In this case, 53 per cent chose option F with no investigation of additional medications.

Another group of family practitioners was given exactly the same scenario except that two rather than one alternative medications were mentioned. The paragraph ended with the sentences 'Before sending him away, however, you check the drug formulary and find that there are two non-steroidal medications that this patient has not tried (ibuprofen and piroxicam). What do you do?' and in this case there were three options:

> G: refer to orthopaedics and also start ibuprofen,
> H: refer to orthopaedics and also start piroxicam, and
> I: refer to orthopaedics and do not start any new medication.

In this case, the option proposing no further investigation of medications was chosen by 72 per cent of the sample. If anything, one would imagine that the possibility of exploring two medicines would tend to reduce, not increase, the likelihood of opting straight away for the surgery option. Yet, instead, about 19 per cent of practitioners who would otherwise have preferred experimenting with another medication in the first scenario reversed their preference under the second scenario and selected the no-medication option.

How can it be that adding one more option to a set of alternatives can change people's preference between two other options? It may be that the added option simply adds confusion to an already complex decision. This is particularly likely when the added option has both advantages and disadvantages as this simply increases the number of conflicting reasons. Another possibility is that decision makers anticipate having to justify their decisions, and an additional option can make this harder to do. Whereas justifying option E in the first family practitioner scenario is straightforward ('it seemed worth trying one last medication') this becomes harder in the second scenario where the justification would have to be developed further to account for choosing one drug over another.

Such an explanation has also been proffered for a related choice anomaly. Imagine that you are faced with a choice between two objects, A and B, which differ on two dimensions. A is better than B on one dimension but worse on the other. For example, A and B might be two people you are considering inviting out on a date, with A being more attractive than B but less intelligent. Let us suppose this is a difficult choice and you are roughly equally inclined to choose A and B. Now we introduce a third person, C, into the equation. Although this superficially makes your decision harder, the good news is that C is 'dominated' by A – which is to say, C is worse than A on at least one dimension and not better on the other (C is less attractive than A and equally intelligent). It would seem straightforward to reject C in comparison with A, and simply focus on the comparison of A with B as before. However, studies have shown that in this sort of 'asymmetric dominance' situation, C's presence is often not neutral: instead, it can increase preference for A.

Sedikides, Ariely, and Olsen (1999) demonstrated this in the context of dating decisions. Participants were presented with descriptions of potential dating partners. Thus person A would be described as scoring 80 for attractiveness, 56 for sense of humour, and 61 for intelligence, while person B might score 60, 61, and 82 on these dimensions, respectively. Choosing between A and B depends, obviously, on how much the participant values the different attributes, which will, naturally, vary from one individual to the next. In Sedikides et al.'s study, 50 per cent of participants preferred person A and 50 per cent person B. When person C, who scored 80, 56, and 51 on the three attributes, was brought into the set, choice of person A increased to 62 per cent. This was despite that fact that C must be inferior to A as they scored equally on two dimensions but A was more intelligent.

This effect has occasionally been exploited by marketing experts to increase the market share of their products. A toothpaste manufacturer, for instance, might introduce a new product alongside their existing one in order to boost the latter's attractiveness to customers. Provided that this new product is clearly inferior to the existing one (more expensive and in cheaper packaging), competitors' products would be harmed in the marketplace. The need to form justifications for one's decisions (even if this is only an internal justification to oneself) may help to explain such asymmetric dominance effects. When it clearly dominates another choice alternative, an object's selection is much easier to justify than when no such dominance is evident.

Effect of experience on preference reversals

We have mentioned several explanations of preference reversals (including the compatability and evaluability hypotheses) in addition to those suggested by Redelmeier and Shafir's experiment. Whatever the merits of these accounts, a key question is, what happens to preference reversals when people have the opportunity to make repeated decisions? Our approach in this book assumes that to the extent that decisions are grounded in experience, they tend to be optimal and hence we would expect preference reversals to be eliminated or at least reduced when choices are made or prices set for 10 or a 100 pairs rather than just one. This is exactly what is observed. In List's (2002) study, for example, professional dealers in baseball cards did not show a statistically significant tendency to value the 10-card bundle higher than the 13-card one in separate evaluation and hence did not make preference reversals to the extent that less experienced collectors did. Presumably their extensive experience with bundles of cards allowed them to develop better weightings of the dimensions on which the bundles varied.

Similarly, Wedell and Böckenholt (1990) found that choice of the option with the higher probability (equivalent to gamble A above) declined when participants were told that the gamble would be played 10 or 100 times, while the tendency to place a higher price on the alternative with a large potential payoff (equivalent to gamble B) also declined. These two effects combined to dramatically reduce the prevalence of preference reversals. Cox and Grether (1996) and Chu and Chu (1990) furnish evidence of reduction (but perhaps not elimination) of reversals in real-world economic settings where experience and expertise play a greater role than in the one-shot tasks often undertaken in the psychology laboratory.

Preference reversals tell us that the axioms of decision theory are inadequate in that preferences are not always stable. Instead, they often seem to be constructed on the fly, are highly context-dependent, and influenced by the individual's goals and expectations. As with many other examples of the 'fluidity' of mental processes, they force us to think of judgments, preferences and decision making as much more contextually embedded than is traditionally assumed in decision theory. A graphic example was described by Ariely, Loewenstein, and Prelec (2003). They asked their (American) business school participants to study everyday commodities such as bottles of wine, computer accessories, and luxury chocolates and to decide whether they would choose to purchase each item for a dollar amount equal to the last two digits of their social security number. Next, they stated how much they were willing to pay for each item. Remarkably, focusing attention on the individuals' social security numbers caused a dramatic change in the amounts they were willing to pay, despite the fact they should have been able to realize this number is random and could not possibly have any bearing on the value of the objects. Participants whose social security numbers were in the top quintile (in the population this would be 80–99) made offers that were typically three times greater than those of participants with numbers in the lowest quintile (00 to 19). It seems that the initial focus on the social security number acted as an 'anchor' that was still active in working memory when the later judgment had to be constructed.

All sorts of judgments are susceptible to anchoring effects. Strack and Mussweiler (1997) found that people estimated Aristotle's birth date to be about 140 BC if they first judged whether he was born before or after AD 1825, but earlier than 1000 BC if they first judged whether he was born before or after 25,000 BC (some further examples are given in chapter 15). Judgments and decisions, such bizarre findings tell us, are based on highly fluid mental states and not on fixed preferences or beliefs.

Summary

This chapter built on the framework for analysing decisions presented in chapter 8 and introduced the main psychological theory of choice behaviour, prospect theory. The principal contribution of prospect theory is in explaining why we observe a variety of departures from EUT when people make choices. The explanation for these characteristic violations – framing, the certainty effect, loss-aversion, the endowment effect – is built on the idea that people base decisions on their mental representations of decision problems. That is, objectively given (or experienced) utilities and probabilities undergo cognitive distortions prior to choice. The second part of the chapter reviewed extensive evidence showing that the preferences on which we act are not fixed, but are subject to numerous external influences. Such influences can lead to preference reversals, historically one of the most compelling violations of the normative theory of decision making.

10 Decisions across time

Confronted with the prospect of marriage to Emma Wedgwood, Charles Darwin famously wrote down lists of pros, such as companionship in old age, and cons, such as disruption to his scientific work, and embarked on a cost–benefit decision analysis to help him make up his mind. Of course, these prospects were all in the future for him, but their remoteness varied enormously. The pleasure to be derived from having a companion in old age was at least 20 years off, whereas disruption to his work (from having to visit his wife's relatives, say) might be only 1 or 2 years in the future. Thus, like many decision problems, time was a critical variable. Alternatives often have to be compared that will be realized at very different points in the future. In this chapter we consider some of the problems raised by these so called 'intertemporal' choice situations. (Thankfully – for the reputation of decision analysis – Charles and Emma were married in 1839.)

We begin, however, by considering an indirect influence of time on choice, namely via its common biasing effects on memory. We do not always remember events in a way that accurately reflects how they were experienced – indeed, our recollections often dramatically distort past events and how enjoyable or unpleasant they were. As an example, when students evaluated the enjoyment they were having during a particular type of vacation, their ratings did not predict how likely they were to repeat that type of vacation. That is to say, ratings taken during the vacation, as it was being experienced, did not determine future behaviour (Wirtz, Kruger, Scollon, & Diener, 2003). However, recollections of how enjoyable the vacation was did predict future behaviour. Moreover, ratings of expected enjoyment given before the vacation influenced later recalled enjoyment independently of experienced enjoyment during the vacation: one's expectations have a long-lasting effect and are not overwritten by the actual experience. This raises the striking paradox that if you want to determine how likely it is someone will repeat an experience such as revisiting a restaurant, asking them during the experience will be less useful than seeking their subsequent remembered experience: How much they are enjoying the meal when they are actually in the restaurant will be less predictive than their later recollections of how enjoyable it was.

Hindsight and other time-related biases

'Hindsight' and related 'self-serving' biases often influence recollections of attitudes and can lead to distortions whereby people tend to be biased to take credit for favourable outcomes and avoid blame for unfavourable ones. For instance, imagine you have to organize a restaurant dinner for a large group of people from work. Beforehand, you are a little anxious about the complexity of the arrangements and whether the evening will be successful (will everyone like the food?). If asked, you would rate the likelihood of a good meal at about .7. The meal in fact turns out to be a success. Congratulating you, your boss asks you how confident you were that it would all work out. Your reply ('Oh, about 95 per cent') represents a hindsight (or 'I knew-it-all-along') bias: knowing the outcome makes it very difficult to imagine what your judgment would have been if you had not known the outcome. You also feel a warm glow of satisfaction that the evening was a success *because* of you. But if it had been a failure, you would have blamed the restaurant (the service was poor) or the people in your party (they had no sense of humour). This is a 'self-serving' bias: the tendency to take credit for good outcomes while avoiding blame for bad ones.

In the context of financial purchase decisions, Louie (1999) asked individuals to decide whether or not to purchase a company stock prior to giving them information that the stock either increased or decreased in value. When the stock value increased, participants overestimated what they thought they would have judged the likelihood of an increase to be (hindsight bias) and they credited themselves with the favourable outcome (self-serving bias).

Similarly, Conway (1990) asked a group of students to report prior to an exam how well prepared they thought they were for the exam and what their expected grade was. After the exam they were asked to recall as accurately as possible their earlier ratings. Conway found that students who did worse than they expected reported having prepared less and having expected a lower grade than they truly had. These students were motivated to avoid blame for a poor outcome by misremembering a smaller amount of preparation. In contrast, students who did better than they expected reported having prepared more and having expected a higher grade than they actually had.

It seems likely that these biases are often due to the more general difficulty people have with counterfactual thinking (i.e., thinking about something that's inconsistent with reality). When you learn something, this doesn't simply add one piece of information to your memory, but instead it causes a cascade of inferences that are often automatic and hence difficult to reverse. When your restaurant meal turns out to be successful, a lot of information in your memory changes over and above the fact that the evening was a success: you learn that the food in the restaurant is exceptional, that the people in your party are very relaxed, and so on. Accurately gauging what the prior likelihood was of a successful evening requires negating all these new facts you've learned and, hardly surprisingly, this is extremely hard to do.

Further examples of biased recall are very easy to find (see Hawkins & Hastie, 1990). For instance, several studies reviewed by Ross (1989) asked people to report their attitudes on two occasions separated by several years to such things as state spending, equality for women, and political opinions. Most people's views on such things tend to change over long time periods but Ross's key finding was that when the individuals were asked on the second occasion to recall their earlier attitudes, those recollections were biased towards their later attitudes. Thus someone who is initially some-what liberal politically but becomes more conservative is subsequently likely to misremember themselves as having previously been more conservative than they actually were. To recall accurately what one's earlier attitudes were requires undoing several years of new inferences and perspectives, an unfeasible act.

Given this evidence for biased recall of attitudes and judgments, it is perhaps not surprising that similar distortions pervade recall of decisions and of the criteria used for reaching those decisions (Pieters, Baumgartner, & Bagozzi, 2006). Situations often occur in which we consider a range of reasons for or against a particular choice, make our choice, and then later try to recall what our reasoning was. Can we accurately recall why we selected a degree course that turned out well, or why we accepted a job offer that didn't? If we hope to learn from our experiences and avoid repeating poor decisions, accurate recall would seem crucial. One clear result is that people's current views of how they should have reasoned tend to colour their recall of how they actually reasoned – in other words, people reconstruct their memory for a decision on the basis of their current beliefs and attitudes. Of course the decision can turn out to be a good or a bad one and this also appears to influence recall.

Galotti (1995) studied these issues in a naturalistic setting by asking high-school students to describe the criteria they were using to decide which university to go to, and for each criterion, they rated how important it was in their decision making and how each of the universities they were considering scored on that measure. Thus one university might have scored well on cam-pus appearance and another poorly on financial aid. When they were at university some 8–20 months later the students were asked to recall the fac-tors they had considered as well as the factors in retrospect they felt were most important. Galotti's key finding was that while recall of the factors was moderate (about half were recalled), there was a significantly greater ten-dency to recall factors that the students *now* thought were important. For example, students rated type of institution (public/private/single sex, etc.) as quite an important factor at the time they were making their decisions, but after arriving at university they believed this to be much less important and tended not to recall basing their decisions on it, despite the fact that they patently had. Conversely, campus atmosphere was not heavily weighted initially but was thought later to be an important factor, and the students were much more likely to recall (or more accurately, falsely recall) taking this into consideration in their original decision. People hence are prone to 'recall' factors that in truth they did not put emphasis on but that after the fact seem significant to them.

Distortions of recollection are only one type of biasing mechanism in people's judgments and choices. People may sometimes also be influenced by their own (incorrect) lay theories about how their preferences change over time. People are poor, for example, at predicting how much they will enjoy future events such as eating yogurt every day for a week, believing that their enjoyment will decline when objectively it will not (Kahneman & Snell, 1992). But being able to predict one's future preferences is very important in many decision contexts. Consider a person who, having enjoyed a skiing holiday, is considering buying an apartment in that location. Will her enjoyment of skiing on subsequent visits be equally positive? Or will she become bored with skiing and regret the purchase? Unless one can make accurate forecasts of one's future likes and dislikes, significant mistakes about property purchases, job decisions, marriage, or other major choices might ensue. Loewenstein and Angner (2003) have suggested that a common reason why people make unsatisfactory decisions is that they tend to regard their current preferences as much more stable and intrinsic than they actually are. In truth, many of our likes and dislikes are highly fluid (as discussed above) and are determined by ever-changing external and cultural influences (think of clothes). This means that our preferences are likely to change with external drivers, yet we may underestimate the extent of this change and believe ourselves to be more immune to the vagaries of external influences than we truly are. This in turn leads us to believe that our future self will be more like our current self in terms of likes and dislikes than it in fact will be.

Examples of this sort of 'projection' bias abound. For instance, people appear unable to predict the change in their future valuation of an object that will accompany owning it. People tend to place higher values on things when they own them than when they do not – recall the discussion of the 'endowment' effect with the coffee mugs in the previous chapter. Another example relates to the effects of visceral influences on decision making. We are often not very good at taking account of the ways in which our future states of hunger, thirst, sexual arousal, and so on will motivate our behaviour. Read and van Leeuwen (1998) gave a choice of healthy or unhealthy snacks to office workers at times when they were either hungry or satiated. The choice was for a snack to be consumed in a week's time, which would be handed over at a point during the day in which the individual was likely to be either hungry (late afternoon) or satiated (after lunch). Read and van Leeuwen found, as might be expected, that individuals who expected to be hungry at the point of obtaining the snack were more likely to select an unhealthy one than those expecting to be satiated at the point of obtaining it. More interestingly, individuals who were hungry at the time of making the choice were also more likely to select the unhealthy snack than ones who weren't, suggesting that they projected their current desire onto their future selves and assumed that they would be hungrier at the point of obtaining the snack than they objectively would be.

Predicting pleasure and pain

What is interesting about such examples is that they illustrate another type of irrationality, namely when a decision is inconsistent with an objective benchmark. The students in Wirtz et al.'s (2003) study of vacation enjoyment, for instance, genuinely enjoyed some holidays more than others and should, on any reasonable grounds, have sought to repeat those vacations more than ones they enjoyed less. Yet their 'true' enjoyment did not determine their future choices. A famous experiment by Kahneman and his colleagues (Kahneman, Fredrickson, Schreiber, & Redelmeier, 1993) illustrates this kind of irrationality even more graphically. Suppose you are asked to decide between the following two alternatives:

A: submerge your hand in very cold water for 60 seconds, or
B: submerge your hand in very cold water for 60 seconds, and then in mildly cold water for 30 seconds.

Presumably we will all agree that option A is preferable as it contains less total pain (30 seconds in mildly cold water is not as bad as 60 seconds in very cold water, but is still unpleasant). Normatively, to determine the pleasure or pain of an extended experience, one should simply add up (integrate) across all its constituent moments. Yet Kahneman et al. found that people forced to experience both options tended to prefer option B when they had to decide which one to repeat – hence this is another example of a preference reversal, in this case a reversal between what people would reflectively choose when fully briefed, and what they actually choose. The reason for this behaviour is that people (mis)remembered the longer episode as being less unpleasant (they were not given and had no access to objective information about the duration or temperature), presumably because the 30 seconds of mildly cold water partially overshadowed their recall of the earlier minute in very cold water (the 'happy end' effect). It is the passage of time that seems crucial here in introducing distortion between experience and recollection.

Kahneman and his colleagues (Redelmeier, Katz, & Kahneman, 2003) have shown similar paradoxical choices in a much more painful real-world setting, where people are undergoing a colonoscopy for the detection of colorectal cancer. Some patients were given an extra period of a couple of minutes at the end of the procedure in which the colonoscope remained inserted in the rectum, but in a way that was less painful than in the preceding period. Despite the fact that this extra period was undoubtedly unpleasant and made the longer procedure 'objectively' more painful, patients recalled the procedure as being less painful and were more likely to return for a follow-up colonoscopy when the additional period had been added. This behaviour seems irrational because if one were to calculate the 'total pain' by integrating the moment-by-moment pain levels across the whole experience, the shorter procedure would yield less total pain.

The enjoyment or displeasure we obtain from everyday experiences such as eating an expensive meal, waiting in a queue, or having a medical procedure are of course important not only in their own right but also insofar as they shape our likelihood of repeating these and similar experiences. Yet, as the examples above show, this relationship is far from straightforward. What is it precisely that determines the mapping between the pleasure or pain experienced during an event and the subsequently recalled level of pleasure/ pain? Quite a lot of evidence (see Ariely & Carmon, 2003) suggests that there are two particularly important features of any extended experience, namely its peak level of pleasure/displeasure and its end level. Research has suggested that these are subjectively combined to produce an overall weighting. This function explains the results of the experiments of Kahneman and his colleagues because whereas the contrasting conditions are equated for their peak displeasure, adding a less unpleasant period at the end reduces the end level of displeasure. The fact that the peak level of pain or pleasure is heavily weighted in global judgments of pleasantness or unpleasantness may seem entirely reasonable, and indeed it is. However, the combination of and reliance on peak and end levels can lead to strikingly irrational behaviour, such as preference for sequences that include more total pain (described above) and for relative neglect of the duration of a pleasant or unpleasant event (discussed below).

Although the peak/end formula provides a good account of retrospective judgments of pleasantness or unpleasantness, additional complex features having to do with the ordering of events come into play when people make judgments ahead of time about how attractive an event will be. People tend, for instance, to have a very strong preference for improving sequences over ones that get worse. Varey and Kahneman (1992), for instance, obtained judgments of the overall unpleasantness of sequences of aversive events, such as exposure to loud drilling, which were hypothetically experienced by individuals. Each sequence was described in terms of the individual's discomfort rating every 5 minutes (e.g., 2–4–6) where larger numbers indicate greater discomfort. Judgments were much greater for sequences of increasing discomfort such as 2–4–6 than for corresponding decreasing ones such as 6–4–2, possibly because in the latter each period is an improvement on what came before it. (Although this may appear to be consistent with the peak/end formula, in that 2–4–6 ends with a worse level of discomfort than 6–4–2, it is important to bear in mind that we are considering here judgments made ahead of time, before the events are experienced, rather than recollections.) If experiences are evaluated in a relative rather than an absolute way, then such an outcome makes sense. Varey and Kahneman also found, consistent with the studies described above, that adding a painful period at the end of the sequence made the whole experience seem less painful, provided the added period was less aversive than what came before: sequences such as 2–5–8–4 were rated (again, ahead of time) as less unpleasant than ones like 2–5–8, which are subsets of them. In the case of positive events, like consuming foods or receiving money, improving sequences are again more attractive. People prefer jobs, for example, with increasing rather than decreasing wage profiles, even when the latter are objectively better.

A factor that seems to play a surprisingly small role in judgments of pleasure/displeasure is the duration of an experience. Indeed, so minimal is this role in many circumstances that the term 'duration neglect' has been coined. In Kahneman et al.'s (1993) cold water experiment, for instance, participants were generally accurate in recalling the relative durations of the two episodes, but recalled duration was only slightly correlated with recalled discomfort. Varey and Kahneman reported something similar: profiles of discomfort such as 2–3–4–5–6–7–8 (lasting for 35 minutes) were judged barely more unpleasant than ones like 2–5–8 (lasting 15 minutes) despite more than doubling the total duration of the discomfort.

However, the extent to which duration is neglected or underweighted, and the implications of this for normative theories, has been the subject of some controversy (Ariely, Kahneman, & Loewenstein, 2000). Ariely and Loewenstein (2000) have suggested that duration may be neglected when retrospective judgments about single extended experiences are made, but that this is often understandable. If someone asks you how painful a visit to the dentist was, the questioner is likely to be more interested in the peak pain level than in the duration. Furthermore, Ariely and Loewenstein argued that duration is much less likely to be underweighted when the experience is compared to some reference point. More research is needed on this important topic.

Section summary

The preferences on which we act are not fixed but are subject to numerous external influences. One of these is the distorting influence of memory, which can misrepresent events in striking ways: we can misremember the enjoyment of a vacation or the pain of a surgical procedure. We can misrecall the reasons why we made a decision. Moreover, people tend to be quite poor at anticipating their future preferences. What unites these distortions is that memory often tries to 'rewrite' the past in a way that is more congenial with our lay theories, expectations, desires, and so on. Thus our recall of a vacation is closer to how much we expected to enjoy it beforehand than to the actual pleasure it afforded us. Our recall of the reasons behind a decision is driven more by our current values than by the ones we actually held at the time.

Direct effects of time

Whereas the influence of time in these studies is indirect in being mediated by memory, the bulk of research on intertemporal choice looks at more direct time-based influences. This reflects very many real decision problems in which the outcomes of different choices may be realized at different points in time. Any decision involving a choice between saving and spending is of this nature, as are decisions about whether to have a medical procedure now or in the future, whether eating a chocolate bar now will reduce the pleasure of this evening's meal, and so on. Addictions are probably the most unfortunate illustrations of the difficulties we face when making time-based choices: whether to consume a drug or carry out some behaviour that will have rewarding effects immediately but longer term harmful effects on our health and wealth.

Economists propose a simple extension of choice theory to deal with time-based decisions. Basically, the value of an outcome or commodity should be discounted as a function of how far into the future it is delayed, with the discount rate being like a subjective interest rate. Thus $10 in the future is equivalent to $10 × $d(t)$ now where t is the delay and d is the discount function, assumed to be exponential in economic theory (i.e., $d(t) = e^{-\delta t}$). In other words, the present value of $10 at a delay of t is $10 × $e^{-\delta t}$, where δ, the discount rate, is a constant. The concept of discounting of future events makes sense when one considers monetary assets and liabilities, for example. A bill that is due tomorrow does not have the same 'cost' as one due next year, and most people would pay to exchange the former for the latter (at least, if the amount involved was sufficiently large). This makes perfectly good economic sense. Rather than using your current wealth to pay the bill tomorrow, it would be financially beneficial to delay the bill and invest the wealth in something that accumulates interest. So long as the earned interest is greater than the cost of delaying the bill, it is prudent to choose the delayed bill. In other words, time dilutes the value of future outcomes. A discount rate (of say, 100 per cent) should be read as referring to the percentage increase in the magnitude or value of an immediate reward that would be required to make a person indifferent between having that reward now versus delaying it for 1 year.

A straightforward implication of the classic exponential model of discounting is that an individual's rank ordering of the value of various future outcomes cannot change with the passage of time. To see what this means, consider the choice between $100 in a year versus $120 in 13 months. Many people will prefer the latter. Exponential discounting implies that this preference ordering should be maintained regardless of when the events will occur, so long as they are separated by a month: counter-intuitively, $120 in a month should be preferred to $100 today. To see this graphically, Figure 10.1 shows discount curves for these two monetary amounts. The horizontal axis of the graph indicates time, hence one moves rightwards along this axis as time passes. The vertical axis shows the current value of a future reward. Note that when the two monetary amounts are actually delivered (the vertical lines at the right of the graph), more value will be obtained from receiving $120 than from $100 – the bar for the former is higher. At the

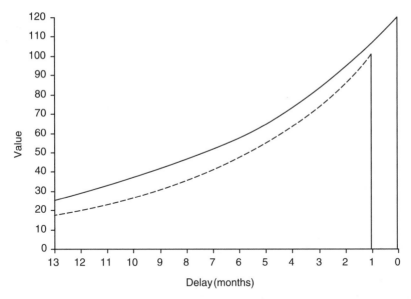

Figure 10.1 Exponential discount functions. In this example a choice is offered
between $120 delayed by 13 months from today and $100 delayed by
12 months. Hence today is the point labelled 13 on the *x*-axis, and as
time passes and the payoffs get nearer, one moves rightwards along the
axis. The bars at the right indicate the value of each of the outcomes at
the point of delivery. The black line plots the discounting of the larger,
more delayed outcome by the function $d(t) = e^{-\delta t}$ where δ, the discount
rate, is 0.12, while the dotted line plots that for the smaller, less delayed
one with $\delta = 0.15$. The important point to note is that these functions
cannot cross.

point at which the delayed alternatives are being considered (month 13 on
the *x*-axis), the two monetary amounts are a long way off in the future,
13 and 12 months respectively, and the larger amount is preferred. As time
passes the exponential curves reflecting their value gradually rise as receipt
of the money becomes more imminent, but they never cross. Hence at month
1, when the smaller amount can be taken, it is not chosen because the larger
amount is still preferred even though it is delayed for a further month.
Choices between the same outcomes separated by the same amount of time
must always be consistent on this model.

Several violations of this normative account have been documented.
Consider a simple example from Rachlin (2000) that will undoubtedly
resonate with all of us. You set your alarm clock to wake up at 7am, but when
the time comes and your clock rings, you turn it off and go back to sleep. In
the evening, your preference is to wake up at 7am rather than later but in the
morning your preference has reversed and you would rather stay in bed until
later. Given the prevalence of preference reversals as discussed in the previous
chapter, it will perhaps come as no surprise that reversals such as this

one can be demonstrated in intertemporal choices too. Such inconsistencies cannot be explained by any model of choice that incorporates exponential discounting. Returning to our monetary example, it is also common to find reversals such that a person who prefers $120 in 13 months to $100 in a year will also prefer $100 today to $120 in a month.

Such findings require that discount rate is descriptively modelled with something other than an exponential function, something that will allow the value curves to cross. One such function that has been applied to many studies of intertemporal choice is the hyperbolic function (in which $d(t) = 1/(1 + kt)$), where t is again the delay and k is a constant). Although this might seem like a mathematical detail, in fact it has quite profound consequences as the exponential form is the only one that guarantees the avoidance of certain choice anomalies. Hence from a rational economic perspective, hyperbolic discounting is non-normative. However, these anomalies become perfectly understandable given a hyperbolic function. Figure 10.2 shows hyperbolic functions and the consequences that ensue when the value functions can cross. When the payoffs are a long way off, the larger and more remote one ($120) is preferred to the closer but smaller one. However, after about 10 months have elapsed (month 2 on the x-axis), the smaller reward is preferred. The rank ordering of different outcomes can reverse with the passage of time, yielding the sorts of preference reversals described above.

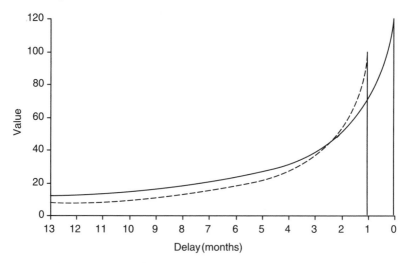

Figure 10.2 Hyperbolic discount functions plotting the same choice as in Figure 10.1 between $120 delayed by 13 months and $100 delayed by 12 months. The black line plots the discounting of the larger, more delayed outcome by the function $d(t) = 1/(1 + kt)$ where k is 0.7, while the dotted line plots that for the smaller, less delayed one with $k = 0.9$. Unlike the exponential curves in Figure 10.1, hyperbolic curves can cross. Hence the larger payment is preferred at all delays until about a month before the smaller payment becomes available, at which point the latter is preferred.

Discount rates

A second general finding from studies of intertemporal choice that is inconsistent with the normative exponential model is that discount rates tend to be larger for lower valued outcomes than for higher valued ones, larger for more immediate outcomes than for longer delayed ones, and greater for gains than for losses of the same magnitude (see Frederick, Loewenstein, & O'Donoghue, 2003). Chapman and Winquist (1998) asked participants to imagine they had won a lottery and to indicate how much they would accept in 3 months instead of taking their winnings immediately. Conversely, in another condition participants imagined they had received a speeding fine and could either pay an amount now or a larger amount in 3 months. The average discount rates were about 400 per cent for the fine (a loss) but around 2000 per cent for the lottery (a gain). Hence with a loss of $100, indifference is reached when the fine is $500 at 3 months, while with a gain of $100, indifference is not reached until the delayed winnings reach $2100 (perhaps with real money outcomes participants would have been slightly more conservative!). However these average effects were moderated by a magnitude effect such that the discount rates were far higher for small than for large amounts.

It is important to realize that this magnitude effect could lead to highly anomalous behaviour. An interest rate that would be unacceptable to a customer on a large bank loan would become acceptable if the loan was broken down into several smaller loans. In other work, Chapman (1996) has found that influences such as delay have very different effects on discount rates in different domains such as money versus health. Even when money and health are matched to be of equal value, the utility that results from money is not the same as that from health in decisions across time, and does not yield comparable discount functions. Indeed, Chapman found very little correlation between discount rates in these domains. It must be emphasized, however, that the normative model only anticipates identical discount rates across all domains if the outcomes are what economists call 'fungible', that is freely exchangeable for one another. Although this is approximately the case for many domains (e.g., money and food), it is probably not true of money and health. One cannot simply trade a given amount of money for a given change in health level.

This might explain why, despite the fact that very low correlations between money and health discount rates are found, monetary discounting does correlate with another very important health-related behaviour, namely addiction. Indeed, quite a number of studies have documented this. In a typical experiment, money discount rates are measured in the usual way by offering varying (often hypothetical) amounts delivered either immediately or at a delay, and these rates are compared in sample groups of addicts and non-addicts. Studies of this sort have shown, for instance, that heroin addicts, heavy drinkers, and smokers all have steeper money discount functions (see

Chapman, 2003). This makes sense if one assumes that individual differences in susceptibility to substance abuse relate to the relative weighting given to events occurring at different time horizons: heroin offers an immediate highly pleasurable reward at the expense, inevitably, of future costs in terms of health, wealth, work, relationships, and so on.

The issue of cross-domain generalization aside, the observed properties of discount rates are plainly inconsistent with the normative model. In fact there are even examples of negative discount rates for some non-monetary losses: people often prefer to take a loss immediately rather than to delay it, implying that a delayed loss is more painful than an immediate one, perhaps because the delay creates the unpleasantness of dread. Conversely, in the domain of gains, people sometimes prefer to delay a pleasurable event, presumably in order to savour it, but nonetheless demonstrating a negative discount rate. When students were asked when they would most like (hypothetically) to kiss their favourite film star, the median response was 3 days in the future rather than immediately (Loewenstein, 1987). These examples raise issues about visceral or emotional influences on decision making, which we return to later.

A third non-normative finding is that people will pay less to bring forward an outcome than they will accept to delay it. Loewenstein (1988) found that people would pay on average $54 to receive immediately a video cassette recorder that they didn't expect to receive for a year, while others who expected to receive it immediately demanded an average of $126 to delay receipt for a year. This is inconsistent with the normative model as the same change in value should be measured regardless of the method.

To what extent should these many deviations from the normative exponential discounting model cause us concern? Do they constitute clear examples of irrational behaviour or are they better viewed as 'anomalies' rather than mistakes? This of course depends on how strongly one believes the exponential model to be normatively justified. In many domains of judgment and decision making, individuals will often agree, when the situation is fully explained to them, that their behaviour is irrational. For example, someone who is induced in an experiment to judge that a conjunction ('it will rain tomorrow and the next day') is more probable than either of its disjuncts ('it will rain tomorrow') is very likely to admit the invalidity of this on reflection. For deviations from the normative model of time-based decisions, however, this seems rather less likely. To explain why the individual should discount money and food equally would not be an easy task. Many behavioural economists now dispute the normative status of the model (e.g., Frederick et al., 2003) and have turned their attention instead to more descriptive approaches to intertemporal choice. With great variability as a function of seemingly insignificant experimental details (e.g., the amounts under consideration or their delays), it has proved extremely difficult to find any stable measures of discount rates and this calls into question the whole normative approach to discount rates.

Anticipated emotions

As alluded to above in the context of savouring the prospect of a kiss or bringing forward an unpleasant and dreaded event, emotions seem to play an important role in decision making, and in particular may be critical in causing time-based preference reversals when an imminent event gains control of our behaviour against our more long-term objectives. This is reflected in the fact that as one moves away from the point of delivery of a valued event, the hyperbolic discount function is steeper than the exponential one, implying a greater impact of imminent events. There is now quite a lot of evidence that there is something special about immediate outcomes. McClure, Laibson, Loewenstein, and Cohen (2004) have shown, by way of illustration, that immediate and delayed outcomes evoke brain activity in two quite distinct brain regions and that the relative magnitude of activity in these regions predicts whether the individual will choose an immediate or a delayed outcome. Their participants chose between small but immediate monetary amounts (immediate here meaning at the end of the experiment) and larger delayed amounts (up to 6 weeks later). When a choice involved an immediate outcome, the striatum and orbitofrontal cortex (limbic structures innervated by dopamine cells) became particularly active. With delayed outcomes, a different network including parts of lateral prefrontal and parietal cortices became active, irrespective of the delay involved. McClure and his colleagues referred to these systems as the β and δ systems, respectively.

The fact that immediate rewards can often have an excessive pull on our behaviour leads to many highly undesirable behaviours, such as addictions. A craving for instantaneous pleasure from a drug often co-exists with a strong desire to give up the drug in the future. This is exactly what is depicted in Figure 10.2: a preference is one way round at a point in the future (not having the drug is preferred to having it) but is reversed when immediate consumption is at issue (having the drug is preferred to not having it). Among young people, about 30 per cent report that they expect to be still smoking in 5 years time, but the true figure is about 70 per cent, indicating a strong but erroneous tendency to believe they will give up. A smoker prefers a cigarette today to no cigarette and plans to give up next month, without realizing that the choice next month will be the same as the one faced today. This is the paradox of addiction, that a desire to quit can coincide with continued consumption.

In an extensive theoretical treatment of the effects of immediate events on behaviour, Loewenstein (1996) has suggested that what he calls 'visceral' influences have several significant properties that distinguish them from other, more coldly valued, events. One is that they have a disproportionate effect on behaviour, and of course this is very obvious in the case of drug cravings, sexual compulsion, or the urgent desire to escape pain. The brain imaging data described above suggest a biological basis for this exaggerated influence, which often runs counter to the individual's more reflective judgment.

Another feature is that these punishing or rewarding events tend to alter the attractiveness of other events or actions. A drug addict loses concern with career, social relationships, and so forth in the desire to obtain a drug. A particularly vivid illustration of this is the behaviour of rats in the famous experiments of Olds and Milner (1954) when allowed to self-administer electrical stimulation of the brain. This stimulation can be so pleasurable that some animals will ignore food and water to the point of death. Third, Loewenstein pointed out that visceral influences on behaviour, although extremely powerful 'in the moment,' are often profoundly underweighted in memory and downplayed when future courses of action are under consideration. Someone who contemplates a future visit to the dentist may sincerely intend to avoid the use of anaesthetic despite on a previous occasion having abandoned such a resolution at the first sight of the dentist's drill. Memory for pain (e.g., during childbirth) is notoriously poor. Thus there are a variety of reasons to believe that immediate emotional or visceral events have a singular influence on behaviour, one that is often not easily accommodated within classical decision theory.

The extent to which the immediate rewarding or punishing attributes of an object influence behaviour can also depend on the focus of one's attention. This notion is captured in models of 'attentional myopia' developed in the context of alcohol consumption and eating behaviour. These models apply to any situations in which behaviours are subject to conflicting forces, with some influences promoting the behaviour and some inhibiting it. We have all had the experience of letting our best intentions slip and succumbing to temptation when our attention is diverted. Suppose one is considering consuming a highly attractive but unhealthy chocolate milkshake. In normal circumstances, a whole range of features may be attended to and weighted in the course of forming a decision about whether to consume it: its perceptual qualities, the current context, one's mood and motivational state, as well as its dietary impact. Under conditions of low attention, in contrast, where attentional resources are partially diverted away from the milkshake, some of these attributes will fall outside the narrower focus of attention and only the most salient features will remain under consideration. If those features, as will often be the case, happen to be strongly tied to the visceral attractiveness of the object, then consumption is more likely to occur. For example, Ward and Mann (2000) showed that increased cognitive load (i.e., requiring participants to attend to another task concurrently) caused dieters to become disinhibited and consume foods they would not have done under conditions of full attention.

If, however, the more salient aspects of the object are inhibitory ones, then narrowing one's attention may make it easier to avoid consumption. Just as decreased attention will increase selection of the object when the preponderance of salient features are promoting ones, so should it decrease selection when the majority of such features are inhibiting ones. Mann and Ward (2004) provided convincing evidence in support of this prediction in a study in which dieters were required to taste a milkshake unobserved and the amount consumed was measured. Under conditions of reduced attention, participants had to remember a 9-digit number during the test. The critical manipulation was that some subjects were primed before the test to think about features of the milkshake associated with its visceral properties (specifically, they were led to believe they were taking part in a taste memory experiment and therefore focused on the milkshake's taste) whereas others were primed to think about inhibiting factors – specifically their own diets and the high fat content of the drink. Consistent with the attentional myopia model, when diet was made salient, participants consumed *less* of the milkshake under conditions of distraction than when devoting full attention. The opposite trend was observed, as in the earlier Ward and Mann (2000) study, when the visceral properties were made salient.

These results have both theoretical and practical implications. On the theoretical front, they emphasize again that visceral events can have a powerful sway on behaviour and that this sway can be increased when an individual cannot fully weigh up all the relevant factors in reaching a decision. But they extend this by suggesting that the reason for this outcome is that the most powerful and attractive features of an object tend to be highly salient in decision making. If, in contrast, the salience of inhibiting features can be enhanced, then reduced attention will tend to cause greater weighting of those features in the choice process and hence avoidance of the object. From a practical perspective, the findings suggest a simple method for helping people to avoid attractive foods, drugs, and so on, when they come under attentional pressure by enhancing those attributes associated with avoidance.

Setting deadlines

Returning to the issue of temporal discounting, one important way to avoid the consequences of crossing discount functions and addictive behaviour is to make a commitment. In the example of setting an alarm to wake yourself up in the morning, you could decide to place the alarm clock on the other side of the room in order to force yourself to get up. You know when you set the clock in the evening that your preferences will reverse during the night and that at 7am, staying in bed will be preferable to getting up. However, when you set the alarm your preferences are the other way round and hence you might thwart your future self by doing something that will change the value of the alternatives when they are available. Putting the clock on the other side of the room will reduce the pleasure of staying in bed (as it will be ruined by having the clock going off) and will increase the value of getting up (it's easier to stay up once you're forced by the clock to get out of bed). Commitments such as this are very common ways of controlling our intertemporal decision making. Putting aside a regular savings amount each month is a form of commitment if it prevents you from impulsive spending.

Commitment does, however, require self-awareness. You have to be aware that your future preferences may not coincide with your current ones. Some people are more insightful about this than others. Perhaps one can learn to be more insightful in an appropriately structured environment. Some would doubtless argue that this is part of the value of education in general. There has not been a great deal of research on this topic, but some evidence suggests that people are sometimes aware of the value of costly commitments but perhaps not optimally so.

Evidence for this claim comes from Ariely and Wertenbroch's (2002) study of self-imposed deadlines, a form of commitment used to overcome the tendency for value functions to cross. We commonly face situations where we agree to do some task by a particular time, such as agreeing to write a book or organize a party or have a difficult confrontation with a colleague, yet don't start the task immediately because with the deadline far in the future the pleasure to be gained from doing the task is lower than that of all other activities. That is to say, at time t_0 the value function for doing the task is lower than that of everything else. As time passes, however, the value functions cross as in Figure 10.2 until a point is reached (t_1) where the value of doing the task exceeds that of all other activities that can substitute for it, and we finally get around to doing it. Setting a deadline is a way of committing to do the task. For example, you might organize a meeting with your co-authors on a particular deadline day to discuss the draft of your book. A co-author who fails to meet this deadline risks embarrassment and opprobrium – in other words, the deadline is costly in the same way that having to get out of bed to switch off an alarm clock is costly.

Ariely and Wertenbroch recruited participants to proofread long essays containing grammatical and spelling errors. These individuals were set the task of correcting three such essays at weekly deadlines, or they were allowed to submit all the corrected essays at the end of 3 weeks, or they were required to commit to their own deadlines for the three pieces of work in advance. Participants in this last condition could have chosen to give the final day of the 3-week period as their deadline for all pieces of work, but in fact chose to set deadlines spaced throughout the period despite the fact that this was costly for them: by having the latest possible deadline, they would have had more time to do the work and more flexibility about their workload. This suggests some awareness that a deadline is needed to avoid having to do all the work at the last minute. Consistent with this, participants who set themselves deadlines detected more errors in the essays, missed fewer deadlines, and earned more from the task (their earnings related both to errors detected and to getting the work in on time). Hence there are tangible benefits to commitments, and people seem to be aware of this and are able to use commitments to boost their performance. Yet they are not always perfect at this: the participants in Ariely and Wertenbroch's study who set their own deadlines did not perform as well as those who were forced to abide by external deadlines (one essay marked per week). Thus, by an objective measure, they could have improved their performance and earnings but failed to do so because they did not space their deadlines in the most efficient way. Lastly, and in accord with experiences that we doubtless all share, the participants who worked towards a single final deadline put less time into the task in total than those who committed to deadlines (who in turn worked less than those with evenly spaced deadlines). As we all know, waiting until the last minute usually means that a job is done poorly.

Summary

In the context of time-based decisions, violations of the normative theory (in this case, the exponential discounting model) are easy to find. Crossing discount functions, which describe many problems of self-control such as dieting and addiction, can be modelled by hyperbolic discount functions. In addition, an important concept for understanding behaviour in these circumstances is the notion of visceral influences on behaviour, those influences that are associated with powerful biological drives. In the past few years a considerable body of research has illustrated how these may affect behaviour.

This discussion of the effects of time on decision making brings us to the end of the chapters concerned with analysing and describing models of choice. In the next two chapters our attention turns to the fundamental processes underlying learning. We examine how we learn about the environments in which we make decisions and how this learning can improve our decision making. Put another way, we investigate the mechanisms that facilitate *straight choices*.

11 Learning to choose, choosing to learn

Imagine you're at a horse racetrack and want to bet on the outcome of a two-horse race. What factors are likely to determine the winner? Of course, the horses themselves will differ in ability and their past records will give some clues about how they compare. But just because horse A has a better recent record than horse B does not mean that it will prevail – its wins may have been against poor horses while B's losses may have been against good ones, in which case past record will be a very poor clue as to the race outcome. Other factors will include the ability of the respective jockeys, the weather conditions, and so on. In a striking study, Ceci and Liker (1986) showed that expertise at predicting the outcome of such races can develop even in individuals of low intelligence (as measured by IQ) and can be based on extraordinarily complex decision rules that take account of numerous cues, with the cues often interacting with each other. How can such learning be accomplished?

The goal in this chapter is to describe developments over the last few years in our understanding of learning in decision problems and the way this has influenced theories of decision making. The review, however, will be conceptual rather than historical. Learning models now exist that encompass an enormous range of empirical phenomena. Of course, the horse-race scenario is just one of a potentially endless catalogue of examples that range from complex medical, financial and legal decision learning at one extreme to the basic ability all of us possess to make category decisions about unfamiliar objects or situations: recognizing an object as a chair or a facial expression as an example of jealousy involve learning about subtle cues and combining them to make a decision.

It will be useful in this chapter to focus on a simple choice situation in which an individual is faced with a repeated choice between two alternatives or commodities, A_1 and A_2. On each trial A_1 is the correct choice with probability $p(A_1)$ and A_2 is correct with probability $p(A_2)$. Often (but not always) it will be the case that the options are exclusive and only one alternative is correct, that is $p(A_1) = 1 - p(A_2)$. If the correct alternative is selected, a reward or reinforcer is delivered. This basic set-up distils the key decision learning aspects of numerous real-life choice situations. Examples would be a doctor choosing between two alternative diagnoses for a patient, with the reinforcer being the alleviation of the patient's symptoms, or a financial expert choosing whether to buy or sell a particular stock, with the reinforcer being financial gain or loss.

The starting point for understanding how learning proceeds in such situations is the so-called *linear* model of Bush and Mosteller (1955), which serves as a parent of almost all subsequent models (see Bower, 1994 for a historical overview; Yechiam & Busemeyer, 2005 describe recent developments and tests of this model). What we would like to know is how the individual's probability of choosing A_1 on trial t, which we denote $P(A_1)_t$, is related to the actual probability $p(A_1)$ of A_1 being the correct choice. The basic idea is simple: if A_1 is chosen and rewarded, then there should be a small increment to the probability of it being emitted on the next trial, and this increment depends on how far the probability is from a value of 1 (if $P(A_1)_t$ is close to zero on the current trial, the increment should be larger than if it is already close to 1). Conversely, if A_1 is chosen but not rewarded, then there should be a small decrement to the probability of it being emitted on the next trial. Specifically, in this model it is assumed that

$$P(A_1)_t = P(A_1)_{t-1} + \lambda[1 - P(A_1)_{t-1}]$$

on rewarded or correct trials and

$$P(A_1)_t = (1 - \lambda) P(A_1)_{t-1}$$

on non-reinforced or incorrect trials, where λ is a learning rate parameter that is assumed to vary from task to task and from one person to another. The probability of choosing A_2 is simply $1 - P(A_1)_t$. These two equations can be rewritten as a single one:

$$P(A_1)_t = P(A_1)_{t-1} + \lambda[d - P(A_1)_{t-1}] \tag{11.1}$$

in which d codes the magnitude of the reinforcer: $d = 1$ on rewarded trials and $d = 0$ on non-rewarded ones. Note that although $p(A_1)$ does not appear in this equation, it is nonetheless the case that it influences the evolution of $P(A_1)$. It does so via determining the distribution of d across trials, with d in turn influencing the individual's behaviour.

The simplicity and elegance of this model masks a deceptively broad degree of empirical power. Note, first, that the model captures basic properties of rewarded choice. Assuming that the individual guesses on the first trial, chooses A_1, and is rewarded, then $P(A_1)$ is incremented and A_1 accordingly becomes the more likely choice on the next trial. This will continue, with $P(A_1)$ approaching 1, until reward is omitted, at which point $P(A_1)$ is reduced and the choice of A_1 becomes slightly less likely (choice of A_2 becoming correspondingly more likely). With repeated trials, it can be shown that the asymptotic value of $P(A_1)$ is $p(A_1)$, the true probability of a reinforcer on trials on which A_1 is chosen. If the alternatives are exclusive $[p(A_1) = 1 - p(A_2)]$, then the asymptotic likelihood of selecting A_2 is $p(A_2)$. The learning rule therefore allows the individual to track the true reward probabilities, homing in on a pattern of behavioural allocation that perfectly matches the true probabilities. If these happen to change during the course of learning, the rule will allow adaptation to the new probabilities with the speed of adaptation being governed by the parameter λ.

Fifteen or so years after the introduction of the linear model, Rescorla and Wagner (1972) introduced a small but important modification. They proposed that the primary goal of mathematical models of learning is not to predict response probabilities per se, but internal association strengths or weights. It is a person's belief about an association between an action and an outcome that we want to understand, rather than the superficial manifestation of that belief. After all, many factors having nothing to do with learning (such as one's level of motivation) will determine whether a response is made. Whereas response probability is a purely behavioural descriptor, the idea of a weight is intended to refer to an internal mental construct something like the preference for choosing A_1. Hence Rescorla and Wagner rewrote the model with weights w replacing response probabilities. With this change, it is easier to see how the model incorporates one of the truly great discoveries of modern cognitive and biological psychology, namely the idea that learning is driven by a process of error correction or gradient descent. This insight was hit on independently by a number of researchers in different fields but credit is usually given to Widrow and Hoff (1960). The model computes an error in the sense that the critical term $[d - P(A_1)]$, now written as $(d - w_1)$, represents the error or discrepancy between the actual outcome of a learning episode, d, and the person's expectation of that outcome, w_1. The idea therefore is that learning should proceed via the very elementary process of trying to minimize this error, and the linear model achieves this by adjusting w across trials. Another way of thinking about this is that learning always moves in the steepest direction down a gradient towards a point that minimizes the discrepancy between expectancy and outcome. An enormous amount is now known about the computation of error signals in the brain in terms of the neuroanatomy of the reward and error-calculation systems (Schultz & Dickinson, 2000). Signals can be detected in brain imaging studies that function exactly as expected on the basis of error detection (Fletcher et al., 2001).

As noted above, the asymptotic pattern of behavioural allocation in the model perfectly matches the true reward probabilities. Unfortunately, this means that the model predicts *probability matching*. As we will see in the next section, this is a serious problem with the model. It can be remedied however by a further modification that greatly expands its explanatory scope.

Probability matching

Imagine you are in Caesar's Palace and are simultaneously playing two slot machines. You feed coins into each machine, pull the levers, watch the reels spin, and occasionally win. You notice that the machine on the left pays off more regularly than the one on the right. In terms of the amounts you feed into each machine, what should you do? A striking violation of rational choice theory is commonly observed in simple repeated binary choice tasks like this in which a payoff is available with higher probability given one response than another. In such tasks people often tend to 'match' probabilities: that is to say, they allocate their responses to the two options in proportion to their relative payoff probabilities. In the slot machine example, this amounts to feeding money into the machines in proportion to how often they are paying out. Suppose that a payout of fixed size is given with probability $P(L) = .7$ for choosing the left machine and with probability $P(R) = .3$ for choosing the one on the right. Probability matching refers to behaviour in which coins are inserted into the left machine on about 70 per cent of trials and into the right one on about 30 per cent. In fact, the optimal thing to do is to put all your money into the higher paying machine.

This is easy to see. After an initial period of experimentation and assuming that the payoff probabilities are stationary, the best strategy for *each separate decision* is to select the machine associated with the higher probability of payoff. On any trial, the expected payoff for choosing the left machine is higher than the expected payoff for choosing the right one. There is never a time at which the expected payoff is higher for the lower yielding machine. Even if the payoff probabilities are very close (say .31 versus .29) it is still irrational to put *any* money into the lower yielding machine (except to explore its payoff behaviour).

Choice behaviour in this sort of game has been studied in a huge number of experiments, and demonstrations of probability matching are very robust (in the statistics literature these situations are called *bandit problems* by analogy with slot machines). For instance, in Neimark and Shuford's (1959) study one response alternative was correct on 67 per cent of trials and the other on 33 per cent, and at the end of 100 trials participants were choosing the former on about 67 per cent of trials. However, there are also many studies reporting 'overmatching', that is, a tendency to choose the option with the higher probability of payoff with probability closer to 1.0. In Edwards' (1961) study, for example, participants' asymptotic choice probability for a response that had a payoff probability of .7 was .83.

The fact that participants fail to maximize their payoffs in these choice tasks has attracted the interest of many theorists concerned with the implications of this phenomenon for rational choice theory. Thus the Nobel Prize-winning economist Kenneth Arrow (1958, p. 14) noted that:

The remarkable thing about this is that the asymptotic behavior of the

individual, even after an indefinitely large amount of learning, is not the
optimal behavior ... We have here an experimental situation which is
essentially of an economic nature in the sense of seeking to achieve a
maximum of expected reward, and yet the individual does not in fact, at
any point, even in a limit, reach the optimal behavior.

What is particularly striking is that participants fail to maximize despite
the apparent simplicity of the problem facing them. Keeping track of payoff
probabilities across two response options should hardly tax working memory,
and one would not expect the comparison of these probabilities to be very
demanding. Moreover, unlike many examples of apparently irrational choice
behaviour, such as preference reversals, participants make repeated choices
and receive a steady flow of feedback from their behaviour that should
provide a strong impetus to help them find the optimal choice strategy.

In response to this somewhat pessimistic perspective, a number of objections can be raised to the conclusion that people inherently behave irrationally
in these probability learning tasks. First, many studies used sequences that
were not truly random (i.e., not independent and identically distributed)
and this often means that the optimal strategy is no longer to choose one
option with probability 1.0 (see Fiorina, 1971). Second, quite a large number
of studies used either non-monetary outcomes or else payoffs of such low
monetary value that the difference in expected cumulative earnings from
maximizing compared to matching was negligible, and there is some evidence
that monetary payoffs promote responding that is more nearly optimal (see
Vulkan, 2000). Third, given participants' common suspicion about psychological experiments, they may be reluctant to believe that the payoff probabilities are constant and may seek sequential dependencies and predictable
patterns across trials (Peterson & Ulehla, 1965; Wolford, Newman, Miller,
& Wig, 2004). Fourth, almost all studies have reported group rather than
individual participant data, with the obvious danger that probability matching at the group level masks wide variations at the individual participant
level.

How does all this relate to the linear model? As mentioned earlier, the
linear model predicts matching, and early studies that appeared to demonstrate matching were therefore taken as supportive of it. But demonstrations
of overmatching, and the demonstrations of maximizing we describe below,
clearly present a challenge to the model.

Friedman's (1998, p. 941) has asserted that 'every choice "anomaly" can
be greatly diminished or entirely eliminated in appropriately structured learning environments'. This appears to be the case with probability matching.
Shanks, Tunney, and McCarthy (2002) presented evidence against the pessimistic conclusion that people's natural behaviour in probability learning tasks
is suboptimal. They explored simple probability learning tasks in which large
performance-related financial incentives were provided, together with meaningful and regular feedback, and extensive training in the hope of obtaining

evidence that this particular choice anomaly, like others, can be eliminated. Participants were given an enormous number of learning trials (up to 1800 in one experiment). The results were fairly clear in demonstrating that large proportions of participants (about 70 per cent) can maximize their payoffs when maximizing is defined as a run of at least 50 consecutive choices of the optimal response. Many participants quite comfortably exceeded this criterion. Each of the three factors mentioned above contributed to participants' ability to maximize: the Shanks et al. study demonstrated that both feedback and payoffs affected the overall likelihood of exclusively choosing the best alternative and that stable performance is not reached until after many hundreds of trials.

The linear model

Returning to the linear model, it is clear that the ability of people to maximize under appropriate conditions is a problematic result as the model necessarily predicts matching. This can be handled however by assuming a non-linear transformation of beliefs into behaviour. In terms of weights, the model is:

$$w_t = w_{t-1} + \lambda(d - w_{t-1}) \tag{11.2}$$

and we now explicitly incorporate a separate decision function to translate weights into behaviour:

$$P(A_1)_t = 1 / [1 + \exp(-\theta w_t)] \tag{11.3}$$

In this equation, θ is a scaling parameter. If θ is small (< 1), responding is predicted to be quite close to probability matching, but provided θ is sufficiently large, maximizing is predicted since $P(A_1)$ follows a step function with the step at 0.5.

This, then, is the essence of the linear model. It has been remarkably influential in the history of learning research stretching back over more than 30 years. The remainder of the chapter attempts in a non-technical way, first, to show how it can be expanded to deal with situations involving multiple predictive cues, and second, to highlight some of the ways in which additional processes might need to be added to construct a more complete model of decision learning.

Choices informed by multiple cues

The classic probability learning task is one of the most stripped-down decision problems it is possible to imagine and hence omits numerous features of significance in real decision making. In real life we are rarely confronted with exactly the same problem repeatedly; instead, there are usually cues that vary from occasion to occasion and give us information about the likely correct choice at that particular moment. A stock analyst, for instance, does not make a decision on whether or not to purchase a stock simply on the basis of past history of success with that stock: he or she takes into account numerous cues such as the overall economic climate, the company's financial position, and so on, some of which increase the analyst's belief that the stock will increase in value and others of which predict it will decrease. Decision making therefore needs to be situated within a framework for determining the role that such cues have on behaviour. The simple situation we have considered thus far needs to be generalized to include the informational role of such cues. In chapter 3 we introduced multiple-cue tasks in the context of the lens model framework for thinking about the stages involved in judgment, but now we examine the specific learning mechanisms underlying performance in these situations.

Research on probability matching dwindled considerably after the mid-1970s, but since a seminal article by Gluck and Bower (1988), a growing number of studies have used versions of a multiple-cue probability learning (MCPL) task to examine rational choice in probability learning situations. In the prototypical experiment resembling the horse-race example described earlier, participants are presented with a cue or a set of cues that vary from trial to trial and that signal independent reinforcement probabilities for the choice alternatives. For example, in one condition of a study by Myers and Cruse (1968), one cue signalled that left was correct with probability .85 and right with probability .15, while another cue signalled probabilities of .15 and .85 for left and right, respectively.

In a common cover story, participants imagine themselves to be medical practitioners making disease diagnoses about a series of patients. Each patient presents with some combination of the presence or absence of each of four conditionally independent symptoms (e.g., stomach cramps, discoloured gums) and is either suffering or not suffering from a disease. Thus each symptom pattern can be described by a set of 1s and 0s referring to whether each symptom is present or absent. The person's task is to predict whether the disease is present ($d = 1$) or absent ($d = 0$) for each of many such patients, receiving outcome feedback (the actual value of d) on each trial. The structure of the task is such that for each of the possible symptom patterns there is some fixed probability that patients with that pattern have the disease and the complementary probability that they have no disease. The standard probability learning experiments reviewed in the last section can be thought of as degenerate cases of this sort of task in which the number of symptoms (cues) is zero.

To maximize the number of correct diagnoses, participants should always choose the outcome (disease or no disease) that has been more frequently associated with that particular symptom pattern. Just as with the basic probability matching problem, there has been a lot of debate about whether people are capable of achieving optimal performance or whether instead they are inevitably drawn towards suboptimal decisions. Recent evidence has tended to paint a more encouraging picture with behaviour approaching – if not actually reaching – optimality so long as enough learning periods are included, and informative feedback and significant incentives are provided.

The linear model can be applied fairly straightforwardly to MCPL tasks. All that is required is an algorithm for specifying how the propensity or weight w for each of the various choice alternatives varies as a function of the set of cues present on a given occasion. Suppose again that there are two choice options, A_1 and A_2. Picking up on another key proposal introduced by Rescorla and Wagner (1972), Gluck and Bower (1988) proposed that the weight for one of these options is the linear sum of the weights of the individual cues for that alternative, Σw. That is to say, the total propensity to choose alternative A_1 is simply the sum of the weights for A_1 of all the cues present on that occasion. This combined weight is converted to a response probability via the same rule as previously:

$$P(A_1)_t = 1 / [1 + \exp(-\theta \Sigma w_t)] \tag{11.4}$$

where θ is a scaling parameter. The only difference between this and equation 11.3 is that we now sum all the weights of the separate cues. As before, if θ is small (< 1), responding is predicted to be quite close to probability matching, but provided θ is sufficiently large, maximizing is predicted. Lastly, each individual weight is updated by the original linear rule, that is:

$$w_t = w_{t-1} + \lambda(d - \Sigma w_{t-1}) \tag{11.5}$$

where λ is a learning rate parameter and d is the reinforcement (1 if the payoff is positive, 0 otherwise). Figure 11.1 provides a graphical illustration of the contributions of the cue weights to choice between the alternatives.

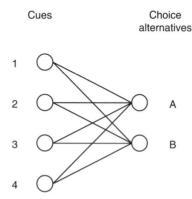

Figure 11.1 Application of the linear model to a multiple-cue probability learning (MCPL) situation. Each cue possesses weights for each of the choice alternatives and these weights are incremented and decremented as a function of the error term in equation 11.5.

The linear model bears a very important relationship to the classic cue integration model of MCPL (Juslin, Olsson, & Olsson, 2003b). This 'normative' regression model proposes that people adopt a linear independence assumption (i.e., that the outcome is a linear function of the input values). The linear model is essentially a learning model for this cue integration approach (Stone, 1986).

Despite its simplicity, the linear model of MCPL has been strikingly successful in predicting decision behaviour in laboratory learning experiments (although, as we discuss below, it also faces several problems). In a sense this success should not be surprising as the model is a very close relative indeed of a model, the Rescorla-Wagner (RW) theory, that has been enormously influential in another domain of simple learning, namely Pavlovian conditioning. The linear model can be thought of as extending the RW theory to situations in which associations are concurrently learned between multiple cues and outcomes rather than to a single cue (the conditioned stimulus) and outcome (the unconditioned stimulus). The reason why Gluck and Bower's (1988) study was so influential was because it drew attention to this connection.

Gluck and Bower introduced the medical decision-making task described above in which hypothetical patients present with some combination of four symptoms (bloody nose, stomach cramps, puffy eyes, discoloured gums). The participant's task was to decide for each patient whether he or she had fictitious disease R or C, and having made a choice, feedback was provided (each patient had one disease or the other). Participants saw 250 such patients and thus had extensive opportunity to learn the basic probabilistic structure of the task; that is, the probabilities of the two diseases given each symptom combination. One symptom was particularly associated with disease C, another with disease R, while the other two fell in between. These probabilities however were never 0 or 1 so, as in many real decision problems, participants could never be 100 per cent correct. The presence and absence of each of four symptoms means there were 16 different patterns in total, but Gluck and Bower eliminated cases in which no symptoms were present, leaving 15 patterns in the experiment.

Figure 11.2 shows participants' choices of disease R across the final 50 cases. Each symptom pattern is denoted by a string of 0s and 1s, where 0 means the symptom is absent and 1 means it is present; hence pattern 1010 means the patient in question had bloody nose and puffy eyes but not stomach cramps or discoloured gums. The figure shows the true objective probability of the disease, together with participants' mean choice of the disease and the predicted probability from the linear model with θ set to a value of 3.2. This value implies fairly deterministic responding in this situation; later in the chapter we consider some of the determinants of the value of this parameter. It is clear not only that participants were quite good at this task – choosing the alternatives in approximate accord with the true probabilities – but also that the model did a good job of predicting their behaviour. This fit was supported in a number of follow-up studies.

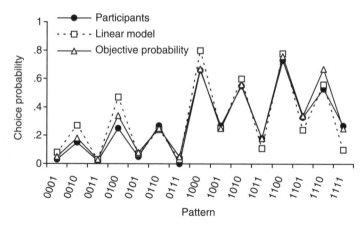

Figure 11.2 Results of Gluck and Bower's (1988) simulation using the linear model.
The graph shows the objective probability of disease R given each symptom pattern. These are denoted by a string of 0s and 1s representing the
four symptoms, where 1 means the symptom is present and 0 means it is
absent. Also shown is the mean probability with which participants chose
the disease and the corresponding probability predicted from the linear
model. Adapted from Table 1 of Gluck and Bower (1988).

Several of these studies also examined the role of base rates in learning
about cue weights. Base rate refers to the overall probability of an event
within a population, independently of any cues that might signal the presence
of that event. As we saw in chapter 6, much research has been concerned with
evaluating people's sensitivity to base rates (Koehler, 1996).

Gluck and Bower's study incorporated a base rate manipulation and this
allowed a strikingly simple but compelling prediction of the linear model to
be tested. In the basic design employed by Gluck and Bower the two diseases
did not occur equally often: one was much more common than the other
(indeed the labels R and C mean 'rare' and 'common'). This allows a situation to be created where a particular symptom *s* is paired with these diseases
with equal probability,

$$P(C/s) = P(R/s) = .5$$

but where the probabilities of these diseases in the absence of the symptom
are not equal. For instance, in a study by Shanks (1990) they were:

$$P(C/\neg s) = .86, P(R/\neg s) = .14$$

From a normative point of view, when seeing a patient who only has symptom *s*, the two diseases are equally likely. However participants did not
choose them with equal frequency: instead they chose the rare disease on
about 63 per cent of occasions in Shanks' (1990) experiment.

Importantly, this is precisely what the linear model predicts. Why is this? The reason is that although the rare and common diseases were equally likely given the target symptom, this symptom was in another sense a much better predictor of the rare disease because the latter occurred only rarely in the absence of this symptom. An analogy may help to explain this. Think of the influence of a particular player on the success of a football team. Objectively, the team is as likely to win as to lose when he plays. However, when he is not playing the team is overwhelmingly more likely to lose than to win. It seems clear that the player is having an influence on the success of the team, raising P(win) from a low level when he is absent to a much higher level (.5) when he is playing. What Gluck and Bower (1988), Shanks (1990), Nosofsky, Kruschke, and McKinley (1992) and others found was that such a situation induces a decision 'error' whereby people tend to select the event that is rarer overall (winning in this example, disease R in the laboratory experiments) when the cue is present, despite the fact that on such occasions the two outcomes are objectively equally likely.

Another illustration of the same effect was provided by Kruschke (1996). The basic design is shown in Table 11.1. Each row in the table can be thought of as representing a case such as a patient. The cues across the top refer to cues such as medical symptoms. Concentrating first on the top part of the table, it can be seen that three out of four patients have the common disease C1 while one has the rare disease R1. Thus the base rate of C1 is higher than that of R1. All patients have symptom X, which is therefore unpredictive. In contrast symptom Y is a perfect predictor of C1. The critical symptom is Z, which occurs with equal prevalence in the two diseases. Kruschke trained participants on this structure by showing them hypothetical patient records

Table 11.1 Design of Kruschke's (1996) experiment

Symptoms			*Disease*
X	Y	Z	
1	1	0	C1
1	1	0	C1
1	1	1	C1
1	0	1	R1
1	1	0	C2
1	1	0	C2
1	1	0	C2
1	0	1	R2

Note: The top half illustrates a situation in which a cue (Z) is objectively equally associated with two alternatives (C1 and R1), but where one of the alternatives (C1) is more common than the other in the absence of that cue. Presented with cue Z alone, people tend to choose alternative R1 over C1. The bottom half illustrates the conditions necessary to evoke an 'inverse' base rate effect. Here people tend to choose alternative R2 over C2 when shown a case with both cues Y and Z, which never co-occurred in the training corpus. This is an inverse base rate bias because people's choices go against the true base rates.

indicating the symptoms and requiring them to predict the correct disease prior to feedback. After many such training trials Kruschke presented the critical case, which comprised a patient presenting with just symptom Z. As is clear from the table, the probabilities of diseases C1 and R1 are both .5 in patients with this symptom, yet Kruschke's participants, like those in Gluck and Bower's probabilistic version of this design, were biased to choose disease R1, preferring this nearly six times as often as C1.

The 'inverse' base rate effect

The bottom part of Table 11.1 illustrates another striking base rate anomaly Kruschke observed, which was originally identified by Medin and Edelson (1988) who termed it the 'inverse' base rate effect. In this set of patients symptom X is again non-predictive. Symptom Y is a perfect predictor of disease C2 and symptom Z a predictor of disease R2. Y and Z are mutually exclusive, never appearing together in the training set. Again disease C2 has a higher base rate than disease R2. The critical test in this instance is when a patient is presented who has both symptoms Y and Z. It is hard to reconcile this conflicting pattern but in that case the base rates should predominate: given ambiguous evidence about an instance, one should normatively take base rate information into account. This would lead to prediction of disease C2 in such a case. The striking finding, however, is that people tend to choose R2 instead (Kruschke, 1996; Medin & Edelson, 1988; Shanks, 1992). This effect is even more puzzling in light of the fact that people go with the base rates and tend to select C2 when shown a patient with all three symptoms.

The pattern model predicts the base rate neglect result in the top half of Table 11.1 because it allocates weight to a cue as a function of its predictive value, not merely as a function of the probability of the outcome given the cue. Formal analyses of the linear model (e.g., Stone, 1986) have documented its relationship to statistical methods such as multiple linear regression, in which cues are weighted in accordance with their partial correlations with the outcome event. Clearly the presence of the footballer in the example above is correlated with winning and for this reason would be chosen by a statistical model, such as regression, as a predictor of the outcome. Perhaps the simplest context in which this phenomenon can be observed is in examples of 'blocking', which refers to the finding, first observed in animal conditioning experiments (Kamin, 1968), that a cue will only become weakly associated with an outcome if it is paired with another cue that has previously been associated with that outcome. For example, if two symptoms X and Y occur together and are associated with some disease, then the extent to which people will learn to predict the disease given symptom Y will be reduced if symptom X has previously, on its own, been paired with the disease (Chapman, 1991). The blocking effect, which has been enormously influential in animal conditioning research (Dickinson, 1980), is one of the critical phenomena taken as support for error-correcting models such as the linear model. The model predicts blocking because, in the first stage, symptom X will acquire a strong weight for the disease. When X and Y are now paired in the second stage, the term Σw_{t-1} in equation 11.5 will be large and hence the error term $(d - \Sigma w_{t-1})$ will be small: cue X will therefore receive only a small weight change.

The inverse base rate effect (bottom of Table 11.1) requires a slightly more complex analysis but still appears to be broadly consistent with the linear model (Kruschke, 1996; Shanks, 1992). Kruschke's (1996) explanation for the inverse base rate effect as embodied in a model called ADIT has two major principles: (1) asymmetric representation, where the common outcome C2 is represented by its typical features while the rare outcome R2 is represented by the feature that distinguishes it from C2; and (2) normative decision making on the representation, driven by explicit knowledge and use of the outcome base rates in the testing phase.

Broadly, the hypothesized asymmetric representation results from error-driven selective attention that moderates the error-driven learning of associative weights between the cues and the outcomes. Specifically, the asymmetric representation occurs during training because C2 tends to be learned before R2 as a consequence of the difference in their base rates and tends to be encoded in terms of both of its cues, X and Y. That is, in the tradition of cue competition models (Gluck & Bower, 1988; Rescorla & Wagner, 1972), both X and Y share the burden of predicting C2 and as such both have reasonably large associative weights to it. R2 tends to be learned later because it is less frequent. Since X has already been associated with C2, its occurrence on R2 trials generates error. ADIT uses this error to shift attention away from the source of the error, X, and toward Z *before* it then uses the error to update the associative weights between the cues and the outcomes based on the attention-moderated activations of the cues. The effect of this is that most of the burden of predicting R2 is carried by Z, and the associative weight from X is much weaker to R2 than to C2.

In addition to the indirect/implicit influence of the outcome base rates in the formation of the asymmetric representation, Kruschke (1996) also hypothesized that participants *explicitly* know and use the difference in the outcome base rates during the testing phase. That is, participants systematically apply their knowledge of the base rate differences in their decision making on all of the testing trials but, in the case of the critical testing trial YZ, this base rate driven tendency to respond C2 is overridden by the asymmetric representation's tendency to produce R2 responses.

Choice rules

As we have already mentioned, despite the fact that probability matching is often observed in simple choice tasks, people can be induced to maximize or nearly maximize their payoffs via selecting only the higher probability response alternative. Within the linear model this is captured by variation of the θ parameter. Conditions in which participants probability match are characterized by a low value of θ, whereas ones in which they maximize are described by setting θ to a higher value. But is there any direct evidence concerning the psychological reality of this response determinism parameter? In the present section we elaborate on the theoretical interpretation of this aspect of the linear model.

Friedman and Massaro (1998), Friedman, Massaro, Kitzis, and Cohen (1995) and Kitzis, Kelley, Berg, Massaro, and Friedman (1998) reported some important studies using multiple-cue choice tasks that considerably clarify our understanding of the factors that might drive participants towards more nearly optimal performance, or in other words, might influence the value of the θ parameter. In their initial study (Friedman et al., 1995), very clear probability matching was obtained with correlations between asymptotic choice and actual probabilities in excess of .88. In a later study (Friedman & Massaro, 1998; Kitzis et al., 1998), however, the payoff conditions and provision of information about prior relevant cases were systematically varied. Some groups were provided both trial-by-trial and cumulatively with a score based on their accuracy, others were in addition paid on a performance-related basis, and others received neither the score nor monetary payoff. An interesting aspect of the score information was that it included information about how well an ideal Bayesian expert would have done, thus allowing participants to see how close or far their performance was from that achievable by the optimal but unspecified algorithm. Orthogonal to the score and payoff manipulation, some groups were able to access on each trial a summary table providing information about the outcomes of previous cases with the same pattern of symptoms as the current patient. Other groups did not have access to this information.

Friedman and Massaro (1998) found that the provision of history information pushed participants significantly closer to maximizing. The score conditions had a similar beneficial effect, but providing a payoff (somewhat surprisingly) had no such effect. The effects of providing a score, however, strongly suggest that one reason why probability matching occurs in many situations is because participants have not been adequately motivated to search for the optimal response strategy, and that when appropriate outcome feedback is provided, maximizing might be observed.

A natural interpretation of these findings in terms of the θ parameter is that the provision of history and score information increases the effective value of θ. In the study by Shanks et al. (2002) both feedback and monetary payoffs increased the likelihood of maximizing, so these also appear to increase the extent of response determinism. In sum, the linear model seems to fit the results of these studies quite well, provided that allowance is made for variations in the degree of response determinism.

Summary

The basic features of repeated decision learning with feedback are captured by the example of playing slot machines and receiving occasional payoffs. This scenario can be extended by incorporating cues that vary from moment to moment and signal changes in the payoff conditions. For such situations, a formidable body of normative theoretical and statistical work has attempted to describe the ideal learning process, whereas psychological research has concentrated on descriptive models of actual behaviour (the linear model and its variants). Actually, the distinction between normative and descriptive approaches is quite narrow here because the linear model (under certain assumptions) is equivalent to the statistical method of multiple linear regression, a common technique for identifying which cues are predictive of some criterion. The linear model captures many striking properties of people's choice behaviour.

12 Optimality, expertise and insight

At the heart of the debate on the nature of human rationality is the question of whether people are intrinsically bound to commit decision errors or whether in contrast they can make optimal decisions. In the context of our emphasis on the relationship between learning and choice, this translates into a question about the long-term outcome of exposure to a decision environment. With sufficient exposure can people always find the optimal decision strategy, or do they inevitably and unavoidably, even after extensive experience, fall prey to decision errors? Proponents of both sides in this debate have been able to marshal powerful evidence to support their views. The present chapter considers these important issues.

How close can a decision maker get to optimality?

Perhaps the simplest question is, what happens in the long run when people are exposed to simple choice tasks of the sort we focused on in the previous chapter? We have already seen that in binary problems like the slot machine examples people can achieve near-optimal behaviour, that is to say, maximizing (Shanks et al., 2002). A number of factors have to come into alignment for this to happen (e.g., the incentives must be adequate), but the evidence suggests there is no intrinsic limit to people's competence in simple binary-choice tasks.

What about multiple-cue tasks in which cues vary from trial to trial and signal changes in the likelihood of reward? Here there is less evidence, but again there are persuasive examples of optimal behaviour. The work of Gluck and Bower has already been discussed in the previous chapter. In the studies by Friedman et al. (1995) and Kitzis et al. (1998) participants saw cue patterns containing binary information about medical symptoms and on the basis of these cues judged which of two hypothetical diseases a patient had. Friedman and his colleagues compared decision behaviour across 240 learning trials, taking a Bayesian model as the yardstick for optimal behaviour. This model essentially assumes that a record is kept of the frequency with which each cue is associated with each outcome and then combines information across the cues present on each trial. The striking outcome was that behaviour approximated the predictions of the Bayesian model remarkably well.

Another way of specifying what counts as 'optimal' is to use linear regression. In tasks with a dichotomous outcome, participants predict the outcome on a trial-by-trial basis and learning performance is measured in terms of correct predictions. Standard analyses then average across both individuals and trials to produce a mean percentage correct for the whole task. While this kind of approach is useful for broad comparisons across different tasks, it does not provide much information about the learning process. It ignores the possibility of individual differences in judgment or learning strategies, and that these strategies may evolve or change during the course of the task. As we have already seen in chapter 3, a richer approach to the analysis of the judgment process is provided by the lens model framework. This is founded on the idea that people construct internal cognitive models that reflect the probabilistic structure of their environment. A central tenet of this approach is that people's judgmental processes should be modelled at the individual level before any conclusions can be drawn by averaging across individuals. This is done by inferring an individual's judgment policy from the pattern of judgments they make across a task. More specifically, a judge's policy is captured by computing a multiple linear regression of his or her judgments onto the cue values across all the trials in the task. The resultant beta coefficients for each cue are then interpreted as the weights the judge has given to that cue in reaching these judgments (cue utilization weights).

Each judge's policy model can be assessed against the actual structure of the task environment. This is done by computing a parallel multiple linear regression for the actual outcomes experienced by the judge onto the cue values (again across all task trials). The resultant beta coefficients are interpreted as the objective cue weights for the judge's environment. If all the participants have been exposed to the same environment then the objective cue weights revealed by this computation will be the same for everyone. However, this technique allows for the possibility that different individuals experience different environmental structures. A judge's policy (his or her cue utilization weights) can then be compared with the objective weights to see how well he or she has learned the task environment. This is illustrated by a lens model in which one side of the lens represents the structure of the environment, and the other side represents an individual's cue utilization (see Figure 3.1).

The lens model framework thus provides a means to analyse individual judgmental processes. However, although it avoids the loss of information incurred by averaging over participants, it still loses information by averaging over trials. It fails to capture the dynamics of a learning task – in terms of both potential changes in the environment, and potential changes in a judge's policy. In particular, the reliance on global weights ignores the fact that both the actual weights experienced by the judge, and the judge's own subjective weights, may vary across the course of the task. This is a problem even when the underlying structure of the environment is stationary (as it usually is in multiple-cue tasks), because the cue–outcome patterns that someone actually experiences (and therefore the environmental weights) may not be representative of the underlying probabilistic structure, especially early on in a task. Analysing individual judgment policies just in terms of their averaged performance across all the trials ignores this possibility, and as a consequence may underestimate someone's performance. Moreover, it overlooks the possibility that the person's judgment policy may change over trials, and that such changes may track variations in the actual environment.

A related shortcoming is that these global analyses assume that the judge has a perfect memory for all task trials, and that he or she treats earlier trials in the same way as later ones. But both of these assumptions are questionable – people may base their judgments on a limited window of trials, and may place more emphasis on recent trials (Slovic & Lichtenstein, 1971).

The need for dynamic models of optimal performance is now widely recognized, and a variety of different models are being developed. A natural extension to the lens model (and very closely related to the linear model) is the 'rolling regression' technique introduced by Kelley and Friedman (2002) to model individual learning in economic forecasting. In their task participants learned to forecast the value of a continuous criterion (the price of orange juice futures) on the basis of two continuous-valued cues (local weather hazard and foreign supply). Individual learning curves were constructed by computing a series of regressions (from forecasts to cues) across a moving window of consecutive trials. For example, for a window size of 160 trials, the first regression is computed for trials 1 to 160, the next for trials 2 to 161, and so on. This generates trial-by-trial estimates (from trial 160 onwards) for an individual's cue utilization weights, and thus provides a dynamic profile of the individual's learning (after trial 160).

Each individual learning profile is then compared with the profile of an 'ideal' learner exposed to the same trials. Regressions for each ideal learner are also computed repeatedly for a moving window of trials, but in this case the actual criterion values (prices) are regressed onto the cues. The estimates of the ideal learner thus correspond to the best possible estimates of the objective cue weights for each window of trials. The rolling regression technique thus provides dynamic models of both actual and ideal learners, and permits trial-by-trial comparisons between the two as the task progresses. For example, in analysing the results in their orange juice task, Kelley and Friedman (2002) compared actual and ideal learning curves to show that while ideal learners converged quickly to the objective weights, participants learned these weights more slowly, and their final predictions tended to overestimate the objective cue weights.

Lagnado, Newell, Kahan, and Shanks (2006b) applied the rolling regression technique in a slightly more complex task in which participants learned to predict the weather (rainy/sunny) on the basis of four binary predictors. As with the orange juice task, participants learned in a manner that corresponded quite well to the optimal regression model, although their learning was somewhat slower and the final weights overshot the objective ones. This latter finding is consistent with probability maximizing, however. An individual who, on the basis of the regression weights, decides that a particular outcome is more than 50 per cent likely and who then maximizes by selecting that outcome on every trial will appear to have extracted weights that are larger than the true regression weights. Such maximizing behaviour is of course captured by equation 11.4 from Chapter 11.

Answering the question 'Is human decision learning optimal?' requires first of all a specification of what an ideal learner would do. Bayesian and regression models, among others, provide one such set of yardsticks, which can then be used in comparisons with human behaviour. Although much work needs to be done on this important question, the studies described above suggest that we should not be too pessimistic. In many quite difficult learning problems, people's decisions come close to converging with the optimal ones. Moreover, the optimal models we have briefly sketched link back nicely to the linear model: there are very close and deep relationships between learning models based on error correction and rational statistical or Bayesian inference (McClelland, 1998; Stone, 1986).

This perspective – that decision learning approximates optimal behaviour in the long run – implies that in real-world decision settings, experts should be much less susceptible to biases than non-experts. Several studies confirm this prediction. An enormous amount of research has examined expert decision making, and although biases are often obtained, it is also true that experts seem less prone to such biases than non-experts. The tendency to ignore information about base rates (see chapter 6) is largely eliminated in repeated-decision situations in which individuals have enough experience to become 'experts' (Goodie & Fantino, 1999). Proneness to hindsight bias – the tendency to distort one's estimate of the likelihood of an event as a result of knowing how it turned out – is markedly attenuated in experts (Hertwig, Fanselow, & Hoffrage, 2003). Another example relates to the 'sunk cost' effect, the irrational tendency we have to continue with a plan of action in which we have invested resources despite the fact that it has become suboptimal. From a rational perspective, previous investment that has been irretrievably sunk should not influence one's current evaluations of the utilities of the different options, yet we all know that this bias is hard to avoid. The effect is sometimes also called the Concorde fallacy in honour of the supersonic jet. Long after it had become an economic white elephant, politicians in Britain and France continued to invest millions in the development of the airliner because they feared the political consequences of abandoning the project. Such a desire to appear consistent (or to avoid being inconsistent) is not in itself irrational, but that doesn't alter the fact that if one's only motivation is to make a good decision, then past investment should be discounted. Another way in which people sometimes justify sunk cost reasoning is through a desire not to waste resources already committed.

Importantly, there is evidence that the sunk cost effect diminishes with expertise. Bornstein, Emler, and Chapman (1999) asked medical experts (residents) or non-experts (undergraduates) to judge the attractiveness of various options in medical and non-medical settings. For instance, in a medical setting, participants were asked to decide what to do in the case of a patient prescribed a drug that was proving ineffective, either to stick with the treatment or discontinue it. In one case (high sunk cost) the patient was described as having purchased a supply of the drug for $400, in another case (low sunk cost) the supply cost $40. For these medical decisions, the experts showed no sunk cost effect: their choices were unaffected by the investment. This is heartening as it suggests that experience can help people to avoid decision biases. However, this only applies to the specific area of expertise. Bornstein et al. found that the experts and non-experts were equally prone to the sunk cost effect in reasoning about non-medical scenarios. Arkes and Ayton (1999) argued that the effect does not occur in animals and that when it occurs in humans, it does so for a simple reason, namely people's keenness to adhere to a 'don't waste' rule. Resources that have already been invested in an option go to waste if a different option is selected and people often find this disagreeable.

A related finding has been described by Christensen, Heckerling, Mackesyamiti, Bernstein, and Elstein (1995) in the context of the framing effect we discussed in chapters 1 and 9. This effect refers to the tendency for decisions to be influenced by the way in which they are couched. For example, when presented with scenarios, students are more willing to accept risk if a medical treatment is described in terms of a potential loss and less willing to accept risk if the very same treatment is described in terms of gain (Tversky & Kahneman, 1981). Yet, Christensen et al. reported that framing effects tend to be small and highly variable from one scenario to another when medical experts are asked to make choices relating to their domain of expertise.

Lastly, recall the evidence (described more fully in chapter 9) that experts are better able than novices to avoid making preference reversals. List (2002) asked professional dealers in baseball cards and less experienced collectors to value a 10-card bundle and a 13-card one that included the same 10 cards plus 3 inferior ones. The less experienced collectors preferred the 10-card bundle when valuing the bundles in isolation, but preferred the 13-card one when comparing them side by side. The professional dealers, in contrast, were able to avoid this irrational preference reversal.

Limitations of the linear model

Despite the many successes of the linear model as applied both to simple choice tasks and to more complex MCPL problems, there are some fairly serious difficulties that this model faces and that have been taken as the starting point for alternative approaches. Perhaps the simplest problem is caused by the fact that the propensity to choose alternative A is an increasing function in equation 11.4 (chapter 11) of the independent weights of the cues present on a given occasion.

It seems natural at first glance to assume that if two cues X and Y each have some positive weight for A – that is to say, they each imply that A is the likely correct choice – then the presence of both X and Y should increase the likelihood of choosing A over and above what would happen if only one cue were present. But it is trivial to set up a situation in which this would not be objectively correct. Suppose cue X indicates A will be reinforced as the correct choice, and cue Y signals the same, but when X and Y are both present A will be the incorrect choice. An example is provided by a classic experiment by Bitterman, Tyler, and Elam (1955): Humans and animals can readily learn discriminations in which two red stimuli are shown on some trials and reward depends on choosing the right hand one, while on other trials a pair of green stimuli are presented and reward is given for choosing the left hand stimulus. Such a discrimination cannot be solved by the linear model because each element (red, green, left, right) should be equally associated with reinforcement.

The linear model is unable to deal with such situations because weights necessarily add together linearly (see equation 11.4 in chapter 11): No set of weights can be constructed that would point towards A in the presence of X or Y but not in the presence of X and Y (this is called an XOR problem). One way around this problem is to assume that in addition to learning direct associations between the outcome and the separate elements that make up the stimulus, intermediate representations of the stimulus can also be involved in associations with the outcome. This is the essence of connectionist models incorporating a layer of 'hidden' units that intervene between the input and output units, as shown in Figure 12.1.

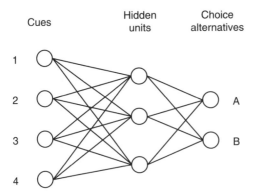

Figure 12.1 Architecture of a backpropagation model to a multiple-cue probability learning (MCPL) situation. Each cue possesses weights but instead of connecting directly with the choice alternatives these are relayed via intermediate hidden units. Connections in both layers are incremented and decremented as a function of the error term shown in equation 11.5 of chapter 11.

One particular type of hidden-unit network has been extremely widely investigated and has been shown to have some very powerful properties. In such a 'backpropagation-of-error' network, the linear rule applies exactly as before except that it is refined in order to determine how much the input-hidden weights and the hidden-output weights should be changed on a given trial. The precise calculations are not critical here, but the key point is that the development of multilayer networks using this generalized version of the delta rule has provided a major contribution to recent connectionist modelling because phenomena such as the learning of non-linear classifications that are impossible for single-layer networks can be easily dealt with by multilayer networks. This class of models has been extremely influential in cognitive psychology (Houghton, 2005; McClelland & Rumelhart, 1986; Rumelhart & McClelland, 1986).

In the context of decision making, neural network models based on the architecture shown in Figure 12.1 and using the backpropagation algorithm have been applied to a broad number of real-world problems. Many of these have involved medical decisions. A common technique has been to use databases of information on predictors of particular medical conditions as training sets for network models. Databases have included predictors of heart disease, diabetes, hepatitis, psychiatric admission, back pain, and many more. In one application, for instance, Baxt (1990) trained a network on 356 cases relating to patients admitted to a hospital emergency department, which included 236 in which myocardial infarction was ultimately diagnosed and 120 in which it was not. Each case provided numerous predictors or cues such as the patient's age, past history variables such as diabetes or high cholesterol, and test results such as blood pressure and electrocardiogram indicators. Half the cases were used as training examples for the neural network, with this corpus being presented repeatedly to the model until the weights were stable, and the model was then tested on the remaining cases. Baxt reported that previous decision models had achieved at best a detection rate of about 88 per cent (patients with the condition correctly diagnosed as such) combined with a false alarm rate of 26 per cent (patients without the condition incorrectly diagnosed as having it) and that this is about the level of accuracy achieved by expert physicians. In contrast, the neural net model achieved a detection rate of 92 per cent and a false alarm rate of 4 per cent. Bear in mind that this highly impressive level of performance is achieved on a sample of cases different from the ones used in training. Numerous similar studies have compared the success of neural network models on real datasets against both human performance and that of statistical models such as logistic regression.

Hence there is no question about the power of this sort of connectionist network for learning predictive relationships and applying this knowledge to make decisions. But the question remains, does it learn in the same way as humans? The fact that such models can outperform human experts hints that the answer might be 'no', and one reason for this seems to be their neglect of important processes concerned with selective attention. This has been taken into account in the construction of a powerful model called ALCOVE (Kruschke, 1992; Nosofsky & Kruschke, 1992), which is a promising alternative to standard backpropagation. Briefly, in models such as ALCOVE it is acknowledged that learning takes place at two levels: there is basic learning about the predictive utility of each cue (or configuration of cues), but there is also more generalized learning about how useful it is to attend to each cue. It is generally helpful to learn to attend more to those cues that have strong connections to an outcome, but learning to attend and learning the weight of a cue are not the same thing: one could ignore a cue – perhaps because it has not been useful in the past – that in fact is now highly predictive. Models that separate out these two types of learning have proven better able to capture aspects of decision learning than standard backpropagation models.

Exemplar theories

Up to this point, we have concentrated solely on associative approaches to decision learning. This family of models is based on the assumption that knowledge of the structure of some decision problem is captured by a set of weights connecting cues to choice alternatives, either directly (in the linear model) or indirectly (in multilayer neural network models). Accordingly, such models construe the learning process as involving the updating of these weights on a case-by-case basis and it is almost universal that such updating is based on the sort of error term captured in equation 11.5 in chapter 11. An entirely different approach to decision making, in contrast, emphasizes memory processes rather than learning. So-called 'exemplar' models conceive of decisions as being based on retrieval of past cases from memory, with the decision being pulled towards more similar previous cases. The exemplar approach is also known in the machine learning literature as 'case-based' reasoning. Hence we turn now to a consideration of the successes of such models in simulating and predicting human performance. At the end of the section we discuss the relationship between connectionist and exemplar-based theories.

There is a wealth of evidence that exemplar or instance memorization plays a role in decision making. Much of this evidence comes from studies of categorization, a simple variety of decision making in which a person judges which of several potential categories an object belongs to. An illustration would be making a diagnostic decision in a medical context: on the basis of a set of indicators, a medical expert decides whether a patient belongs to the category of diabetic people, for instance. Indeed, several of the tasks discussed previously, such as that used in Gluck and Bower's (1988) study, are categorization tasks. Categorization research has shown that decisions are heavily influenced by similarity to previously seen cases. Brooks et al. (1991), for example, found that dermatologists were heavily influenced by prior cases in classifying skin disorders. A given disorder was more likely to be diagnosed if a similar case of that disorder had been seen previously, and this influence persisted across several weeks. Such facilitation was not induced by a dissimilar example of the disorder.

On the basis of evidence that memorized exemplars play a crucial role in category decision making, Medin and Schaffer (1978) proposed that a significant component of the mental representation of a category is simply a set of stored exemplars or instances. The mental representation of a category such as *bird* includes representations of the specific instances belonging to that category, each presumably connected to the label *bird*. In a category decision learning experiment, the training instances are encoded along with their category assignment.

The exemplar view proposes that subjects encode the actual instances during training and base their classifications on the similarity between a test item and stored instances. When a test item is presented, it is as if a chorus of stored instances shout out how similar they are to the test item. Research has shown that this sort of conception of decision making can be very powerful, with complex sets of behaviour being well predicted by formal exemplar theories. Recent research by Juslin and his colleagues has also begun to explore factors that might promote instance-based versus cue-integration modes of decision learning. Juslin et al. (2003a) used a task in which participants judged the toxicity of a secretion from a frog. Four binary cues (e.g., the frog's colour), differing in their predictive validity, allowed the level of toxicity to be judged. Juslin and his colleagues found that participants' performance was well reproduced by a version of the linear model when the feedback about toxicity provided on each trial was both binary (harmless/dangerous) and continuous-valued on a scale from 0 to 100 ('its toxicity is 40'). However when only the binary feedback was provided, performance was better modelled by an exemplar process. (You might recall this example from our discussion of feedback effects in chapter 4.)

It thus appears that people can employ different strategies for learning a repeated-choice decision problem: they can either abstract the cue weights according to the sort of process captured by the linear model, or they can memorize specific training exemplars. Other processes may be possible too. Juslin et al.'s work suggests that various features of the task, such as the type of feedback provided, may encourage one process or another. But perhaps there is another way to think about these findings. Rather than adopting a multiple-process account of learning, it may be appropriate to think of cue abstraction and exemplar memorization as emerging from a common mechanism. Indeed, the ALCOVE model briefly mentioned in the previous section is both an associative learning model – in that cue weights are incrementally adjusted according to an error-correcting learning algorithm – and an exemplar model in that hidden units in the network represent specific training items. On this approach, it may be possible to subsume both types of process within a unitary, more general model. Whether Juslin et al.'s data can be adequately accounted for by ALCOVE is yet to be established but considerable effort is currently being put into trying to distinguish between multiple-system versus unitary models of decision learning (e.g., Maddox & Ashby, 2004; Nosofsky & Johansen, 2000).

Search, expertise and insight

Information search

Learning not only involves forming beliefs about the predictive utility of various cues or signals (and learning how much attention to pay to each of them), it also requires the adoption of suitable search strategies to obtain cue information in the first place. As discussed in chapter 3, cue information is not always presented to us on a plate. It is true that a doctor, for example, may occasionally see a patient who straightforwardly presents with symptoms A, B and C, but more often the doctor will postpone making a decision until more information is available, say from test results. The doctor is therefore deciding what sorts of information he or she needs before making a diagnosis. This raises a set of issues such as how to make an appropriate cost–benefit analysis (additional bits of information are inevitably costly to obtain, even if only in the sense that they introduce a delay), and what sorts of strategy to adopt to search for information that might be helpful.

When the decision situation is familiar, as in the case of a doctor making diagnoses, cost–benefit calculations become the primary issue in information search. The doctor knows exactly what the relevant cue or piece of missing information is (a blood test for a specific virus, say) but doesn't know the status of that cue and so has to decide whether to obtain it. Optimally, the decision maker should trade off the increase in the accuracy of his or her decision (and the concomitant gain in utility from making a greater number of correct decisions) against the cost of acquiring the missing information. This, needless to say, can quickly become a very difficult calculation to make. Nevertheless, we saw in chapter 3 that there is good evidence that people are attuned to the relative costs and benefits in deciding whether to wait for more information or to go ahead and make a decision on the available cues (Connolly & Serre, 1984; Edwards, 1965).

When the decision problem is more unfamiliar, a different problem presents itself: one may not know what sort of information is likely to be useful, and hence information search becomes much more open-ended. In these circumstances, what should the decision maker do? One feature of such situations is that cue discovery becomes an important process, as discussed in chapter 3. Another way to think about this problem, however, draws an analogy with animals foraging for food. Like the decision maker, the animal doesn't know it should start foraging where food is available, and hence it has to adopt some strategy for allocating its search time. Optimal foraging theory proposes that evolution has endowed animals with strategies that allow them to maximize the food energy gain per unit of search effort. They do this by moving to a new patch when the gains from the current patch fall below what they can anticipate in other patches. Consider a person searching the World Wide Web for an answer to a particular problem – let us imagine he or she is searching for information about the energy efficiency of various washing machines as a prelude to deciding which one to buy. Search engines such as Google provide an enormous number of information sources (websites) any one of which could contain the piece of information being sought. At any moment the person has to decide whether to keep searching the current website (staying in the current food patch) or to switch to another site (another patch). Research on information search in contexts such as this has found that people are quite good at juggling the costs and benefits in a near-optimal way (Pirolli & Card, 1999).

Expertise

The models of learning discussed so far in this chapter invariably predict improved performance with more and more experience and feedback. Thus it is natural to ask whether the general perspective they give for the development of expertise is empirically correct. We will not attempt to review here the very substantial literature on the development of expertise (which connects with many branches of psychology in addition to judgment and decision making, for instance memory and perception) but will briefly look more at the broad properties of expertise.

One way in which the performance of error-correcting models improves is via steadily increasing discrimination. In the early stages of learning, the same response is often given in response to different cue configurations. A naïve person trying to learn how to determine the sex of day old chicks simply doesn't see differences between them (they all look alike) and hence can't discriminate between them. An expert, in contrast, instantly focuses on the features that tell them apart and hence is able to make different decisions in the face of quite similar objects. Error-correcting models capture this aspect of discrimination quite readily, as feedback provides the driving force for a set of weights to be formed that is sensitive to small but potentially significant differences between objects. Selective attention to the most important attributes or features amplifies this effect.

Weiss and Shanteau (2003) have proposed that discrimination is only one of the critical ingredients of expertise. Another is consistency. An expert in marking student exams, for example, would give approximately the same mark to the same piece of work on two different occasions whereas a novice, whose benchmarks are yet to develop fully, might give quite different marks. In an analysis of doctors, auditors and personnel selectors, Weiss and Shanteau showed that a measure which took both discrimination and consistency into account seemed to distinguish levels of expertise well. The importance of consistency is less well captured in formal models of decision learning, however. As we have couched them, these models would behave in the same way to the same input pattern on different occasions (except insofar as new learning might occur in the intervening period). To deal with this, our models would have to be supplemented by an account of performance error. The idea would be that the output of the linear model is combined with error to generate the observed behaviour, with this error diminishing in influence as the individual becomes more expert in the domain.

Yet a third feature of human expertise is its remarkable narrowness. A chess expert is unlikely to be outstanding at poker, the stock tips of an expert weather forecaster are probably not worth undue attention, and an outstanding golfer will probably be average at soccer. Research has consistently failed to find general skills or abilities that underlie expert performance. For instance, basic cognitive processes such as working memory, attention and learning speed are not *in general* better developed in experts. Put differently, becoming an expert does not entail an improvement in any of these basic processes (Ericsson, 1996). What does improve are the perceptual, memory and cognitive components that the task places demands on. Thus an expert chess player has a vastly superior memory and perceptual capacity for chess positions than a novice. Consistent with the linear model, becoming an expert does not intrinsically require the development of basic cognitive, perceptual or motoric processes – it is specific to the domain in question and the cues and outcomes intrinsic to that domain.

The sorts of laboratory learning experiments reviewed in this chapter induce expertise by their very nature. After many trials in which some decision is made and feedback provided, performance inevitably improves – the participant becomes more expert at that particular task.

But of course real experts have skills that go beyond simple learning, discrimination and consistency. They typically are better teachers than non-experts, they can reflect more deeply on the structure of the environment in which their expertise is embedded, and they usually have deeper insight about their own performance. However, the core of most types of expertise does seem to be some sort of learning process similar to that exemplified by the linear model and its variants.

Insight

An intriguing finding emerging from several recent studies is that even when people perform well in multiple-cue decision learning tasks, they seem to lack insight into how they achieve this (Evans, Clibbens, Cattani, Harris, & Dennis, 2003; Gluck, Shohamy, & Myers, 2002). A larger body of research has documented a similar finding in more naturalistic settings such as medical experts' decision making (Harries, Evans, & Dennis, 2000).

This apparent dissociation is illustrated in Gluck et al.'s (2002) study of multiple-cue learning. They found that while participants attained high levels of predictive accuracy (well above chance), they demonstrated little explicit knowledge about what they were doing. In particular, in questionnaires administered at the end of the task they gave inaccurate estimates of the cue–outcome probabilities, and there was little correspondence between self-reports about how they were learning the task and their actual task performance.

The possibility that learning and insight can be teased apart has been taken as evidence for two separate learning systems (Ashby & Ell, 2002). On the one hand, an implicit (or procedural) system operates in the absence of awareness or conscious control, and is inaccessible to self-report. On the other hand, an explicit (or declarative) system requires awareness, and involves conscious, analytic processing. Multiple-cue tasks, which require the gradual learning and integration of probabilistic information, are generally considered to involve implicit learning. The lack of self-insight on such tasks is thus explained by the operation of an implicit system to which participants lack access.

It is also argued that these two systems are subserved by distinct brain regions that can be differentially impaired (Ashby & Ell, 2002). Thus multiple-cue decision making tasks have been used to reveal a distinctive pattern of dissociations among patient populations. For example, Parkinson's disease patients with damage to the basal ganglia show impaired learning on multiple cue tasks despite maintaining good explicit memory about task features (Knowlton, Mangels, & Squire, 1996). In contrast, amnesic patients with damage to the medial temporal lobes appear to show normal learning but poor declarative memory on such tasks (Reber, Knowlton, & Squire, 1996).

If correct, these conclusions have wide repercussions for understanding everyday judgment and decision making. Indeed, many researchers have been developing 'dual-process' theories of judgments and decision making (e.g., Kahneman, 2003). However, there are several reasons to be cautious about this dual-process framework. We focus on two fundamental issues: the measurement of insight and the analysis of individual learning.

It is important to distinguish between someone's insight into the structure of a task (*task knowledge*) and their insight into their own judgmental processes (*self-insight*). In the case of a multiple-cue learning task, this translates into the difference between a learner's knowledge of the objective cue–outcome associations, and their knowledge of how they are using the cues to predict the outcome. There is no guarantee that the two coincide. Someone might have an incorrect model of the task structure, but an accurate model of their own judgment process. For instance, think of a pathologist whose job is to screen cell samples in order to detect a particular disease. This person might have complete and accurate awareness of the features she is looking for and how much weight to give them (she might be very good at passing on her understanding to students). She thus has excellent self-insight. However, her actual success in detecting abnormal cells might be poor or non-existent if the features and weights she is using are not objectively valid. This would imply weak task knowledge.

Though distinct notions, there is a tendency in previous research to run the two together. Thus it is not always clear whether claims about the dissociation between insight and learning refer to a dissociation between self-insight and learning, task knowledge and learning, or both. Further, this conflation can infect the explicit tests given to participants. Questions that are designed to tap someone's insight into their own judgment processes may instead be answered in terms of their knowledge about the task. Such confusion needs to be avoided if firm conclusions are to be drawn about the relation between learning and insight.

There are several other problems with the explicit tests commonly used to measure task knowledge and self-insight. First, these measures tend to be retrospective, asked after participants have completed a task involving numerous trials, and this can distort the validity of the assessments that people give. The reliance on memory, possibly averaged across many trials, can make it difficult to recall a unique judgment strategy. This is especially problematic if people's strategies have varied during the course of the task, making it hard if not impossible to summarize in one global response. In general it is better to get multiple subjective assessments as close as possible to the actual moments of judgment (Ericsson & Simon, 1980).

Second, explicit tests often require verbalization, but this can also misrepresent the knowledge someone has about the task. In particular, it can lead to an underestimation of insight, because participants may know what they are doing but be unable to put this into words. This is particularly likely in probabilistic tasks, where natural language may not be well adapted to the nuances of probabilistic inference.

A third problem with previous tests of explicit knowledge, especially in the neuropsychological literature, is that they are too vague (Lovibond & Shanks, 2002). Rather than focus on specific features of the task necessary for its solution they include general questions that are tangential to solving the task. Once again this reduces the sensitivity of the test to measure people's relevant knowledge or insight. This problem can lead to an overestimation of insight (because someone may be able to recall features of the task that are irrelevant to good performance on it) or to underestimation (because the questions fail to ask about the critical information).

Lagnado et al. (2006b) sought to improve the sensitivity of explicit tests on all these counts in their multiple-cue learning task. Separate explicit tests for task knowledge and self-insight were used, and both involved specific questions of direct relevance to the task. In the case of task knowledge these concerned probability ratings about cue–outcome relations, in the case of self-insight, subjective ratings about cue usage. Such ratings-based tests avoided any problem of verbalization. To tackle the problem of retrospective assessments, multiple judgments during the course of the task (either blocked or trial-by-trial) were taken.

The results were clear-cut: There was no evidence of any dissociation between insight and performance. Participants were very accurate in their probability ratings for the various cues, and their cue usage ratings mirrored their objective cue utilization. These findings suggest that previous claims of 'intuitive' decisions being made without insight were premature and that care needs to be taken in decision making studies not to underestimate insight. More research is needed on this relatively unexplored aspect of choice.

Summary

In this chapter we have followed a path through theory development from the original linear model for simple binary choices to models that incorporate internal representations, along the way discussing expertise and optimality, and exemplar representation. The linear model is an extraordinarily compelling yet simple way of accounting for how people learn to assign weights to cues in a decision environment, and its scope suggests that error-driven learning in some form or other plays a central role in the learning process. The model often predicts convergence to optimal behaviour in the long run, and this appears to be consistent with expert performance. In many settings, both in the laboratory and in real life, experts seem able to iron out many biases such as base rate neglect. Although experts can be outperformed by statistical tools (as we saw in chapter 3), we should take heart from the capacity of the brain to incorporate incredible amounts of complex data into accurate decisions.

The final section on insight concludes our discussion of the role of learning and experience in decision problems. In the three remaining chapters of the book we examine some contextual effects on decision making – namely, what happens when emotions influence our decisions, and when we make decisions in groups – and then we finish with a look at some applied techniques for improving our decision making outside the psychology laboratory.

13 Emotional influences on decision making

In January 2005 some tragic events occurred in Italy. A woman drowned herself in the sea off Tuscany, a man from Florence shot his wife and children before turning the gun on himself, and a man in Sicily was arrested for beating his wife. These and many other incidents were connected by the 'Venice 53' – an elusive and unlucky number in the Italian national lotto.

Italians are invited to bet any amount of money on numbers from 1 to 90 in biweekly draws of the lotto. The draws take place in 10 cities throughout Italy, with five numbers picked in each of the 10 cities. By the beginning of February 2005, the number 53 had not been drawn in Venice in almost 2 years. A '53 frenzy' gripped the nation, with €671 million bet on the number in January alone. The unfortunate 'victims of 53' were so convinced that the number's time had come that they bet their entire family savings on '53' – all to no avail. Finally on Wednesday 9 February '53' was pulled from the basket in the Venice lottery and the nation sighed in relief.

The belief that a number's time has come is, of course, fallacious – the lottery has no memory for previous outcomes, so any number is just as likely to be picked on every occasion. Adhering to such a belief is an example of the well-documented 'gambler's fallacy'; that is, believing that after a long run of one outcome – '53' not being drawn – the other outcome – '53' being drawn – is more likely to occur (see Ayton & Fischer, 2004 for a discussion of this phenomenon). The tragic examples illustrate, however, the degree to which people are swayed by such fallacious beliefs. What causes people to hold on to these beliefs so strongly, and to go to such extremes?

In the preceding chapters we have considered several explanations for why, when and how people might fall off the 'straight and narrow' road of good decision making, but in most of our discussions (with the exception of the discussion of visceral influences in chapter 10) we have taken a cognitive perspective and focused on the decision maker as an 'information processor'. But when a person commits suicide because a number has not appeared in a lottery, it seems too simplistic to explain this away as solely due to a misunderstanding of randomness, or in terms of the 'gambler's fallacy'. For such an extreme action to be provoked, feelings and emotions must have played a fundamental role.

For quite some time, several decision researchers have been making this point, urging that decision making does not occur in an emotional vacuum and that therefore it should not be studied in one either (e.g., Finucane, Peters, & Slovic, 2003; Loewenstein, Weber, Hsee, & Welch, 2001). In this chapter we move away from the 'cold' analysis of the learning underlying decision making that was the focus of the last two chapters and examine the effects of emotions on judgment and choice. Our change in focus is in acknowledgement of the fact that if we want to improve our decision making in the 'real world' then we need to understand more about 'hot' cognition – that is, cognition influenced by emotion and affect.

Decisions and emotions

One of the first people to emphasize the importance of understanding the link between decision making and emotion was Robert Zajonc. In a classic paper published in 1980 Zajonc argued that affective reactions to stimuli may precede cognitive reactions and thus require no cognitive appraisal; or as Zajonc (1980) rather pithily described it: 'preferences need no inferences'. He went on to argue that we sometimes delude ourselves into thinking that we make rational decisions – weighing all the pros and cons of various alternatives – when in fact our choices are determined by no more than simple likes or dislikes: 'We buy the cars we "like", choose the jobs and houses we find "attractive" and then justify these choices by various reasons' (p. 155). If Zajonc's 'primacy of affect' argument is correct then it has strong implications for our understanding of how we make decisions effectively and efficiently in our increasingly complex world (see Finucane et al., 2003).

One highly influential account of the role of affect in decision making comes from the work of Damasio, Bechara and colleagues (Bechara, Damasio, Damasio, & Anderson, 1994; Bechara, Damasio, Tranel, & Damasio, 1997; Damasio, 1996, 2000). In a series of experiments these researchers investigated the reasons behind the defective choices made by some brain-damaged individuals. Specifically, they were interested in why some individuals with damage to the prefrontal cortex of the brain are unable to learn from their mistakes, and often make decisions that lead to negative consequences, despite displaying intact general problem-solving and intellectual abilities. To investigate the reasons underlying this 'myopia' for future consequences of decisions, Bechara et al. (1994) developed a simple gambling task that they argued simulated many real-world decisions in the way it involves uncertainty of premises and outcomes as well as rewards and punishments.

In the task participants (both normal and brain damaged) sit in front of four decks of cards and are asked to turn over cards one at a time from any of the four decks. The trick to learning the task is to discover what kind of monetary reward or punishment is associated with each deck. Two of the decks (A and B) have a reward/punishment schedule that results in a net loss over the course of the experiment; the other two decks (C and D) have a schedule that results in a net gain. However, the key feature of the design is that the immediate reward associated with decks A and B is higher than that associated with decks C and D. The interesting question is whether participants learn to choose from the decks that are advantageous in the long term (C and D) or are more influenced by the immediate gains from the disadvantageous decks (A and B).

The results showed a clear difference between the performance of normal and brain-damaged individuals. While normal participants learned to choose from the 'good decks' – choosing from C or D on approximately 70 per cent of the trials – brain-damaged individuals showed the reverse pattern choosing from A or B on around 70 per cent of trials (Bechara et al., 1994). Why are the brain-damaged individuals insensitive to future consequences? Damasio (2000) has suggested that in these individuals 'the delicate mechanism of reasoning is no longer affected ... by signals hailing from the neural machinery that underlies emotion' (p. 41). According to Damasio, the damage these individuals have suffered to specific areas in the brain results in the loss of a certain class of emotions and the loss of the ability to make rational decisions.

These ideas are encapsulated in what Damasio describes as the 'somatic marker hypothesis'. The central claim of the hypothesis is that in normal individuals, somatic or bodily states provide a 'mark' indicating the affective valence (positive or negative) for a cognitive scenario. Although Damasio further assumed that these somatic markers are unconscious, that need not be the case (Maia & McClelland, 2004), but whether conscious or unconscious, individuals with prefrontal cortex damage have lost the ability to mark scenarios with positive or negative feelings and so do not exhibit the appropriate anticipatory emotions when considering the future consequences of decisions. Put simply, the hypothesis explains the gamble task behaviour by suggesting that the patients failed to anticipate the catastrophic losses incurred by perseverance on the bad decks.

The affect heuristic and risk as feelings

Slovic and colleagues have built on Damasio's idea of emotional markers for decision making and suggested that 'mental representations of decision stimuli evoke on-line affective experiences that influence people's perceptions and consequently their judgments and decisions' (Finucane et al., 2003, p. 341). They propose an 'affect heuristic', arguing that in the same way as memorability and imaginability might be used as rules of thumb in probability judgment (e.g., the availability heuristic), so affect can be used as a cue for a variety of important judgments.

Empirical evidence supporting the operation of such a heuristic is not yet extensive but Finucane, Alhakami, Slovic, and Johnson (2000) reported some supportive results. In one study, they demonstrated that participants' judgments regarding the risks and benefits of an item could be altered by manipulating the global affective evaluation of that item. For example, they suggest that nuclear power may appear more favourable in the light of information indicating that it has either high benefit or low risk. The notion here is that if you are given information about the benefits of nuclear power, your affective evaluation of nuclear power rises and so you infer – via an 'affect heuristic' – that the risks associated with nuclear power are low. In a similar fashion, if you are told that risks are high, your affective evaluation is lowered and you infer that nuclear power has low benefit. Finucane et al. contrast this affective account with a more cognitively derived prediction that inferences pertaining to the attribute you did not receive any information about would remain unaffected (i.e., if you only learned about the risks of nuclear power your attitudes to its benefits should remain unchanged).

To test this idea Finucane et al. (2000) presented participants with vignettes designed to manipulate affect by describing either the benefits or the risks of nuclear power. They then collected perceived risk and benefit ratings. The general pattern in the results was that providing information about one attribute (e.g., risk) had a carryover effect on the attribute about which nothing had been learned directly (e.g., benefit). Finucane et al. (2000) interpreted this pattern in terms of people 'consulting their overall affective evaluation of the item when judging its risk and benefit' (p. 13) – in other words, people relied on an affect heuristic to make risk/benefit judgments.

A similar notion to the affect heuristic has been proposed by Loewenstein and colleagues (Loewenstein et al., 2001) with the 'risk-as-feelings' hypothesis. The hypothesis overlaps with the affect heuristic in proposing that often emotional reactions and cognitive evaluations work 'in concert to guide reasoning and decision making' (p. 270); but the hypothesis also states that cognitions and emotions may diverge and emotions may sometimes lead to behavioural responses that depart from ones that a purely cognitive appraisal might lead to.

A good example of the kind of evidence that Loewenstein and colleagues draw on in formulating the risk-as-feelings hypothesis is their interpretation of one of the most robust findings in the decision making under uncertainty literature – the overweighting of small or extreme probabilities. As we saw in chapter 9, a change of .01 in the probability of an event occurring is deemed trivial if the probability of occurrence is already .49, but if it is a change from 0 to .01 it is interpreted as far more important. Kahneman and Tversky (1979a) described these non-linearities in probability weights in terms of a *certainty effect*. Loewenstein et al. (2001) argue that by including emotion in the 'prediction equation' this effect can be readily explained. Their suggestion is that an increase from 0 to .01 represents the crossing of a threshold from a consequence of no concern to one that becomes a source of worry (or hope depending on the context); once this threshold has been crossed any subsequent increments in probability have a much lower emotional impact and thus tend not to influence choice (recall the Russian roulette example from chapter 9 as an extreme illustration of such an effect).

An empirical investigation of the relation between emotion and over-weighting was reported by Rottenstreich and Hsee (2001). They were interested in whether the affective quality of an outcome influenced people's choices under conditions of certainty and uncertainty. Rottenstreich and Hsee's study had two conditions: a certainty condition in which participants were offered the choice between the opportunity to meet and kiss their favourite movie star or $50 in cash, and an uncertainty condition in which participants chose between two lotteries offering a 1 per cent chance to win either the cash or the movie-star kiss. The authors proposed that if emotions impact on choice, then participants would prefer the more affect-laden option (kiss) to the affect-poor option (cash) – despite the chance of winning either prize being equal (1 per cent). Note that a purely psychophysical analysis of this choice focuses solely on the probabilities and not on the outcomes to which they are attached. This means that both expected utility theory and prospect theory (see chapters 8 and 9), which posit separate functions for the evaluation of outcomes and probabilities, predict no impact of the affective quality of the outcome on choice.

The results provided overwhelming support for Rottenstreich and Hsee's contention that the affective quality of the outcome would impact choice. In the uncertainty condition 65 per cent of participants preferred the kiss lottery over the cash lottery. This was despite the fact that in the certainty condition 70 per cent of participants preferred the $50 cash. This striking probability–outcome interaction (another example of a preference reversal) was interpreted as indicating that the weight assigned to a 1 per cent probability is greater for the affect-rich kiss than for the affect-poor cash. In two follow-up experiments, Rottenstreich and Hsee replicated this same basic finding using more comparable prizes (a $500 coupon redeemable for either tuition fees or a European holiday) and negative outcomes (an electric shock). Overall the results provided strong support for the notion that people are more sensitive to departures from certainty and impossibility for affect-rich than for affect-poor prizes. It appears that probabilities and outcomes are not independent, as proposed in standard theories, but interact as a function of the emotional reactions evoked via the outcomes.

Imagery, affect and decisions

An important thread running through the approaches we have reviewed so far is the role of vivid imagery in determining emotional reactions and the decisions based on those reactions. Damasio's somatic marker hypothesis has at its core the notion that 'images' (loosely constrained to include real and imaginary visual images, as well as sounds and smells) are marked with positive and negative feelings throughout the course of our lives. Finucane et al. (2003) describe the 'basic tenet' of the affect heuristic as being the idea that positive and negative feelings are attached to images that sub-sequently influence judgments and decisions. The risk-as-feelings perspective

(Loewenstein et al., 2001) proposes that a key influence on the determinant of feelings is the vividness of evoked imagery.

One factor, discussed by both the affect heuristic and risk-as-feelings perspective, that is claimed to influence the vividness of images, is whether statistical information is presented in terms of frequencies or in terms of probabilities. For example, Slovic, Monahan, and MacGregor (2000) demonstrated that clinicians provided with recidivism risks presented as frequencies (e.g., 20 out of 100) judged mental patients as posing higher risks than when the same information was presented as probabilities (e.g., 20 per cent). The explanation was that only the frequency presentation generated a 'terrifying image' of the recidivist in the mind of the clinician, and the affect associated with this imagery led to the more extreme judgments (Slovic et al., 2000). In a similar vein, Purchase and Slovic (1999) reported that individuals were more frightened by information about chemical spills framed as frequencies (e.g., out of 1,000,000 exposed people, there will be 1 additional cancer death) than as probabilities (e.g., each exposed individual has an additional chance of .0001 per cent of getting cancer). In a related set of findings Yamagishi (1997) demonstrated that participants rated a disease that kills 1286 people out of every 10,000 as more dangerous than one that kills 24.14 per cent of the population (despite the former number obviously being equivalent to only 12.86 per cent!).

It is worth noting that although these format effects are interpreted as due to evoked imagery there is often no independent evidence that participants given frequency formats do indeed experience more vivid imagery than those given probability formats. However, Slovic et al. (2000) refer to an unpublished study that does provide support for this interpretation. Participants were given scenarios in which patients were described as having either a '10 per cent probability of committing a violent act' or in frequentist terms as '10 out of 100 similar patients are estimated to commit an act of violence'. They were then asked to 'write a few brief thoughts or images that come to mind as you evaluate the risk posed by this patient' (p. 289). The frequency format produced images of violent acts in participants' reports, whereas the probability format did not.

Koehler and Macchi (2004) speculated that particular statistical formats need not necessarily evoke terrifying or affectively rich imagery to influence probability judgment; it may be sufficient for the statistics to simply evoke thoughts about other examples of the target event. Their 'exemplar cuing theory' states that, 'the weight decision makers attach to low probability events is, in part, a function of whether they can easily generate or imagine exemplars for the event' (p. 540). They suggest, for example, that a lottery ticket might be more appealing if a potential purchaser is induced to think about other winning lottery tickets.

According to exemplar cuing theory, however, the use of a frequency format is not the crucial factor underlying the imaginability of exemplars. Koehler and Macchi propose a 'multiplicative' mechanism for the facilitation of exemplar generation. This mechanism cues exemplars when the product of the size of the reference class for the event and the incidence rate of the event is greater than 1. For example, a lottery ticket described as having a 1 per cent chance of winning, with a reference class of 500,000 tickets sold in a day, generates 5000 exemplars of winning tickets. Such a ticket is deemed to be more appealing than a ticket with a 1 per cent chance in a lottery in which only 50 tickets are sold in a day because this arrangement only generates 0.5 of a winning ticket. Importantly, this mechanism is unaffected by the format of the information; that is, by whether incidence rates are provided as percentages (1 per cent) or frequencies (1 out of 100). The reason that format does not affect exemplar generation is that the format does not identify a relevant sample space within which to search for exemplars (Koehler & Macchi, 2004). This sample space is provided by the reference class (e.g., the number of other tickets sold), a factor common to both formats.

Koehler and Macchi tested their exemplar cuing model in the context of DNA evidence in mock jury trials. Participants rated the evidence against a defendant as weaker when the product of the reference class cued exemplars of other possible matches. However, Newell, Mitchell, and Hayes (2005) were unable to find any evidence for a multiplicative mechanism in other situations involving low probability events. In fact, in situations where the event was positive (e.g., winning a lottery), participants were more willing to play when, according to exemplar cuing theory, no exemplars of winning tickets were cued. Newell et al. explained their results in terms of participants anchoring on the reference class (i.e., preferring lotteries in which fewer tickets are sold) rather than any multiplicative process.

Newell et al. (2005) also found strong evidence for a frequency format effect, contrary to the prediction of exemplar cuing theory. Specifically Newell et al. found that when the low probability event was positive (e.g., winning a lottery), participants were more willing to engage in the proposed behaviour when frequency formats were used, but when the low probability event was negative (e.g., suffering a side-effect of a vaccine), participants were less willing to engage in the behaviour when frequency formats were used. Overall the results were better explained by the simple frequency format account than by the more complicated exemplar cuing theory.

One final piece of evidence concerning the effect of imagery that is relevant to our discussion is the tendency for people to 'image the numerator' when presented with probability ratios. Consider the following problem: in front of you are two bowls containing different numbers of jelly beans. The small bowl contains 1 red bean and 9 white beans; the large bowl contains 7 red beans and 93 white beans. If you select a red bean you will win $1. The bowls will be shielded from view when you make your selection (it is not that easy!) but you have to decide which bowl you would like to select from – the large one or the small one?

We hope that by this stage of the book, most readers will be able to see that the probability of selecting a red bean is higher for the small bowl (.10) than it is for the large bowl (.07) so the rational choice is to select the small bowl. Denes-Raj and Epstein (1994) gave a series of problems like this one to undergraduate students and found that over 80 per cent of them made at least one non-optimal choice (i.e., selected the larger bowl). Furthermore, participants made these non-optimal choices despite knowing that the probabilities were stacked against them. What prompted this irrational behaviour?

Denes-Raj and Epstein explain the effect in terms of participants 'imaging the numerator' – that is focusing on the overall number of red beans in the bowl rather than the probability ratio. They noted that participants often made statements such as 'I picked the one with more red jelly beans because it looked like there were more ways to get a winner, even though I knew there were more whites and the percents were against me' (1994, p. 823). Thus the affect associated with winning combined with the images of winning beans appears to drive participants to make non-optimal choices – even when they know they shouldn't.

Koehler and Macchi (2004) reported similar effects again using DNA statistics. They found that participants were more convinced by DNA evidence when a probability ratio was expressed as 1 out of 1000 than as 0.1 out of 100. The interpretation: innocent matches can only be imagined with the integer numerator (1) not with the fractional numerator (0.1) (i.e., what does 0.1 of a person look like?).

Providing the image

Our focus in this section has been on how different numerical formats affect judgments and decisions through evoked imagery. However, as we noted, the evidence for imagery is often indirect (i.e., the images are assumed to be in participants' heads). What happens if the image is provided to the participant? How do graphical representations of statistics influence judgment? A study by Stone, Yates, and Parker (1997) asked this question in relation to perceived risk. Stone et al. (1997) described the following scenario to participants:

> A set of four standard tires cost $225. The risk of a serious injury from a tire blowout is 30 per five million drivers. How much extra would you be willing to pay for a set of improved tires in which the injury risk is halved to 15 per five million drivers?

The key manipulation was that in one condition the risk was conveyed in numbers (e.g., 30 per 5,000,000) but in the other 'graphical' condition the numerator of the risk statistic (i.e., either 30 or 15) was conveyed using figures of 'stick men' drawn on the page. Stone et al. found that participants in the stick figures condition were willing to pay significantly more ($125 in addition to the $225) for the improved tyres than those in the numbers only condition ($102). Stone et al. explained the effect in terms of the graphical display increasing participants' estimate of the risk of the standard tyres relative to the improved ones. In follow up work (Stone, Sieck, Bull, Yates, Parks, & Rush, 2003) the boundaries of this effect have been explored, with the evidence suggesting that when both the numerator and the denominator are displayed graphically the difference between graphical and numerical displays disappears. Thus it seems that the increase in risk perception might operate in the same way as the 'image the numerator' mechanism, and unsurprisingly, when the image of the numerator is *provided* rather than evoked the effects are stronger.

Summary

An increasing number of researchers are beginning to recognize the importance of studying the role of affect and emotion in decision making. Empirical evidence collected to date suggests that affect plays a part in heuristic judgment as well as in the evaluation of the probabilities and outcomes involved in choice. A common mechanism underlying these effects appears to be the emotional reactions evoked via vivid imagery. Further research is needed to understand how, when and why such imagery is evoked and how it influences decision making.

Our coverage of this fascinating topic has been necessarily rather brief; readers interested in learning more should take a look at the special issue of the *Journal of Behavioral Decision Making* on 'The role of affect in decision making' (edited by Peters, Västfjäll, Gärling, & Slovic, 2006). This collection of papers examines many facets of the relation between emotions and decisions, from investigations of how sexual arousal influences our willingness to engage in various sexual practices, to how thinking about our mood influences everyday choices.

14 Group decision making

Imagine you are a contestant on the popular TV game show 'Who wants to be a millionaire?' You have answered a few questions and have some money 'in the bank' but now you are facing a tricky question. You still have all three 'lifelines' in hand so to get help with the answer you can phone a friend, ask the studio audience or use the 50:50 to eliminate two of the four multiple-choice answers. Which lifeline should you opt for?

The choice between 'phone a friend' and 'ask the audience' requires deciding whether to rely on the intelligence of a single person or on the 'wisdom of the crowd' (Surowiecki, 2005). Intuitively, we might expect that the expert friend at home would be a better bet than the collection of individuals who just happen to be in the studio. Is this intuition correct? Surowiecki (2005) obtained statistics from the US version of 'millionaire' and discovered that in fact the opposite was true: experts were right on average 65 per cent of the time, but the audience picked the correct option on an impressive 91 per cent of occasions!

Surowiecki acknowledges that this anecdotal evidence would not necessarily stand up to scrutiny – for example it may simply be the case that the audience are asked easier questions than the experts – but the data do appear to suggest that several heads might be better than one when it comes to making certain types of decision. (An interesting footnote to Surowiecki's observation is that the most successful contestant on the Australian version of the show (at the time of writing) used his 'ask the audience' lifeline on the penultimate and thus very difficult question, and chose the option voted for by the *fewest* members of the audience. Presumably, the contestant reasoned that for very difficult questions the obvious answer is often wrong so it is reasonable to go against the audience choice – he was right (or lucky) and went on to win the million dollars.) These observations from game shows are all very interesting, but as the saying goes, the plural of 'anecdote' is not 'data' – what do we know from controlled empirical tests about the merits or otherwise of group decision making?

Intellective and judgment tasks

The received wisdom concerning group decision making is that by working together on a problem we will arrive at a better solution than if we ponder the problem alone. Why else would we have invented juries, think-tanks or brainstorming sessions? However, the literature on group decision making does not always concur with this 'wisdom'. In a review of over 50 years' worth of research on group decision making, Hill (1982) concluded that group judgments were about as accurate as the second best individual member of the group. In a later analysis, Gigone and Hastie (1997) echoed the earlier conclusion, stating that: 'For the most part group judgments tend to be more accurate than the judgments of typical individuals, approximately equal in accuracy to the mean judgments of their members, and less accurate than the judgments of their most accurate member' (p. 153). The same basic conclusion was drawn by Kerr and Tindale (2004) in a recent review of the literature.

So what is the empirical basis for these conclusions about group performance? One class of problems commonly used to compare individual and group performance is known as 'eureka-type' problems or intellective tasks because they have a demonstrable solution (e.g., Laughlin, 1999; Lorge & Solomon, 1958; Maier & Solem, 1952). A good example of one of these problems is the rule induction task used by Laughlin and colleagues (Laughlin, 1999; Laughlin, Vanderstoep, & Hollingshead, 1991). Laughlin's task requires participants to induce a rule involving standard playing cards. The task begins with one rule-following card exposed face up on the table; participants are then asked to select a new card from the deck in order to test their hypotheses about the rule. For example, the eight of diamonds might be face up and the to-be-discovered rule might be 'Two diamonds followed by two clubs'. If a participant selects a card consistent with the rule, it is placed to the right of the first card; if it is inconsistent it is placed underneath the first card. Participants continue these trial-by-trial tests of their hypotheses and attempt to use the feedback to infer the rule. The interesting manipulation in the experiments reported by Laughlin et al. (1991) is whether participants are invited to test their hypotheses individually or as part of a cooperative four-person group.

Laughlin et al. (1991) found that the best individual participants generated significantly higher proportions of correct hypotheses than did the groups or second, third or fourth best individuals. The groups and second best individuals did not differ significantly from each other, but they did produce more correct hypotheses than the third and fourth best individuals (who did not differ significantly from each other). This pattern showing group performance to be equal to the second best individual is consistent with most previous research (e.g., Gigone & Hastie, 1997; Hill, 1982; Kerr & Tindale, 2004). Laughlin et al. conjectured that the poorer performance of the group may have been due to restrictions in the amount of evidence available for hypothesis testing and the time available to discuss potential rules. In a follow-up study they tested this idea by allowing groups 10 extra minutes to solve the problem and providing the opportunity to obtain more information about the rule on each trial. These manipulations led to equivalent performance for the groups and best individuals: both produced the same proportion of correct hypotheses. Thus it appears that given sufficient time and information groups can solve intellective tasks at least as well as the best of an equivalent number of individuals (Laughlin, 1999; Laughlin et al., 1991).

At the opposite end of the spectrum from intellective tasks are those commonly referred to as judgmental tasks. These tend to involve evaluative, behavioural or aesthetic judgments and have no demonstrable solution (e.g., sales forecasting) (Laughlin, 1999). How does the performance of groups and individuals compare on these types of task? Can the group perform as well as the best individual, as they seem to be able to do in the intellective tasks? A study reported by Sniezek (1989) addressed this question. Sniezek presented sales forecasting problems to four groups of five undergraduate students. The task involved predicting sales volumes for a general store on campus. The groups received time-series data for the preceding 14 months and were asked to predict sales for the following month. Sniezek was interested not only in the comparison of individual and group performance but also in different methods of group interaction.

First, all members of the group provided an independent individual sales estimate – these estimates were then collated to provide a 'collective mean' judgment for the group. Second, one of four different group decision techniques was imposed on the group: dictator, consensus, dialectic or Delphi. The dictator technique required group members to decide, through face-to-face discussion, who was the best member of the group and then to submit his or her estimate as the group estimate. The consensus technique was a straightforward discussion aimed at coming to group agreement on the estimate. For the dialectic technique members were provided with the collective mean estimate and then asked to think of all possible reasons why the actual sales volume might be higher or lower than the estimate, following this discussion a revised group estimate was decided on. Finally the Delphi technique required group members to provide estimates anonymously in a series of rounds, with no face-to-face discussion, until a consensus was reached. (This technique is supposed to maximize the benefits of group decision making and minimize possible adverse effects such as one person monopolizing discussion.)

To measure accuracy Sniezek looked at the absolute percent error (APE) between the collective mean estimate and the group estimates. All the group interaction techniques led to slightly more accurate forecasts than the simple aggregation of individual estimates. The greatest improvement was shown by the dictator group (reduction of 7.5 per cent) followed by the Delphi (2.3 per cent), dialectic (1.3 per cent) and consensus (0.8 per cent) groups. However, the APE reduction achieved by the best members was 11.6 per cent, indicating that the best members considerably outperformed all the group decision techniques. It is also worth noting that although groups seemed to be successful in identifying their best member – hence the relatively good performance of the dictator group – the dictators tended to change their judgment following group discussion, and these changes were all in the direction of the collective mean and hence more error. On average the final dictator estimates had 8.5 per cent higher APE than the initial ones.

Sniezek took care to point out that the generality of these results is not known. The groups were small, the participants were undergraduates, and the techniques were only tested in a single context (sales forecasting); nevertheless the results suggest that group interaction and discussion can sometimes lead to improvements in judgment accuracy – at least to a level that is better than the collective mean judgment. If this is the case, then it is important to consider how these interactions might occur – that is, how is the consensus achieved?

Achieving a consensus

Sniezek and Henry (1990) describe consensus achievement in terms of a revision and weighting model. They argue that this two stage model involves the conceptually distinct processes of revision and weighting, which can both operate to transform the distribution of individual judgments into a consensus group judgment. Sniezek and Henry suggest that the fundamental difference between these two processes is that revision occurs at the level of the individual within a group, whereas weighting (i.e., the combination of multiple judgments) occurs at group level. The evidence from two experiments that were similar in design to the Sniezek (1989) experiment discussed earlier, suggested that the weighting process was the more important one for achieving consensus and improving group accuracy (Sniezek & Henry, 1989, 1990). Social interaction of group members during the revision process had little appreciable impact on judgment accuracy; only when the revision process ended and the group engaged in weighting and combining multiple individual judgments were the improvements in accuracy observed.

Gigone and Hastie (1997) built on the ideas of the revision and weighting model, but introduced a Brunswikian lens model framework for conceptualizing the group judgment process. In chapter 3 we encountered the lens model and discussed how the idea of a 'lens of cues' through which a decision maker sees the world is a metaphor that has inspired many researchers (e.g., Hammond & Stewart, 2001). Gigone and Hastie extended the metaphor to think about how groups might arrive at consensus judgments. Figure 14.1 is a graphical representation of their model. Its similarity to the individual lens model shown in Figure 3.1 should be immediately apparent. The far left hand side in both diagrams represents the environment containing the to-be-judged criteria (C); the centre represents the cues that are probabilistically related to the criteria; the far right is the consensus group judgment (G) in Figure 14.1 and the individual judgment in Figure 3.1.

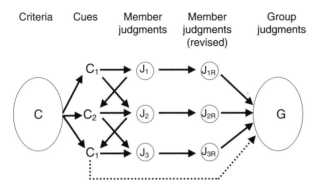

Figure 14.1 A lens model of the group judgment process. From Gigone, D., & Hastie, R. (1997). Proper analysis of the accuracy of group judgments. *Psychological Bulletin, 121,* 149–167. Copyright 1997 by the American Psychological Association. Adapted with permission.

The clear difference between the individual model and the group model is that the latter has two extra layers or stages. In the group model the cues give rise to the initial member judgments and these are then revised before being combined into the group judgment. The advantage of using a lens model framework for thinking about group judgment is that the model lends itself readily to a variety of statistical techniques for analysing judgmental accuracy. For example, the 'lens model equation' (e.g., Cooksey, 1996), can be used to investigate the correlation between the best linear model of the environment (taking into account the validities of all the cues present) and the linear model used by each member of the group. Gigone and Hastie (1997) argue that a group's judgment accuracy depends fundamentally on the accuracy of individual member judgments, so examining individual judgments should be the starting point for understanding group performance.

The model can also be used to think about how accuracy is affected when the group convenes and discusses its judgment. For example, in group discussion a member might learn about a previously unknown judgment-relevant cue. If the member then weights this newly discovered cue appropriately the result will be an increase in the overall correlation between the member's judgment and the environment. Successful combination of members' judgments depends partly on the way in which errors are distributed across the group (Hogarth, 1978). If group judgments converge towards a member whose judgment is highly correlated with the environment then the group judgment will be accurate. However, if there is systematic bias in members' judgments, or a particularly persuasive individual in the group has low accuracy, then the combination process could result in poorer group judgment (Gigone & Hastie, 1997). Therefore if a group adopts an unequal weighting scheme (e.g., one that weights some members' judgments more highly than others) it is very important for the group to be able to identify which of its members are most accurate. Recall that the Delphi technique, in which there is no interaction and judgments are made anonymously, was developed, in part, to counteract the negative impact of domineering but potentially inaccurate group members.

One final aspect of the model in Figure 14.1 that warrants mentioning is the possible direct influence a cue can have on group judgments (depicted by the dashed line connecting the cues and the group judgment). There are at least two ways in which a cue might exert direct influence on the group judgment. One possibility is that there is an 'unshared' cue – that is, one that was only known by a single member of the group and did not come to light until the weighting and combination process. If that cue is a valid predictor then its addition in the group judgment policy will increase the overall correlation with the environment. A second possibility is that during discussion the group might decide a particular cue is very important and thus assign it more weight than did any group member in their individual judgments. Again, if the cue is valid correlational accuracy should improve.

These suggestions for how cue weights might be adjusted and integrated in group judgments are by no means exhaustive. As Plous (1993) notes it is somewhat ironic that the complexity and richness of group research can hinder theoretical progress. The variety of different variables (tasks, group sizes, group members, decision rules) used in experimental studies often makes it very difficult to compare results or draw general conclusions. Gigone and Hastie's (1997) model is very useful in this regard as it provides a framework for applying a common methodology and for improving the ability to make precise comparisons of individual and group accuracy.

Despite the difficulty in drawing general conclusions about group performance, one factor that does appear to be consistent in both intellective and judgmental tasks is the importance of identifying the best individual member of a group. In intellective tasks, like the rule-induction task described earlier, identification of the best member should be straightforward because the solutions to these tasks are demonstrable. Once one member has 'got it' (a 'eureka moment') he or she should be able to demonstrate the 'truth' of the solution. Indeed such a strategy is often described as a 'truth-wins' or 'truth-supported-wins' strategy (Hastie & Kameda, 2005). In judgmental tasks the identification of best members is more difficult because there is not a demonstrable solution. In such tasks groups have to rely on intuitions about a member's credibility or likelihood of being able to generate an accurate estimate (Henry, 1993). An everyday example of this kind of phenomenon can be seen in group attempts to come up with an answer in trivia quizzes. Many of us will be familiar with the experience of being asked a general knowledge question at a trivia night and then trying to achieve a consensus by pooling the resources of the team. For example, if your team was asked 'How long is the river Nile?' different members might attempt to justify their own estimates by claiming that they have been to Egypt and seen the Nile, or that they know the Amazon is so many kilometres and that the Nile is longer, and so on. In an experimental study using general knowledge questions, Henry (1993) provided evidence that groups were able to identify their best members at levels far exceeding chance expectations, and that group members tended to engage in this process of identification as a normal part of the group judgment process.

One finding that appears to contradict the general pattern of accurate identification of best members comes from a study of group decision performance on a conjunction error problem. Recall from chapter 5 that the conjunction error is made when the probability of a conjunction, (e.g., *P*(heart attack and over 55), is rated as more probable than one of its conjuncts (e.g., *P*(heart attack)) (Tversky & Kahneman, 1983). Tindale, Sheffey, and Filkins (1990, as cited in Kerr, MacCoun, & Kramer, 1996) identified the number of persons in four member groups who did and did not commit a conjunction error in individual pretesting and then examined whether the group itself (following discussion of the problem) committed the error. Conjunction problems are intellective because they have a clear demonstrable solution – drawing a Venn diagram like the one shown in Figure 5.1 seems to convince most students – so one might expect that provided at least one member of each four-person group had not committed the error in pretesting, the group as a whole would not commit the error.

This was not what Tindale et al. (1990) found. Seventy-three per cent of the groups containing one member who had not committed the error in pretesting and three members who had, committed the error when making a group judgment. Even those groups with even numbers of members who had and had not committed the error as individuals fared poorly – 69 per cent still rated the conjunction as higher in probability.

Kerr et al. (1996) explained the results in terms of the normatively incorrect alternative (committing the error) exerting a 'strong functional pull' on groups. They argue that when a functional model of judgment (loosely defined as a 'conceptual system . . . that is widely shared and accepted in a population of judges' (p. 701)) operates in opposition to a normative model, the group discussion will tend to exacerbate any bias present in individual members. As we saw in chapter 5, conjunction problems are often interpreted in ways that are at odds with the normative model but consistent with everyday conceptions of language use (e.g., Gigerenzer, 1996; Hilton & Slugoski, 1986) and so it is quite plausible that a group member who knows the demonstrably correct answer might be persuaded that he or she has misinterpreted the question, thereby leading to a group tendency to commit the fallacy.

Groupthink: Model and evidence

One aspect of Tindale et al.'s (1990) results that was abundantly clear was that when all the members in a group committed the conjunction error in individual pretesting, the group had very little hope of coming up with the correct answer – 90 per cent of these groups committed the error. This tendency to be sure as a group that the best decision has been made, even when that decision is demonstrably incorrect, is one of the identifiable dangers of group decision making. Consensus seeking is a good thing, providing all relevant and valid evidence is considered in the discussion (e.g., the dialectic technique used by Sniezek, 1989), but when there is a tendency to seek evidence that serves only to confirm an initial hypothesis or to support a predetermined course of action, it can lead to disastrous consequences (see Wason, 1960).

The most provocative and influential work exploring such a tendency is that of Irving Janis. Janis (1972) coined the term 'groupthink' to describe the type of decision making that occurs in groups that are highly cohesive, insular and have directed leadership. Through the detailed analysis of a number of historical fiascos (the Bay of Pigs, President Johnson's decision to escalate the war in Vietnam, President Truman's decision to do the same in North Korea) and a comparison with major decisions that were successful (the implementation of the Marshall Plan after World War II), Janis identified the characteristics of groupthink-affected decision making: 'groupthink-dominated groups were characterized by strong pressures towards uniformity, which inclined their members to avoid raising controversial issues, questioning weak arguments, or calling a halt to soft-headed thinking' (Janis & Mann, 1977, p. 130).

More specifically, Janis (1972), proposed a model of groupthink with five antecedent conditions, eight symptoms of groupthink, and eight symptoms of defective decision making that result once groupthink has taken grip. The antecedents are those mentioned earlier: cohesiveness, insularity, directed leadership, along with two others – a lack of procedures for search and appraisal of information, and low confidence in the ability to find an alternative solution to the one favoured by the leader. The symptoms of groupthink are:

- the illusion of invulnerability creating excessive optimism and encouraging extreme risk taking;
- collective efforts to rationalize in order to discount warnings that might lead members to reconsider their assumptions;
- an unquestioned belief in the inherent morality of the group, inclining members to ignore the ethical or moral consequences of decisions;
- stereotyped views of rivals and enemies as too evil to warrant genuine attempts to negotiate;
- direct pressure on any members that express strong arguments against any of the group stereotypes;
- self-censorship of doubts or counterarguments that a member might have in order to create an illusion of unanimity within the group; and
- the emergence of self-appointed 'mindguards' who protect the group from adverse information that might shatter shared complacency about the effectiveness and morality of the group's decision.

The groupthink concept has had a huge impact in both the academic literature (see for example the 1998 special issue of the journal *Organizational Behavior and Human Decision Processes, 73* (2)) and popular culture (a search via the internet search engine Google produced an incredible 1,520,000 hits for 'groupthink'; 1 September 2006). It is easy to understand the appeal of such a seductive concept. The eight symptoms of groupthink seem applicable to a vast variety of decision contexts, and appear to provide a useful framework for thinking about how defective decision making arises. Indeed, two of us were so struck by the similarities between the groupthink symptoms and the characteristics of the decision making leading up to the invasion of Iraq in 2003 that we wrote to the *Psychologist* magazine stating that, 'at the time of writing [March 2003] it may just be the heads of state and government who are the victims, but if war results many more heads may be lost to groupthink' (Newell & Lagnado, 2003, p. 176). Tragically our predictions were correct and post-invasion Iraq is now suffering from many of the symptoms of defective decision making that Janis identified as resulting from groupthink-dominated decisions (e.g., the failure to work out the risks of a preferred strategy and the failure to develop contingency plans). We were not alone in our assessment of the influence of groupthink on the decision to go to war. After the invasion the US Senate Intelligence Committee reported the following:

> Conclusion 3: The Intelligence Community suffered from a collective presumption that Iraq had an active and growing weapons of mass destruction (WMD) program. This 'group think' dynamic led Intelligence Community analysts, collectors and managers to both interpret ambiguous evidence as collectively indicative of a WMD program as well as ignore or minimize evidence that Iraq did not have active and expanding weapons of mass destruction programs. This presumption was so strong and formalized that Intelligence Community mechanisms established to challenge assumptions and group think were not utilized.
>
> (Source: http://intelligence.senate.gov/conclusions.pdf)

However, the seductiveness and applicability of the groupthink concept may also be its weakness. Aldag and Fuller (1993; Fuller & Aldag, 1998) have questioned whether groupthink is merely a convenient and overused label and argued that direct empirical support for the groupthink model is almost non-existent. In a characteristic quote they stated, 'Our contention is that even the most passionately presented and optimistically interpreted findings on groupthink suggest that the phenomenon is, at best, irrelevant. Artificially gathering a sampling of decision-relevant factors into a reified phenomenon has only resulted in the loss of valuable information' (Fuller & Aldag, 1998, p. 177). The lost information Fuller and Aldag refer to is the advances they suggest could have been made in understanding deficiencies in group decision making if so much research had not been constrained to fit within the groupthink framework. Fuller and Aldag go as far as suggesting that some researchers have unwittingly acted as virtual 'mindguards' of the groupthink phenomenon.

To explain the lasting popularity of groupthink Fuller and Aldag invoke a rather esoteric but nevertheless instructive metaphor. They describe groupthink as an 'organizational Tonypandy' after the Welsh mining village that was reportedly the site of violent riots in 1910–11. The official story of the riots describes hordes of miners, who were striking for better pay and conditions, clashing with police and soldiers in a series of bloody incidents. In fact there was apparently no serious bloodshed and some doubt that army troops were even involved. Despite these doubts, stories about the riots have been perpetuated over time, and in some circles have taken on legendary status. Fuller and Aldag (1998) argue that the same thing has happened with groupthink. Proponents of the phenomenon, despite being aware of the lack of empirical evidence supporting it, continue to 'herald its horrors . . . building a mosaic of support from scattered wisps of ambiguous evidence' (pp. 165–166).

The truth about groupthink probably lies somewhere in between the colourful language use by Fuller and Aldag (1998) and the rhetoric of its proponents. There is little doubt that the concept has proved to be very useful in focusing attention on the potential flaws of group decision making (e.g., Turner & Pratkanis, 1998), but the time to move on to testing other potential models of group functioning (e.g., the General Group Problem Solving model, Aldag & Fuller, 1993) and to break free from the constraints of groupthink theorizing is almost certainly long overdue.

Summary

Research on group decision making is both appealing and frustrating. The richness of the environments tends to make controlled empirical testing difficult and thus theory advances slowly. Most research is concentrated on eureka/intellective tasks and judgmental tasks. In both types of task, group performance tends to exceed the collective mean but not reach the level of the most talented individuals in the group. The Brunswikian lens model provides a useful metaphor for conceptualizing the processes of group discussion, consensus seeking and revisions of estimates in judgmental tasks. One of the dangers of blinkered consensus seeking is groupthink, a concept that has inspired a great deal of research despite claims that empirical evidence for the phenomenon is scarce.

15 Going straight: The view from outside the laboratory

One of the aims of this book, and indeed the aim of many decision researchers, is to discover and highlight ways to improve decision making (e.g., Hogarth, 2001). With this aim in mind, this final chapter introduces three different approaches to improving decision making. The goal is to tie these approaches to specific examples that we have covered in the preceding chapters, and to provide some practical advice that can be used in the world outside the psychology laboratory. One of the major strengths of research into judgment and decision making is its applicability. Many of the researchers involved in the discipline are motivated by the potential for experimental findings to have real influence on the way decisions are made by individuals, companies and even governments, every day. We consider three approaches to improving or debiasing decision making that can be loosely grouped under the headings: individual, cultural (or institutional), and tools or resources.

Individual techniques for improving decision making

One of the most prevalent types of decisions we face is predicting or forecasting the future on the basis of past experience. We have emphasized throughout this book that the probabilistic nature of the world makes such predictions difficult. Information in the environment can only be used as an imperfect indicator of an outcome of interest because cues and outcomes are typically only probabilistically related (e.g., Hammond, 1955). There is, however, one important technique we can all adopt that can help to mitigate the effects of our uncertain world.

Adopting the outside view

An example used by Daniel Kahneman (e.g., Kahneman & Lovallo, 1993; Kahneman & Tversky, 1979b; Lovallo & Kahneman, 2003) provides an excellent introduction to our first technique. Kahneman tells the story of how he was involved in a project to design a curriculum on judgment and decision making for use in schools in Israel. About 1 year into the project the collection of academics and teachers that comprised the small group turned to the issue of how long they thought the project would take. Each member of the group was invited to make individual estimates of the number of months required to bring the project to completion. The estimates ranged from 18 to 30 months. Kahneman recounts that at this point he asked the senior expert on curriculum development in the group the following question: 'We are surely not the only team to have tried to develop a curriculum where none existed before. Please try to recall as many such cases as you can. Think of them as they were in a stage comparable to ours at present. How long did it take them, from that point, to complete their projects?' (Kahneman & Lovallo, 1993, pp. 24–25). The answer was rather sobering and completely at odds with the estimates provided by the individuals. The expert first stated that around 40 per cent of the groups given such a task eventually gave up and furthermore that those that did complete successfully took between 7 and 10 years! He also noted that there was nothing about the composition of the current group that led him to believe their performance would be any better than previous groups.

Kahneman and Lovallo (1993) argue that this story serves to illustrate the adoption of two distinct modes of prediction. The individuals spontaneously adopted an 'inside view' to the problem, in which they tended to focus solely on the particular problem at hand, paying special attention to its unique or unusual features and extrapolating on the basis of its current status (see Lovallo & Kahneman, 2003). In contrast the expert, having been prompted by Kahneman's question, adopted an 'outside view' in which the details of the current project were essentially ignored and the emphasis was placed on generating a reference class of cases deemed to be similar to the current one, and then placing the current project somewhere in that distribution of similar cases.

So which mode of prediction turned out to be more accurate? The 'results' could not have been more compelling: the team finally completed the curriculum 8 years later (and even then the resulting curriculum was rarely used; Lovallo & Kahneman, 2003)! Thus the outside view with its prediction of 7 to 10 years was much more accurate than the optimistic estimates of 18 to 30 months generated via the inside view. Lovallo and Kahneman (2003) make a particular case for adopting the outside view in the context of managerial and executive decision making. They argue that many of the disastrous decisions made by executives can be traced to the 'delusional optimism' that results from taking an overly inside view of forecasting (see March & Shapira, 1987). They propose a straightforward five step methodology for adopting the outside view; steps that they argue will improve forecasting accuracy considerably in organizational settings (see also Kahneman & Tversky, 1979b). The basic ideas are to identify a reference class of analogous past initiatives or projects, to determine the distribution of outcomes for those initiatives, and to place the current project at an appropriate point along that distribution.

Lovallo and Kahneman (2003) illustrate the five step methodology with the example of a studio executive attempting to forecast the sales of a new film. In this context, the five steps would be something akin to the following:

(1) *Select a reference class*: Perhaps the most difficult step – this involves determining a set of other instances that are sufficiently similar and thus relevant to the problem you are considering, but sufficiently broad to allow for meaningful statistical comparison. For the studio executive this would amount to formulating a reference class that included recent films of a similar genre (e.g., action blockbuster), starring similar actors (e.g., Tom Cruise) and with comparable budgets (e.g. £50 million), and so on.

(2) *Assess the distribution of outcomes*: Attempt to document the outcomes of all members of your reference class as precisely as possible. This should involve working out an average outcome as well as some measure of variability. For the film example, the executive might find that of the films in the reference class the average amount of money made through ticket sales was £30 million, but that 10 per cent made less than £5 million and 5 per cent made more than £100 million.

(3) *Make an intuitive prediction of your project's position in the distribution*: Use your own judgment to rate how the current project compares with all those in the reference class and position it accordingly. In other words the executive should try to weigh up everything he or she knows about the new film, compare it to all the others in the reference class and try to predict where sales of the new film would fall in the distribution. Lovallo and Kahneman (2003) suggest that the intuitive estimate made by the executive is likely to be biased (recall all the reasons why intuitive judgment may be poor that we discussed in chapter 3) and so propose two further steps to adjust this intuitive forecast.

(4) *Assess the reliability of your prediction*: The aim of this step is to estimate the correlation between the forecast and the actual outcome. The correlation can be expressed as a coefficient between 0 (no correlation) and 1 (perfect correlation) This can either be done on the basis of historical precedent (the accuracy of past similar forecasts) or through a subjective comparison with similar forecasting situations. For example, the studio executive might have the sense that the sales forecast would be more accurate than, say, the ability of a sports commentator to predict the score in next year's FA Cup Final but not as accurate as a meteorologist's prediction of the temperature the day after tomorrow. By thinking carefully about the correlations between predictions and outcomes for these different types of domains, the executive should be able to estimate where the predictability of sales forecasts for films lies on an overall scale of predictability.

(5) *Correct the intuitive estimate*: As noted, the estimate made in Step 3 is likely to be biased, and probably optimistically so (i.e., predictions will deviate too far – in an upward direction – from the average outcome of

films in the reference class), so in Step 5 the aim is to adjust the estimate back toward the average by using the analysis of predictability conducted in Step 4. The less predictable the executive believes the environment to be, the less reliable the initial forecast and the more the forecast needs to be regressed toward the mean for the reference class. In the film example, the mean grossing of films in the reference class is £30 million; if the executive estimated £75 million worth of ticket sales, but a correlation coefficient between forecast and outcome of only .55, then the regressed estimate of sales would be calculated in the following way:

$$£30M + [0.55 (£75M - £30M)] = £54.75M$$

The reduction from an estimate of £75 million to just over £50 million illustrates how the adjustment for an optimistic bias in Step 3 can be substantial – especially when the executive is not confident in the reliability of the prediction (i.e., in highly uncertain environments) (Lovallo & Kahneman, 2003). The studio executive example illustrates the applicability of the outside view in the organizational context, but it is relatively simple to see how the procedures could be applied to many of the judgment and decision making tasks we face (see Lagnado & Sloman, 2004b). One important caveat to the general applicability of the approach is the difficulty in selecting the appropriate reference class. As we discussed in chapter 5, generating the correct reference class is not a trivial problem (recall the example of introducing the congestion charge in London), but if we can generate an appropriate class, then following the five steps advocated by Lovallo and Kahneman (2003) should serve to improve our forecasts and judgments in a range of different areas.

Consider the opposite

Another individual technique for improving decision making that is closely related to the 'outside view' is to 'consider the opposite' (Larrick, 2004; Mussweiler, Strack, & Pfeiffer, 2000). As Larrick (2004) notes this strategy simply amounts to asking oneself, 'What are some of the reasons that my initial judgment might be wrong?' It is effective because it counters the general tendency to rely on narrow and shallow hypothesis generation and evidence accumulation (e.g., Heath, Larrick, & Klayman, 1998; Klayman, 1995; McKenzie, 2004). An experimental example of the 'consider the opposite' principle in action comes from a study on judgmental anchoring by Mussweiler and colleagues (Mussweiler et al., 2000). Anchoring – the process by which numeric estimates are assimilated to a previously considered standard of comparison (e.g., Tversky & Kahneman, 1974) – is one of the most robust judgment heuristics. Mussweiler et al. (2000) demonstrated that the magnitude of the anchoring effect could be reduced simply by asking people to list anchor-inconsistent arguments. Mussweiler et al. presented

60 car experts with an actual car and an anchor estimate of its value. The anchor was either set to be high (5000 German marks) or low (2800 German marks). The expert was first asked to state whether he thought the anchor was too high or too low, and then to provide his own estimate. (This is the standard procedure in anchoring experiments.)

The novel manipulation was that before providing an estimate, half of the experts were asked to consider possible reasons for why the anchor value might be inappropriate, while the other half made their own estimate directly after the comparative judgment. The results indicated a clear effect of this manipulation: when the experts were instructed to generate anchor-inconsistent arguments the effect of anchoring was much weaker. For example, experts given the high anchor and not asked to generate arguments provided a mean estimate of 3563 German marks, whereas those asked to consider the arguments provided an estimate of only 3130 German marks. Mussweiler et al. (2000) suggest that considering the opposite mitigates anchoring because it 'debiases the informational basis for the judgment' (p. 1146). In other words using a technique that overcomes the tendency to only consider a narrow sample of evidence can greatly improve judgment. The general strategy of considering the opposite has also proved to be effective in reducing hindsight bias and overconfidence (Arkes, 1991; Soll & Klayman, 2004).

Cultural techniques for improving decision making

We have seen throughout this book that there are myriad ways in which individual decision making can divert from the straight and narrow road. Although some of these errors and diversions may be more apparent than real (i.e., products of the artificial experimental situations – see Gigerenzer, 1996; Hogarth, 1981), many are ubiquitous even in real-world situations (the anchoring effect described above is a good example).

However, we have also emphasized how, in many situations, the opportunity to learn and be exposed to useful feedback on our performance can reduce or eliminate some of these errors. Given that these shortcomings in individual decision making can be alleviated, are there any practices that a culture or institution can encourage to provide opportunities for learning and to counter the defective individual tendencies? Heath et al. (1998) suggest a number of practices that they argue can be used by institutions to 'effectively repair the cognitive shortcomings of individuals' (p. 1). In this section we briefly review some of these practices.

Heath et al. note that when faced with a problem decision makers often generate too few hypotheses and tend only to search for information confirming their initial diagnosis (e.g., Klayman, 1995; Wason, 1960; see McKenzie, 2004 for a detailed discussion). To combat this tendency in individuals the Toyota Company introduced the 'Five Whys' technique, encouraging employees to analyse problems in depth rather than superficially. For example, an employee faced with a broken machine might ask him or herself the following type of questions (Imai, 1986; cited in Heath et al. 1998): Q1: Why did the machine stop? A1: Because the fuse blew due to an overload. Q2: Why was there an overload? A2: Because the bearing lubrication was inadequate. Q3: Why was the lubrication inadequate? A3: Because the lubrication pump malfunctioned, and so on. By asking a series of questions the employee is more likely to discover the root cause of the problem (in this case grime in the lubrication pump) rather than stopping the search for information when the first plausible hypothesis was generated (the blown fuse).

Although not noted by Heath et al. it is clear that the Five Whys technique resonates strongly with Kahneman and Lovallo's (1993) recommendation to take the 'outside view' and Mussweiler et al.'s (2000) suggestion to 'consider the opposite'. In asking the first question the employee might invoke a detail that is specific to the problem at hand, but by delving deeper, the subsequent whys are likely to lead the employee to think about the problem in a broader situational context and thus to come up with a better solution.

A further problem with information search and evaluation that Heath et al. discuss is the tendency for individuals' samples of information to be biased by information that is readily available in memory. Tversky and Kahneman (1973) and many other researchers since (see Schwarz & Vaughn, 2002, for a more recent summary) have shown that information that is available is also perceived to be more frequent, probable and causally important. There is now some debate over whether availability effects are a result of bias in the cognitive process or bias in the external sample of information (see Fiedler, 2000; Fiedler & Juslin, 2006, and the discussion in chapter 6), but regardless of the location of the biasing effects, the effects are problematic if they result in erroneous judgments. Heath et al. (1998) describe a technique used by Motorola to overcome the effects of availability. Motorola had come to realize that a division developing equipment for cellular phones was devoting all its time and energy to their large clients while neglecting the large number of smaller customers. Presumably larger clients were more salient and came to mind more easily and thus their needs were at the fore when new products were being developed. To overcome this 'availability bias' Motorola developed a Feature Prioritization Process in which they surveyed *all* their customers – not just the larger 'more available' ones — several times a year and then weighted the inputs based on customer volume and priority. By employing such a technique the company ensured that all relevant information was considered in the product evaluation process.

The final 'cognitive repair' that we consider is closely related to the mechanisms underlying some of the emotional effects that were reviewed in chapter 13. Recall that many researchers have found evidence showing information formats that support vivid imagery, or decision options that have high emotional content (and are thus vividly imagined), tend to have a disproportionately strong influence on decision makers (e.g., Rottenstreich & Hsee, 2001; Slovic et al., 2000). Heath et al. (1998) describe a technique used by Microsoft that capitalizes on this tendency for vivid information to be weighted more heavily than pallid information. According to Cusumano and Selby (1995; cited in Heath et al., 1998), software developers at Microsoft were reluctant to believe the statistics obtained by the usability group on the ease of using particular programs and features. The developers often dismissed the statistics as being based on a non-representative sample of 'stupid' people who should just 'look in the manual' if they didn't understand something. In an attempt to repair this tendency to ignore statistical information, Microsoft made the information more vivid by forcing developers to watch customers learning to use the new products. A 'usability lab' was set up with a one-way mirror allowing software developers to receive real-time and extremely vivid feedback about how people actually used new programs. The use of the lab led to much greater empathy between developers and customers. Heath et al. (1998) observe that this cognitive repair is interesting because it uses one kind of bias (the tendency to overweight vivid information) to counteract another (the tendency to underweight statistical information). Experimental data consistent with the overweighting/underweighting effect of vivid/statistical evidence was reported by Borgida and Nisbett (1977).

In summarizing their review of cognitive repairs Heath et al. (1998) conclude that the most successful repairs are likely to be those that are relatively simple, domain specific, and emergent (bottom-up) rather than imposed (top-down). Simplicity and domain specificity are encouraged for the straightforward reason that a strategy that is easy to memorize and implement, and for which the applications (domains) are easy to recognize, is more likely to be put into practice than a complex procedure with non-obvious applicability. The emergent property of repairs is emphasized because of the need for decision makers to have a sense of ownership and input into generating solutions. A strategy imposed by management may be viewed with scepticism, but if a particular team has identified a bias or deficiency and developed their own repair it is likely to be viewed in a much more positive light. As we will see in the next section, the lack of transparency and human input has been one of the major sources of resistance to many of the standard 'tools' for improving decision making (see Yates et al., 2003).

Tools for improving decision making

The esteemed decision theorist Ward Edwards told the following story of how he helped a student to decide between two university courses (a problem that is probably pertinent to many readers). The student was trying to decide between two advanced courses (one in international relations and one in political science) that were being offered at the same time thus preventing her from doing both. Both courses satisfied the student's degree requirements. In order to help her decide, Edwards (Edwards & Fasolo, 2001) used a decision-analytic technique called multi-attribute utility measurement (often called MAU for short, Raiffa, 1968; see also Keeney & Raiffa, 1976; Pidgeon

& Gregory, 2004; von Winterfeldt & Edwards, 1986). The core assumption of MAU is that the value ascribed to the outcome of most decisions has multiple attributes. The technique employed by MAU allows for the aggregation of the value-laden attributes. This aggregated value can then act as input for a standard subjective utility maximizing framework for choosing between alternatives (see chapter 8). The particular rule for aggregation depends on the interactions among attributes, but we need not concern ourselves too much with the details.

Let's return to the student's 'choice-of-course' dilemma. Edwards began by eliciting attributes for the two course options from the student – attributes included whether the student felt she would learn something, the amount of work involved, and feelings about the interpersonal interactions with the professor and other students. The next step was to assign weights (degree of importance) to the attributes. Again, the exact method used is not important but part of the process involved a method called SMARTER (Edwards & Barron, 1994) in which rank orders of the weights are elicited and then the ranks are used as the basis for approximating the actual weights. The final step of elicitation required the student to score each of the two courses on a 0–100 scale for each attribute. For example, the student rated international relations as 42 but political science as 80 on the 'interpersonal interactions' attribute, reflecting her stated dislike for the professor teaching the former course. Edwards was now ready to compute the MAU for each course. This was done simply by multiplying the weight of each attribute by its score and summing across all the attributes. The result was clear cut – the MAU for international relations was 37.72 but for political science it was 54.57. Edwards made the obvious recommendation – according to this analysis if the student wanted to maximize her subjective expected utility she should choose political science. The student said she intended to choose the course; history does not relate whether she actually did.

To many of us the MAU procedure might seem rather complicated, time consuming and opaque (How exactly are the weights derived? How do we decide what attributes to consider?). Perhaps pre-empting these kinds of criticism, Edwards (Edwards & Fasolo, 2001) justifies the use of the MAU tool by saying that the student showed a clear understanding of the methodology (even endorsing the 'rank order centroid weights' as being representative of her own values) and that the whole procedure, including explanation time, took less than 3 hours to complete. Moreover, the MAU tool is widely applicable and could be used in many of the situations we have discussed throughout this book, such as buying a car, choosing an apartment to rent, deciding where to invest our money, even the decision to marry. In all these situations options can be defined (e.g., cars, financial institutions, people), attributes elicited (e.g., engine type, account type, sense of humour) and weighted for importance, and scores assigned to each attribute – just like in the student's course example. The MAU method provides a clear principled way to make good, rational decisions.

Nevertheless, the time taken to implement such a process (3 hours in the student example) is often more than we have available to make important decisions (e.g., Gigerenzer et al., 1999). Are there any automated procedures that employ the same rational principles as decision-analytic techniques but take the 'hard yards' out of the process? As Larrick (2004) points out, perhaps the ultimate standard of rationality might be the decision to use superior tools.

The generic label for automated procedures for aiding decision processes is 'decision support systems' (DSSs). Yates et al. (2003) define such systems as 'a computer based system, typically interactive, that is intended to support people's normal decision making activities' (p. 39). The systems are not intended to replace a decision maker, or indeed to make a decision exclusively, but rather to aid in the decision-making process. Yates et al. (2003) describe the systems as having three main components: a data component that can provide substantial amounts of information at the touch of a button; a model component that can perform operations on retrieved data that are often far more complicated than a decision maker alone could perform; and a dialogue component that allows interaction with the system (e.g., through a search engine).

Although we might associate DSSs with major industry or government bodies (e.g., road and transport authorities, finance groups), now that searching for information and indeed purchasing products on-line is so prevalent, we often find ourselves interacting with such systems (Edwards & Fasolo, 2001; Yates et al., 2003). Given that consumer websites now commonly display information about a vast range of goods, a person wishing to buy a new product – say a digital camera – might first access some on-line resource to discover what is available (see Fasolo et al., 2005, discussed in chapter 3). Yates et al. (2003) suggest that the information contained in these sites can be considered to be the output from the data component of the consumer's 'shopping decision-support system'. The dialogue component could be thought of as comprising the consumer's computer, the software used to navigate the web and the site's facilities for displaying information in different orders and categories (e.g., listed by price, by number of mega pixels, etc.). The model component is then represented by any functions that a consumer might use to decide on a favoured model. For example, overall ratings might be computed by summing weighted averages of the different attributes (in much the same way as Edwards did for his student). By engaging with the shopping DSS in this way the consumer can compare any number of given products and choose whichever one achieves the highest rating.

Edwards and Fasolo (2001) provide an excellent summary of the advantages and disadvantages of various web-based DSSs, comparing, for example, compensatory sites (those that focus on alternatives) with non-compensatory sites (those that focus on attributes). (Recall our discussion of information combination strategies of these types in chapter 3.) Edwards and Fasolo note that decision makers on the internet tend to prefer non-compensatory sites because these are more time-efficient than compensatory ones. The time efficiency is due largely to the fact that non-compensatory sites eliminate ('winnow out') options more quickly than compensatory sites. Although time-efficient, there is an associated risk of 'winnowing out winners' – that is, eliminating an option early on in the process, which had it remained in the choice set, would have been the eventual winner (see the apartment renting example in chapter 3). The conclusion seems to be that compensatory sites should be used to make decisions, but because of time pressure decision makers often opt for the less effective non-compensatory sites. The simple lesson is that when using web-based DSSs you should take time, and only eliminate an option if you are absolutely sure it could never be included in your choice set (e.g., if you knew you'd never pay more than £500 for a camera). Despite some of the limitations with web-based DSSs, Edwards and Fasolo (2001) draw an upbeat conclusion, stating that 'decision tools will be as important in the 21st Century as spreadsheets were in the 20th'(p. 581).

Yates et al. (2003) are similarly optimistic about decision support systems. They suggest one of the reasons why these systems have been relatively successful and proved far more popular than some other basic decision-aiding tools (e.g., traditional decision analysis, social judgment theory, debiasing techniques) is that they place a clear emphasis on improving outcomes. Many of the other techniques are more concerned about the normativity of a decision process (e.g., decision analysis) or the statistical properties of multiple repeated instances rather than one-shot decisions (e.g., social judgment analysis). In Yates et al.'s analysis of the reasons decision makers give for a decision being 'good' or 'bad' (see chapter 2) a key finding was the role played by the experienced outcome. Eighty-nine per cent of bad decisions were described as bad because they resulted in bad outcomes; 95.4 per cent of good decisions were described as good because they yielded good outcomes. DSSs are probably successful because they retain the decision maker as an integral part of the decision process (see Heath et al., 1998), but emphasize improving outcomes. This is done principally by providing information that the decision maker may not otherwise have been aware of (e.g., the models and specifications of the cameras on the market), and by assisting in the process of winnowing out undesired options.

Summary

We can improve our decisions through a variety of simple cognitive mechanisms such as adopting an outside view, considering the opposite, or challenging ourselves to discover the root cause of a problem. Additional support can be found in standard decision-theoretic techniques such as multi-attribute analysis, or the more user-friendly decision support systems that many of us now use in our interactions with the internet. Recognizing when it is appropriate to rely on our own thinking and when we should turn over our decision making to a superior tool might be one important standard of rationality.

This exploration of the techniques on offer to improve our decision making brings us to the end of our examination of the psychology of decision making. We hope you have gained an appreciation for the breadth and depth of this exciting field, and have some sense of the importance of examining the learning environment to properly understand the judgments and decisions we make. Armed with your new knowledge and insight you are well placed to stay on the straight and narrow road of good decision making and to keep your choices straight!

References

Adelman, L. (1981). The influence of formal, substantive, and contextual task properties on the relative effectiveness of feedback in multi-cue probability tasks. *Organizational Behavior and Human Performance, 27*, 423–442.

Agnoli, F., & Krantz, D. H. (1989). Suppressing natural heuristics by formal instruction: The case of the conjunction fallacy. *Cognitive Psychology, 21*, 515–550.

Aldag, R. J., & Fuller, S. R. (1993). Beyond fiasco: A reappraisal of the groupthink phenomenon and a new model of group decision processes. *Psychological Bulletin, 113*, 533–552.

Allais, M. (1953). La psychologie de l'homme rationnel devant le risque: Critique des postulats et axiomes de l'école Américaine. *Econometrica, 21*, 503–546.

Anderson, J. R. (1991). The adaptive nature of human categorization. *Psychological Review, 98*, 409–429.

Ariely, D., & Carmon, Z. (2003). Summary assessment of experiences: The whole is different from the sum of its parts. In G. Loewenstein, D. Read, & R. Baumeister (Eds.), *Time and decision: Economic and psychological perspectives on intertemporal choice* (pp. 323–349). New York: Russell Sage Foundation.

Ariely, D., Kahneman, D., & Loewenstein, G. (2000). Joint comment on 'When does duration matter in judgment and decision making?' (Ariely & Loewenstein, 2000). *Journal of Experimental Psychology: General, 129*, 524–529.

Ariely, D., & Loewenstein, G. (2000). When does duration matter in judgment and decision making? *Journal of Experimental Psychology: General, 129*, 508–523.

Ariely, D., Loewenstein, G., & Prelec, D. (2003). 'Coherent arbitrariness': Stable demand curves without stable preferences. *Quarterly Journal of Economics, 118*, 73–105.

Ariely, D., & Wertenbroch, K. (2002). Procrastination, deadlines, and performance: Self-control by precommitment. *Psychological Science, 13*, 219–224.

Arkes, H. R. (1991). Costs and benefits of judgment errors: Implications for debiasing. *Psychological Bulletin, 110*, 486–498.

Arkes, H. R., & Ayton, P. (1999). The sunk cost and Concorde effects: Are humans less rational than lower animals? *Psychological Bulletin, 125*, 591–600.

Arrow, K. J. (1958). Utilities, attitudes, choices: A review note. *Econometrica, 26*, 1–23.

Ashby, F. G., & Ell, S. W. (2002). Single versus multiple systems of learning and memory. In J. Wixted & H. Pashler (Eds.), *Stevens' handbook of experimental psychology: Vol. 4. Methodology in experimental psychology* (3rd ed., pp. 655–691). New York: John Wiley & Sons.

Ayton, P., & Fischer, I. (2004). The hot hand fallacy and the gambler's fallacy: Two faces of subjective randomness? *Memory & Cognition, 32*, 1369–1378.

Ayton, P., & Önkal, D. (2004). *Effects of ignorance and information on judgmental forecasting.* Unpublished manuscript. City University, London, UK.

Balzer, W. K., Doherty, M. E., & O'Connor, R. (1989). Effects of cognitive feedback on performance. *Psychological Bulletin, 106*, 410–433.

Bar-Hillel, M., & Neter, E. (1993). How alike is it versus how likely is it: A disjunction fallacy in probability judgments. *Journal of Personality and Social Psychology, 65*, 1119–1131.

Baron, J. (2000). *Thinking and deciding* (3rd ed.). Cambridge: Cambridge University Press.

Batchelor, R. A. (2004). The pros and cons of technical analysis: An academic perspective. *The Technical Analyst, 1*, 13–18.

Baxt, W. G. (1990). Use of an artificial neural network for data analysis in clinical decision-making: The diagnosis of acute coronary occlusion. *Neural Computation, 2*, 480–489.

Bechara A., Damasio, A., Damasio, H., & Anderson, S. (1994). Insensitivity to future consequences following damage to human prefrontal cortex. *Cognition, 50*, 7–15.

Bechara, A., Damasio, H., Tranel, D., & Damasio, A. (1997). Deciding advantageously before knowing the advantageous strategy. *Science, 275*, 1293–1295.

Benartzi, S., & Thaler, R. H. (2001). Naïve diversification strategies in defined contribution savings plans. *American Economic Review, 91*, 78–98.

Benartzi, S., & Thaler, R. H. (2002). How much is investor autonomy worth? *Journal of Finance, 152*, 1593–1616.

Bergert, F. B., & Nosofsky, R. M. (in press). A response time approach to comparing generalized rational and take-the-best models of decision making. *Journal of Experimental Psychology: Learning, Memory, and Cognition.*

Bernoulli, D. (1954). Exposition of a new theory on the measurement of risk. *Econometrica, 22*, 23–36. (Original work published 1738)

Berry, D. C., & Broadbent, D. E. (1984). On the relationship between task performance and associated verbalizable knowledge. *Quarterly Journal of Experimental Psychology, 36*, 209–231.

Berry, D. C., & Broadbent, D. E. (1988). Interactive tasks and the implicit–explicit distinction. *British Journal of Psychology, 79*, 251–272.

Bitterman, M. E., Tyler, D. W., & Elam, C. B. (1955). Simultaneous and successive discrimination under identical stimulating conditions. *American Journal of Psychology, 68*, 237–248.

Bjorkman, M. (1972). Feedforward and feedback as determiners of knowledge and policy: Notes on a neglected issue. *Scandinavian Journal of Psychology, 13*, 152–158.

Borges, B., Goldstein, D. G., Ortmann, A., & Gigerenzer, G. (1999). Can ignorance beat the stock market? In G. Gigerenzer, P. M. Todd, & the ABC Research Group (Eds.), *Simple heuristics that make us smart* (pp. 59–72). New York: Oxford University Press.

Borgida, E., & Nisbett, R. (1977). The differential impact of abstract versus concrete information on decisions. *Journal of Applied Social Psychology, 7*, 258–271.

Bornstein, B. H., Emler, A. C., & Chapman, G. B. (1999). Rationality in medical treatment decisions: Is there a sunk-cost effect? *Social Science and Medicine, 49*, 215–222.

Bower, G. H. (1994). A turning point in mathematical learning theory. *Psychological Review*, *101*, 290–300.

Brehmer, B. (1979). Preliminaries to a psychology of inference. *Scandinavian Journal of Psychology*, *20*, 193–210.

Brehmer, B. (1980). In one word: Not from experience. *Acta Psychologica*, *45*, 223–241.

Brehmer, B. (1999). Reasonable decision making in complex environments. In P. Juslin, & H. Montgomery (Eds.), *Judgment and decision making: New-Brunswikian and process-tracing approaches* (pp. 9–21). Hillsdale, NJ: Lawrence Erlbaum Associates, Inc.

Brehmer, B., & Allard, R. (1991). Dynamic decision making: The effects of task complexity and feedback delay. In J. Rasmussen, B. Brehmer, & J. Leplat (Eds.), *Distributed decision making: Cognitive models for cooperative work* (pp. 319–334). Brisbane: John Wiley & Sons.

Brenner, L., Griffin, D., & Koehler, D. (2005). Modeling patterns of probability calibration with random support theory: Diagnosing case-based judgment. *Organizational Behavior and Human Decision Processes*, *97*, 64–81.

Brenner, L. A., Koehler, D. J., & Rottenstreich, Y. (2002). Remarks on support theory: Recent advances and future directions. In T. Gilovich, D. Griffin, & D. Kahneman (Eds.), *Heuristics and biases* (pp. 489–509). New York: Cambridge University Press.

Brier, G. W. (1950). Verification of forecasts expressed in terms of probability. *Monthly Weather Review*, *78*, 1–3.

Briggs, L. K., & Krantz, D. H. (1992). Judging the strength of designated evidence. *Journal of Behavioral Decision Making*, *5*, 77–106.

Broadbent, D. E., & Aston, B. (1978). Human control of a simulated economic system. *Ergonomics*, *21*, 1035–1043.

Broadbent, D. E., Fitzgerald, P., & Broadbent, M. H. P. (1986). Implicit and explicit knowledge in the control of complex systems. *British Journal of Psychology*, *77*, 33–50.

Bröder, A. (2000). Assessing the empirical validity of the 'take-the-best' heuristic as a model of human probabilistic inference. *Journal of Experimental Psychology: Learning Memory, and Cognition*, *26*, 1332–1346.

Bröder, A. (2003). Decision making with the adaptive toolbox: Influence of environmental structure, personality, intelligence, and working memory load. *Journal of Experimental Psychology: Learning, Memory, and Cognition*, *29*, 611–625.

Bröder, A., & Eichler, A. (2006). The use of recognition information and additional cues in inferences from memory. *Acta Psychologica*, *121*, 275–284.

Bröder, A., & Schiffer, S. (2003). 'Take-the-best' versus simultaneous feature matching: Probabilistic inferences from memory and the effects of representation format. *Journal of Experimental Psychology: General*, *132*, 277–293.

Brooks, L. R., Norman, G. R., & Allen, S. W. (1991). The role of specific similarity in a medical diagnostic task. *Journal of Experimental Psychology: General*, *120*, 278–287.

Brunswik, E. (1952). *The conceptual framework of psychology*. Chicago: University of Chicago Press.

Brunswik, E. (1956). *Perception and the representative design of psychological experiments*. Berkeley, CA: University of California Press.

Buehler, R., Griffin, D., & Ross, M. (1994). Exploring the 'planning fallacy': Why people underestimate their task completion times. *Journal of Personality and Social Psychology*, *67*, 366–381.

Buehler, R., Griffin, D., & Ross, M. (2002). Inside the planning fallacy: The causes and consequences of optimistic time predictions. In T. D. Gilovich, D. W. Griffin, & D. Kahneman (Eds.), *Heuristics and biases* (pp. 250–270). New York: Cambridge University Press.

Busemeyer, J. R., & Johnson, J. G. (2004). Computational models of decision making. In D. Koehler & N. Harvey (Eds.), *The Blackwell handbook of judgment and decision making* (pp. 133–154). New York: Blackwell.

Bush, R. R., & Mosteller, F. (1955). *Stochastic models for learning*. New York: John Wiley & Sons.

Calderwood, R., Klein, G. A., & Crandall, B. W. (1988). Time pressure, skill, and move quality in chess. *American Journal of Psychology, 101*, 481–493.

Casscells, W., Schoenberger, A., & Grayboys, T. (1978). Interpretation by physicians of clinical laboratory results. *New England Journal of Medicine, 299*, 999–1001.

Castellan, N. J. (1973). Multiple-cue probability learning with irrelevant cues. *Organizational Behavior and Human Performance, 9*, 16–29.

Castellan, N. J. (1974). The effect of different types of feedback in multiple-cue probability learning. *Organizational Behavior and Human Performance, 11*, 44–64.

Castellan, N. J., & Edgell, S. E. (1973). An hypothesis generation model for judgment in nonmetric multiple-cue probability learning. *Journal of Mathematical Psychology, 10*, 204–222.

Castellan, N. J., & Swaine, M. (1977). Long term feedback and differential feedback effects in nonmetric multiple-cue probability learning. *Behavioral Sciences, 22*, 116–128.

Ceci, S. J., & Liker, J. K. (1986). A day at the races: A study of IQ, expertise, and cognitive complexity. *Journal of Experimental Psychology: General, 115*, 255–266.

Chapman, G. B. (1991). Trial order affects cue interaction in contingency judgment. *Journal of Experimental Psychology: Learning, Memory, and Cognition, 17*, 837–854.

Chapman, G. B. (1996). Temporal discounting and utility for health and money. *Journal of Experimental Psychology: Learning, Memory, and Cognition, 22*, 771–791.

Chapman, G. B. (2003). Time discounting of health outcomes. In G. Loewenstein, D. Read, & R. Baumeister (Eds.), *Time and decision: Economic and psychological perspectives on intertemporal choice* (pp. 395–417). New York: Russell Sage Foundation.

Chapman, G. B., & Winquist, J. R. (1998). The magnitude effect: Temporal discount rates and restaurant tips. *Psychonomic Bulletin & Review, 5*, 119–123.

Chater, N., Oaksford, M., Nakisa, R., & Redington, M. (2003). Fast, frugal and rational: How rational norms explain behavior. *Organizational Behavior and Human Decision Processes, 90*, 63–80.

Christensen, C., Heckerling, P., Mackesyamiti, M. E., Bernstein, L. M., & Elstein, A. S. (1995). Pervasiveness of framing effects among physicians and medical students. *Journal of Behavioral Decision Making, 8*, 169–180.

Chu, Y.-P., & Chu, R.-L. (1990). The subsidence of preference reversals in simplified and market-like experimental settings: A note. *American Economic Review, 80*, 902–911.

Cobos, P. L., Almaraz, J., & Garcia-Madruga, J. A. (2003). An associative framework for probability judgment: An application to biases. *Journal of Experimental Psychology: Learning, Memory, and Cognition, 29*, 80–94.

Connolly, T., & Gilani, N. (1982). Information search in judgment tasks: A regression model and some preliminary findings. *Organizational Behavior and Human Decision Processes, 30,* 330–350.

Connolly, T., & Serre, P. (1984). Information search in judgment tasks: The effects of unequal cue validity and cost. *Organizational Behavior and Human Performance, 34,* 387–401.

Connolly, T., & Thorn, B. K. (1987). Predecisional information acquisition: Effects of task variables on suboptimal search strategies. *Organizational Behavior and Human Decision Processes, 39,* 397–416.

Connolly, T., & Wholey, D. R. (1988). Information mispurchase in judgment tasks: A task-driven causal mechanism. *Organizational Behavior and Human Decision Processes, 42,* 75–87.

Conway, M. (1990). On bias in autobiographical recall: Retrospective adjustments following disconfirmed expectations. *Journal of Social Psychology, 130,* 183–189.

Cooksey, R. W. (1996). *Judgment analysis: Theory, methods, and applications.* San Diego, CA: Academic Press.

Cooksey, R. W. (2001). Pursuing an integrated decision science: Does 'naturalistic decision making' help or hinder? *Journal of Behavioural Decision Making, 14,* 361–362.

Cosmides, L., & Tooby, J. (1996). Are humans good intuitive statisticians after all? Rethinking some conclusions from the literature on judgment under uncertainty. *Cognition, 58,* 1–73.

Cox, J. C., & Grether, D. M. (1996). The preference reversal phenomenon: Response mode, markets and incentives. *Economic Theory, 7,* 381–405.

Crupi, V., Fitelson, B., & Tentori, K. (2006). *Comparative Bayesian confirmation and the conjunction fallacy.* Unpublished manuscript, University of Trento, Italy.

Cusumano, M. A., & Selby, R. W. (1995). *Microsoft secrets.* New York: Free Press.

Cutting, J. E. (2000). Accuracy, scope, and flexibility of models. *Journal of Mathematical Psychology, 44,* 3–19.

Czerlinski, J., Gigerenzer, G., & Goldstein, D. G. (1999). How good are simple heuristics? In G. Gigerenzer, P. M. Todd, & the ABC Research Group (Eds.), *Simple heuristics that make us smart* (pp. 97–118). New York: Oxford University Press.

Damasio, A. R. (1996). The somatic marker hypothesis and the possible functions of the prefrontal cortex. *Philosophical Transactions of the Royal Society of London, Series B, Biological Sciences, 351,* 1413–1420.

Damasio, A. R. (2000). *The feeling of what happens: Body, emotion and the making of consciousness.* London: Vintage.

Dawes, R. M. (1979). The robust beauty of improper linear models in decision making. *American Psychologist, 34,* 571–582.

Dawes, R. M. (2001). *Everyday irrationality: How pseudoscientists, lunatics, and the rest of us fail to think rationally.* Boulder, CO: Westview Press.

Dawes, R. M., & Corrigan, B. (1974). Linear models in decision making. *Psychological Bulletin, 81,* 95–106.

Dawes, R. M., Faust, D., & Meehl, P. E. (1989). Clinical versus actuarial judgment. *Science, 243,* 1668–1674.

Dawid, A. P. (2002). Bayes's theorem and weighing evidence by juries. In R. Swinburne (Ed.), Bayes's theorem. *Proceedings of the British Academy, 113,* 71–90.

de Finetti, B. (1937). Foresight: Its logical laws, its subjective sources. Translated in H. E. Kyburg & H. E. Smokler (Eds.), *Studies in subjective probability*. Chichester: John Wiley & Sons.

Deane, D. H., Hammond, K. R., & Summers, D. A. (1972). Acquisition and application of knowledge in complex inference tasks. *Journal of Experimental Psychology, 92,* 20–26.

Death odds (1990). *Newsweek,* 24 September.

deGroot, A. D. (1965). *Thought and choice in chess.* The Hague: Mouton Publishers.

Denes-Raj, V., & Epstein, S. (1994). Conflict between intuitive and rational processing: When people behave against their better judgment. *Journal of Personality and Social Psychology, 66,* 819–829.

Desvousges, W. H., Johnson, F. R., Dunford, R. W., Boyle, K. J., Hudson, S. P., & Wilson, K. N. (1992). Measuring nonuse damages using contingent valuation: An experimental evaluation of accuracy. *Monograph 92–1.* Exxon corporation.

Dhami, M., & Ayton, P. (2001). Bailing and jailing the fast and frugal way. *Journal of Behavioral Decision Making, 14,* 141–168.

Dhami, M. K., & Harries, C. (2001). Fast and frugal versus regression models of human judgement. *Thinking and Reasoning, 7,* 5–27.

Dickinson, A. (1980). *Contemporary animal learning theory.* Cambridge: Cambridge University Press.

Doherty, M. E. (2003). Optimists, pessimists, and realists. In S. Schneider & J. Shanteau (Eds.), *Emerging perspectives on judgment and decision research* (pp. 643–678). Cambridge: Cambridge University Press.

Dougherty, M. R. P., Gettys, C. F., & Ogden, E. E. (1999). Minerva-DM: A memory processes model for judgments of likelihood. *Psychological Review, 106,* 180–209.

Dowie, J. (1976). On the efficiency and equity of better markets. *Economica, 43,* 139–150.

Dudycha, A. L., Dumoff, M. G., & Dudycha, L. W. (1973). Choice behavior in dynamic environments. *Organizational Behavior and Human Decision Processes, 9,* 328–338.

Edwards, A., Elwyn, G., Covey, J., Mathews, E., & Pill, R. (2001). Presenting risk information – a review of the effects of 'framing' and other manipulations on patient outcomes. *Journal of Health Communication, 6,* 61–82.

Edwards, W. (1961). Probability learning in 1000 trials. *Journal of Experimental Psychology, 62,* 385–394.

Edwards, W. (1965). Optimal strategies for seeking information: Models for statistics, choice reaction-times, and human information-processing. *Journal of Mathematical Psychology, 2,* 312–329.

Edwards, W. (1968). Conservatism in human information processing. In B. Kleinmuntz (Ed.), *Formal representation of human judgment* (pp. 17–52). New York: John Wiley & Sons.

Edwards, W., & Barron F. H. (1994). SMARTS and SMARTER: Improved simple methods for multiattribute utility measurement. *Organizational Behavior and Human Decision Processes, 60,* 306–325.

Edwards, W., & Fasolo, B. (2001). Decision technology. *Annual Review of Psychology, 52,* 581–606.

Einhorn, H. J. (1972). Expert measurement and mechanical combination. *Organizational Behavior and Human Performance, 7,* 86–106.

Einhorn, H. J., & Hogarth, R. M. (1975). Unit weighting schemes for decision making. *Organizational Behavior and Human Performance, 13*, 171–192.

Einhorn, H. J., & Hogarth, R. M. (1981). Behavioral decision theory: Processes of judgment and choice. *Annual Review of Psychology, 32*, 53–88.

Ellsberg, D. (1961). Risk, ambiguity and the Savage axioms. *Quarterly Journal of Economics, 75*, 643–679.

Enkvist, T., Newell, B. R., Juslin, P., & Olsson, H. (2006). On the role of causal intervention in multiple cue judgment: Positive and negative effects on learning. *Journal of Experimental Psychology: Learning, Memory, and Cognition, 32*, 163–179.

Ericsson, K. A. (1996). The acquisition of expert performance: An introduction to some of the issues. In K. A. Ericsson (Ed.), *The road to excellence: The acquisition of expert performance in the arts and sciences, sports and games* (pp. 1–50). Mahwah, NJ: Lawrence Erlbaum Associates, Inc.

Ericsson, K. A., & Simon, H. A. (1980). Verbal reports as data. *Psychological Review, 87*, 215–251.

Ericsson, K. A., & Simon, H. A. (1984). *Protocol analysis: Verbal reports as data.* Cambridge, MA: Bradford Books/MIT Press.

Evans, J. St. B. T., Clibbens, J., Cattani, A., Harris, A., & Dennis, I. (2003). Explicit and implicit processes in multicue judgment. *Memory and Cognition, 31*, 608–618.

Evans, J. St. B. T., Handley, S. H., Perham, N., Over, D. E., & Thompson, V. A. (2000). Frequency versus probability formats in statistical word problems. *Cognition, 77*, 197–213.

Fasolo, B., McClelland, G. H., & Lange, K. A. (2005). The effect of site design and interattribute correlations on interactive web-based decisions. In C. P. Haugtvedt, K. Machleit, & R. Yalch (Eds.), *Online consumer psychology: Understanding and influencing behavior in the virtual world* (pp. 325–344). Mahwah, NJ: Lawrence Erlbaum Associates, Inc.

Festinger, L. (1957). *A theory of cognitive dissonance.* Stanford, CA: Stanford University Press.

Fiedler, K. (1988). The dependence of the conjunction fallacy on subtle linguistic factors. *Psychological Research, 50*, 123–129.

Fiedler, K. (2000). Beware of samples! A cognitive-ecological sampling approach to judgment biases. *Psychological Review, 107*, 659–676.

Fiedler, K., & Juslin, P. (2006). Taking the interface between mind and environment seriously. In K. Fiedler & P. Juslin (Eds.), *Information sampling and adaptive cognition* (pp. 3–29). Cambridge: Cambridge University Press.

Finucane, M. L., Alhakami, A., Slovic, P., & Johnson, S. M. (2000). The affect heuristic in judgments of risks and benefits. *Journal of Behavioral Decision Making, 13*, 1–17.

Finucane, M. L., Peters, E., & Slovic, P. (2003). Judgment and decision making: The dance of affect and reason. In S. L. Schneider & J. Shanteau (Eds.), *Emerging perspectives on judgment and decision research* (pp. 327–364). Cambridge: Cambridge University Press.

Fiorina, M. P. (1971). A note on probability matching and rational choice. *Behavioral Science, 16*, 158–166.

Fischhoff, B. (2002). Heuristics and biases in application. In T. D. Gilovich, D. W. Griffin, & D. Kahneman (Eds.), *Heuristics and biases* (pp. 730–748). New York: Cambridge University Press.

Fishburn, P. C. (1974). Lexicographic orders, utilities and decision rules. *Management Science, 20,* 1442–1471.

Fitelson, B. (1999). The plurality of Bayesian measures of confirmation and the problem of measure sensitivity, *Philosophy of Science, 66,* 362–378.

Fletcher, P. C., Anderson, J. M., Shanks, D. R., Honey, R., Carpenter, T. A., Donovan, T. et al. (2001). Responses of human frontal cortex to surprising events are predicted by formal associative learning theory. *Nature Neuroscience, 4,* 1043–1048.

Fox, C. R. (1999). Strength of evidence, judged probability, and choice under uncertainty. *Cognitive Psychology, 38,* 167–189.

Fox, C. R., Rogers, B. A., & Tversky, A. (1996). Options traders exhibit subadditive decision weights. *Journal of Risk and Uncertainty, 13,* 5–17.

Fox, C. R., & See, K. E. (2003). Belief and preference in decision under uncertainty. In D. Hardmand & L. Macchi (Eds.), *Thinking: Psychological perspectives on reasoning, judgment and decision making* (pp. 273–314). New York: Wiley.

Fox, C. R., & Tversky, A. (1995). Ambiguity aversion and comparative ignorance. *Quarterly Journal of Economics, 110,* 585–603.

Fox, C. R., & Tversky, A. (1998). A belief-based account of decision under uncertainty. *Management Science, 44,* 879–895.

Frederick, S., Loewenstein, G., & O'Donohue, T. (2003). Time discounting and time preference: A critical review. In G. Loewenstein, D. Read, & R. Baumeister (Eds.), *Time and decision: Economic and psychological perspectives on intertemporal choice* (pp. 13–86). New York: Russell Sage Foundation.

Frensch, P. A., & Funke, J. (1995). *Complex problem solving: The European perspective.* Hillsdale, NJ: Lawrence Erlbaum Associates, Inc.

Fried, L. S., & Peterson, C. R. (1969). Information seeking: Optional versus fixed stopping. *Journal of Experimental Psychology, 80,* 525–529.

Friedman, D. (1998). Monty Hall's three doors: Construction and deconstruction of a choice anomaly. *American Economic Review, 88,* 933–946.

Friedman, D., & Massaro, D. W. (1998). Understanding variability in binary and continuous choice. *Psychonomic Bulletin & Review, 5,* 370–389.

Friedman, D., Massaro, D. W., Kitzis, S. N., & Cohen, M. M. (1995). A comparison of learning models. *Journal of Mathematical Psychology, 39,* 164–178.

Fuller, S., & Aldag, R. (1998). Organizational Tonypandy: Lessons from a quarter century of the groupthink phenomenon. *Organizational Behavior and Human Decision Processes, 73,* 163–184.

Galotti, K. M. (1995). Memories of a 'decision-map': Recall of a real-life decision. *Applied Cognitive Psychology, 9,* 307–319.

Gettys, C. F., Michel, C., Steiger, J. H., Kelly, C. W., & Peterson, C. R. (1973). Multiple-stage probabilistic information processing. *Organizational Behavior and Human Performance, 10,* 374–387.

Gigerenzer, G. (1994). Why the distinction between single-event probabilities and frequencies is relevant for psychology (and vice versa). In G. Wright & P. Ayton (Eds.), *Subjective probability* (pp. 129–161). New York: Wiley.

Gigerenzer, G. (1996). On narrow norms and vague heuristics: A reply to Tversky and Kahneman. *Psychological Review, 103,* 592–596.

Gigerenzer, G. (2002). *Calculated risks: How to know when numbers deceive you.* New York: Simon & Schuster.

Gigerenzer, G., & Goldstein, D. G. (1996). Reasoning the fast and frugal way: Models of bounded rationality. *Psychological Review, 103,* 650–669.

Gigerenzer, G., & Goldstein, D. G. (1999). Betting on one good reason: The take-the-best heuristic. In G. Gigerenzer, P. M. Todd, & the ABC Research Group (Eds.), *Simple heuristics that make us smart* (pp. 75–96). New York: Oxford University Press.

Gigerenzer, G., & Hoffrage, U. (1995). How to improve Bayesian reasoning without instruction: Frequency formats. *Psychological Review, 102*, 684–704.

Gigerenzer, G., Hoffrage, U., & Kleinbölting, H. (1991). Probabilistic mental models: A Brunswikian theory of confidence. *Psychological Review, 98*, 506–528.

Gigerenzer, G., & Selten, R. (2001). Rethinking rationality. In G. Gigerenzer & R. Selten (Eds.), *Bounded rationality: The adaptive toolbox* (pp 1–12). Cambridge, MA: MIT Press.

Gigerenzer, G., Todd, P. M., & the ABC Research Group (1999). *Simple heuristics that make us smart*. New York: Oxford University Press.

Gigone, D., & Hastie, R. (1997). Proper analysis of the accuracy of group judgments. *Psychological Bulletin, 121*, 149–167.

Gilovich, T., Griffin, D., & Kahneman, D. (Eds.) (2002). *Heuristics and biases*. New York: Cambridge University Press.

Girotto, V., & Gonzalez, M. (2001). Solving probabilistic and statistical problems: A matter of information structure and question form. *Cognition, 78*, 247–276.

Gluck, M. A., & Bower, G. H. (1988). From conditioning to category learning: An adaptive network model. *Journal of Experimental Psychology: General, 117*, 227–247.

Gluck, M. A., Shohamy, D., & Myers, C. (2002). How do people solve the 'weather prediction' task? Individual variability in strategies for probabilistic category learning. *Learning and Memory, 9*, 408–418.

Goldberg, L. R. (1968). Simple models or simple processes? Some research on clinical judgments. *American Psychologist, 23*, 483–496.

Goldstein, D. G., & Gigerenzer, G. (2002). Models of ecological rationality: The recognition heuristic. *Psychological Review, 109*, 75–90.

Goldstein, D., Gigerenzer, G., Hogarth, R., Kacelnik, A., Kareev, Y., Klein, G. et al. (2001). Why and when do simple heuristics work? In G. Gigerenzer & R. Selten (Eds.), *Bounded rationality: The adaptive toolbox* (pp. 173–190). Cambridge, MA: MIT Press.

Goldstein, W. M., & Hogarth, R. M. (1997). Judgment and decision research: Some historical context. In W. M. Goldstein & R. M. Hogarth (Eds.), *Research on judgment and decision making: Currents, connections, and controversies* (pp. 3–68). Cambridge: Cambridge University Press.

Goodie, A. S., & Fantino, E. (1999). What does and does not alleviate base-rate neglect under direct experience. *Journal of Behavioral Decision Making, 12*, 307–335.

Goodman, J. (1992). Jurors' comprehension and assessment of probabilistic evidence. *American Journal of Trial Advocacy, 16*, 361–389.

Goodman-Delahunty, J., & Newell, B. R. (2004). One in how many trillion? *Australasian Science, 25*, 14–17.

Gopnik, A., Glymour, C., Sobel, D. M., Schulz, L. E., Kushnir, T., & Danks, D. (2004). A theory of causal learning in children: Causal maps and Bayes nets. *Psychological Review, 111*, 1–30.

Gould, S. (1992). *Bully for brontosaurus. Further reflections in natural history*. London: Penguin Books.

Griffin, D., & Brenner, L. (2004). Probability judgment calibration. In D. Koehler

& N. Harvey (Eds.), *Blackwell handbook of judgment and decision making* (pp. 177–199). New York: Blackwell.

Grove, W. M., & Meehl, P. E. (1996). Comparative efficiency of informal (subjective, impressionistic) and formal (mechanical, algorithmic) prediction procedures: The clinical/statistical controversy. *Psychology, Public Policy, and Law*, *2*, 293–323.

Grove, W. M., Zald, D., Lebow, B., Snitz, B., & Nelson, C. (2000). Clinical versus mechanical prediction: A meta-analysis. *Psychological Assessment*, *12*, 19–30.

Hacking, I. (1975). *The emergence of probability: A philosophical study of early ideas about probability, induction and statistical inference*. Cambridge: Cambridge University Press.

Hammond, J. S., Keeney, R. L., and Raiffa, H. (1999). *Smart choices: A practical guide to making better decisions*. Boston, MA: Harvard Business School Press.

Hammond, K. R. (1955). Probabilistic functioning and the clinical method. *Psychological Review*, *62*, 255–262.

Hammond, K. R. (1971). Computer graphics as an aid to learning. *Science*, *172*, 901–908.

Hammond, K. R. (1996). *Human judgment and social policy. Irreducible uncertainty, inevitable error, unavoidable injustice*. New York: Oxford University Press.

Hammond, K. R., & Adelman, L. (1976). Science, values, and human judgment. *Science*, *194*, 389–396.

Hammond, K. R., & Boyle, P. J. R. (1971). Quasi-rationality, quarrels and new conceptions of feedback. *Bulletin of the British Psychological Society*, *24*, 103–113.

Hammond, K. R. & Stewart, T. R. (Eds.) (2001). *The essential Brunswik: Beginnings explications, applications*. Oxford: Oxford University Press.

Harries, C., Evans, J. St B. T., & Dennis, I. (2000). Measuring doctors' self-insight into their treatment decisions. *Applied Cognitive Psychology*, *14*, 455–477.

Harries, C., & Harvey, N. (2000). Taking advice, using information and knowing what you are doing. *Acta Psychologica*, *104*, 399–416.

Harvey, N. (1997). Confidence in judgment. *Trends in Cognitive Sciences*, *1*, 78–82.

Harvey, N., & Fischer, I. (2005). Development of experience-based judgment and decision making: The role of outcome feedback. In T. Betsch & S. Haberstroh (Eds.), *The routines of decision making* (pp. 119–137). Mahwah, NJ: Lawrence Erlbaum Associates, Inc.

Hasher, L., & Zacks, R. T. (1979). Automatic and effortful processes in memory. *Journal of Experimental Psychology: General*, *108*, 356–388.

Hasher, L., & Zacks, R. T. (1984). Automatic processing of fundamental information. *American Psychologist*, *39*, 1327–1388.

Hastie, R. (1993). *Inside the juror: The psychology of juror decision making*. Cambridge & New York: Cambridge University Press.

Hastie, R., & Dawes, R. M. (2001). *Rational choice in an uncertain world*. Thousand Oaks, CA: Sage.

Hastie, R., & Kameda, T. (2005). The robust beauty of majority rules in group decisions. *Psychological Review*, *112*, 494–508.

Hawkins, S. A., & Hastie, R. (1990). Hindsight: Biased judgments of past events after the outcomes are known. *Psychological Bulletin*, *107*, 311–327.

Hayes, N. A., & Broadbent, D. E. (1988). Two modes of learning for interactive tasks. *Cognition*, *28*, 249–276.

Heath, C., Larrick, R. P., & Klayman, J. (1998). Cognitive repairs: How organizational practices can compensate for individual shortcomings. In B. M. Staw &

L. L. Cummings (Eds.), *Research in organizational behavior* (Vol. 20, pp. 1–37). Greenwich, CT: JAI Press.

Heath, C., & Tversky, A. (1991). Preference and belief: Ambiguity and competence in choice under uncertainty. *Journal of Risk and Uncertainty, 4,* 5–28.

Henry, R. A. (1993). Group judgment accuracy: Reliability and validity of postdiscussion confidence judgments. *Organizational Behavior and Human Decision Processes, 56,* 11–27.

Hershman, R. L., & Levine, J. R. (1970). Deviations from optimal purchase strategies in human decision making. *Organizational Behavior and Human Performance, 5,* 313–329.

Hertwig, R., Barron, G., Weber, E., & Erev, I. (2004). Decisions from experience and the effect of rare events. *Psychological Science, 15,* 534–539.

Hertwig, R., Fanselow, C., & Hoffrage, U. (2003). How knowledge and heuristics affect our reconstruction of the past. *Memory, 11,* 357–377.

Hertwig, R., & Gigerenzer, G. (1999). The 'conjunction fallacy' revisited: How intelligent inferences look like reasoning errors. *Journal of Behavioral Decision Making, 12,* 275–305.

Hertwig, R., & Todd, P. M. (2004). More is not always better: The benefits of cognitive limits. In D. Hardman & L. Macchi (Eds.), *Thinking: Psychological perspectives on reasoning, judgment and decision making* (pp. 213–231). Chichester: Wiley.

Heyes, C. M. (2003). Four routes of cognitive evolution. *Psychological Review, 110,* 713–727.

Hill, G. W. (1982). Group versus individual performance: Are $N+1$ heads better than one? *Psychological Bulletin, 91,* 517–539.

Hilton, D. J. (2003). Psychology and the financial markets. In I. Brocas and J. D. Carillo (Eds.), *The psychology of economic decisions: Vol. I. Rationality and well being* (pp. 273–297). Oxford: Oxford University Press.

Hilton, D. J., & Slugoski, B. R. (1986). Knowledge-based causal attribution: The abnormal conditions focus model. *Psychological Review, 93,* 75–88.

Hintzman, D. L. (1988). Judgments of frequency and recognition memory in a multiple-trace memory model. *Psychological Review, 95,* 528–551.

Hodge, J. (1996). *Trainspotting: The Screenplay.* London: Faber & Faber.

Hoffman, R. R., Crandell, B., & Shadbolt, N. (1998). Use of critical decision method to elicit expert knowledge: A case study in the methodology of expert task analysis. *Human Factors, 40,* 254–276.

Hogarth, R. M. (1978). A note on aggregating opinions. *Organizational Behavior and Human Decision Processes, 21,* 40–46.

Hogarth, R. M. (1981). Beyond discrete biases: Functional and dysfunctional aspects of judgement heuristics. *Psychological Bulletin, 90,* 197–217.

Hogarth, R. M. (2001). *Educating intuition.* Chicago: University of Chicago Press.

Hogarth, R. M., & Einhorn, H. J. (1990). Venture theory: A model of decision weights. *Management Science, 36,* 780–803.

Hogarth, R. M., & Karelaia, N. (2005). Ignoring information in binary choice with continuous variables: When is less 'more'? *Journal of Mathematical Psychology, 49,* 115–124.

Houghton, G. (Ed.) (2005). *Connectionist models in cognitive psychology.* Hove, UK: Psychology Press.

Hsee, C. K. (1996). The evaluability hypothesis: An explanation for preference-reversal between joint and separate evaluations of alternatives. *Organizational Behavior and Human Decision Processes, 67*, 247–257.

Hume, D. (1748). *An enquiry concerning human understanding*. Oxford: Clarendon.

Hux, J. E., & Naylor, C. D. (1995). Communicating the benefits of chronic preventative therapy: Does the format of efficacy data determine patients' acceptance of treatment? *Medical Decision Making, 15*, 152–157.

Jacoby, L. L., & Dallas, M. (1981). On the relationship between autobiographical memory and perceptual learning. *Journal of Experimental Psychology: General, 110*, 306–340.

Janis, I. (1972). *Victims of groupthink*. Boston, MA: Houghton Mifflin.

Janis, I., & Mann, L. (1977). *Decision making: A psychological analysis of conflict, choice and commitment*. New York: Free Press.

Jeffrey, R. (1965). *The logic of decision*. New York: McGraw-Hill.

Jones-Lee, M. W., Loomes, G., & Philips, P. R. (1995). Valuing the prevention of non-fatal road injuries: Contingent valuation vs. standard gambles. *Oxford Economic Papers, 47*, 676–695.

Juslin, P., Jones, S., Olsson, H., & Winman, A. (2003a). Cue abstraction and exemplar memory in categorization. *Journal of Experimental Psychology: Learning, Memory, and Cognition, 29*, 924–941.

Juslin, P., & Montgomery, H. (1999). Introduction and historical remarks. In P. Juslin & H. Montgomery (Eds.), *Judgment and decision making: New-Brunswikian and process-tracing approaches* (pp. 1–6). Hillsdale, NJ: Lawrence Erlbaum Associates, Inc.

Juslin, P., Olsson, H., & Olsson, A.-C. (2003b). Exemplar effects in categorization and multiple-cue judgment. *Journal of Experimental Psychology: General, 132*, 133–156.

Juslin, P., & Persson, M. (2002). PROBabilities from EXemplars (PROBEX): A 'lazy' algorithm for probabilistic inference from generic knowledge. *Cognitive Science, 95*, 1–4.

Juslin, P., Winman, A., & Olsson, H. (2000). Naive empiricism and dogmatism in confidence research: A critical examination of the hard–easy effect. *Psychological Review, 107*, 384–396.

Kahneman, D. (2003). A perspective on judgment and choice: Mapping bounded rationality. *American Psychologist, 58*, 697–720.

Kahneman, D., & Frederick, S. (2002). Representativeness revisited: Attribute substitution in intuitive judgment. In T. D. Gilovich, D. W. Griffin, & D. Kahneman (Eds.), *Heuristics and biases* (pp. 49–81). New York: Cambridge University Press.

Kahneman, D., Fredrickson, B. L., Schreiber, C. A., & Redelmeier, D. A. (1993). When more pain is preferred to less: Adding a better end. *Psychological Science, 4*, 401–405.

Kahneman, D., Knetsch, J. L., & Thaler, R. H. (1990). Experimental tests of the endowment effect and the Coase theorem. *Journal of Political Economy, 98*, 1325–1348.

Kahneman, D., & Lovallo, D. (1993). Timid choices and bold forecasts: A cognitive perspective on risk and risk taking. *Management Science, 39*, 17–31.

Kahneman, D., Ritov, I., & Schkade, D. (1999). Economic preferences or attitude expressions? An analysis of dollar responses to public issues. *Journal of Risk and Uncertainty, 19*, 220–242.

Kahneman, D., Slovic, P., & Tversky, A. (Eds.) (1982). *Judgment under uncertainty: Heuristics and biases*. Cambridge: Cambridge University Press.

Kahneman, D., & Snell, J. (1992). Predicting a changing taste: Do people know what they will like? *Journal of Behavioral Decision Making, 5*, 187–200.

Kahneman, D., & Tversky, A. (1979a). Prospect theory: An analysis of decision under risk. *Econometrica, 47*, 263–291.

Kahneman, D., & Tversky, A. (1979b). Intuitive predictions: Biases and corrective procedures. *TIMS Studies in Management Science, 12*, 313–327.

Kahneman, D., & Tversky, A. (1982a). The simulation heuristic. In D. Kahneman, P. Slovic, & A. Tversky (Eds.), *Judgment under uncertainty: Heuristics and biases* (pp. 201–208). Cambridge: Cambridge University Press.

Kahneman, D., & Tversky, A. (1982b). Variants of uncertainty. In D. Kahneman, P. Slovic, & A. Tversky (Eds.), *Judgment under uncertainty: Heuristics and biases* (pp. 509–520). Cambridge: Cambridge University Press.

Kahneman, D., & Tversky, A. (1984). Choices, values, and frames. *American Psychologist, 39*, 341–350.

Kahneman, D., & Tversky, A. (1996). On the reality of cognitive illusions: A reply to Gigerenzer's critique. *Psychological Review, 103*, 582–591.

Kahneman, D., & Tversky, A. (2000). *Choices, values, and frames.* Cambridge: Cambridge University Press.

Kahneman, D., & Varey, C. A. (1990). Propensities and counterfactuals: The loser that almost won. *Journal of Personality and Social Psychology, 59*, 1101–1110.

Kamin, L. J. (1968). 'Attention-like' processes in classical conditioning. In M. R. Jones (Ed.), *Miami symposium on the prediction of behavior, 1967: Aversive stimulation* (pp. 9–31). Coral Gables, FL: University of Miami Press.

Kaplan, R. J., & Newman, J. R. (1966). Studies in probabilistic information processing. *IEEE Transactions on Human Factors in Electronics, HFE–7*, 49–63.

Keeney, R. L., & Raiffa, H. (1976). *Decisions with multiple objectives: Preferences and value trade-offs.* New York: Wiley.

Keller, L. R. (1985). The effects of problem representation on the sure-thing and substitution principles. *Management Science, 31*, 738–751.

Kelley, C. M. & Jacoby, L. L. (2000). Recollection and familiarity: Process-dissociation. In E. Tulving & F. I. M. Craik (Eds.), *The Oxford handbook of memory* (pp. 215–228). New York: Oxford University Press.

Kelley, H., & Friedman, D. (2002). Learning to forecast price. *Economic Inquiry, 40*, 556–573.

Keren, G. (1987). Facing uncertainty in the game of bridge: A calibration study. *Organizational Behavior and Human Decision Processes, 39*, 98–114.

Kerr, N. L., MacCoun, R., & Kramer, G. P. (1996). Bias in judgment: Comparing individuals and groups. *Psychological Review, 103*, 687–719.

Kerr, N. L., & Tindale, R. S. (2004). Group performance and decision making. *Annual Review of Psychology, 55*, 623–655.

Kitzis, S. N., Kelley, H., Berg, E., Massaro, D. W., & Friedman, D. (1998). Broadening the tests of learning models. *Journal of Mathematical Psychology, 42*, 327–355.

Klayman, J. (1984). Learning from feedback in probabilistic environments. *Acta Psychologica, 56*, 81–92.

Klayman, J. (1988a). Cue discovery in probabilistic environments: Uncertainty and experimentation. *Journal of Experimental Psychology: Learning, Memory, and Cognition, 14*, 317–330.

Klayman, J. (1988b). On the how and why (not) of learning from outcomes. In

B. Brehmer & C. R. B. Joyce (Eds.), *Human judgment: The SJT view* (pp. 115–160). Amsterdam: North-Holland/Elsevier.

Klayman, J. (1995). Varieties of confirmation bias. In J. Busemeyer, R. Hastie, & D. L. Medin (Eds.), *The Psychology of Learning and Motivation* (Vol 32 pp. 385–418). New York: Academic Press.

Klayman, J. (2001). Ambivalence in (not about) naturalistic decision making. *Journal of Behavioral Decision Making, 14*, 372–73.

Klayman, J., & Ha, Y.-W. (1987). Confirmation, disconfirmation, and information in hypothesis testing. *Psychological Review, 94*, 211–228.

Klayman, J., Soll, J. B., Juslin, P., & Winman, A. (2006). Subjective confidence and the sampling of knowledge. In K. Fiedler & P. Juslin (Eds.), *Information sampling and adaptive cognition* (pp. 153–182). Cambridge: University of Cambridge Press.

Klein, G. A. (1993). A recognition-primed decision (RPD) model of rapid decision making. In G. A. Klein, J. Orasanu, R. Calderwood, & C. E. Zsambok (Eds.), *Decision making in action: Models and methods.* Norwood, CT: Ablex.

Klein, G. A. (1998). *Sources of power: How people make decisions.* Cambridge, MA: MIT Press.

Klein, G. A., Wolf, S., Militello, L., & Zsambok, C. E. (1995). Characteristics of skilled option generation in chess. *Organization Behavior and Human Decision Processes, 62*, 63–69.

Knowlton, B. J., Mangels, J. A., & Squire, L. R. (1996). A neostriatal habit learning system in humans. *Science, 273*, 1399–1402.

Koehler, J. J. (1993). Error and exaggeration in the presentation of DNA evidence. *Jurimetrics Journal, 34*, 21–39.

Koehler, J. J. (1996). The base rate fallacy reconsidered: Descriptive, normative, and methodological challenges. *Behavioral and Brain Sciences, 19*, 1–53.

Koehler, J., Chia, A., & Lindsey, S. (1995). The random match probability in DNA evidence: Irrelevant and prejudicial? *Jurimetrics Journal, 35*, 201–209.

Koehler, J. J., & Macchi, L. (2004). Thinking about low probability events. *Psychological Science, 15*, 540–545.

Koriat, A., Lichtenstein, S., & Fischhoff, B. (1980). Reasons for confidence. *Journal of Experimental Psychology: Human Learning and Memory, 6*, 107–118.

Kruschke, J. K. (1992). ALCOVE: An exemplar-based connectionist model of category learning. *Psychological Review, 99*, 22–44.

Kruschke, J. K. (1996). Base rates in category learning. *Journal of Experimental Psychology: Learning, Memory, and Cognition, 22*, 3–26.

Kunda, Z. (1990). The case for motivated reasoning. *Psychological Bulletin, 108*, 480–98.

Lagnado, D. A., Moss, T., & Shanks, D. R. (2006a). *Grouping choices.* Unpublished manuscript. University College London, UK.

Lagnado, D. A., Newell, B. R., Kahan, S., & Shanks, D. R. (2006b). Insight and strategy in multiple cue learning. *Journal of Experimental Psychology: General, 135*, 162–183.

Lagnado, D. A., & Shanks, D. R. (2002). Probability judgment in hierarchical learning: A conflict between predictiveness and coherence. *Cognition, 83*, 81–112.

Lagnado, D. A., & Shanks, D. R. (2003). The influence of hierarchy on probability judgment. *Cognition, 89*, 157–178.

Lagnado D. A., & Sloman, S. A. (2004a). The advantage of timely intervention. *Journal of Experimental Psychology: Learning, Memory and Cognition, 30,* 856–876.

Lagnado, D., & Sloman, S. A. (2004b). Inside and outside probability judgment. In D. J. Koehler & N. Harvey (Eds.), *The Blackwell handbook of judgment and decision making* (pp. 157–176). New York: Blackwell.

Lagnado, D. A., & Sloman, S. A. (2006). Time as a guide to cause. *Journal of Experimental Psychology: Learning, Memory, and Cognition, 32,* 451–460.

Lan, C. H., & Harvey, N. (2006). *Ellsberg's paradoxes: Problems for rank-dependent utility explanations.* Paper presented at 12th International Conference on the Foundations and Applications of Utility, Risk and Decision Theory, LUISS, Rome.

Lanzetta, J. T., & Kanareff, V. T. (1962). Information cost, amount of payoff, and level of aspiration as determinants of information seeking in decision making. *Behavioral Science, 7,* 459–473.

Laplace, P. S. (1812). *Analytical theory of probability.* Paris: Courcier.

Larrick, R. P. (2004). Debiasing. In D. J. Koehler & N. Harvey (Eds.), *The Blackwell handbook of judgment and decision making* (pp. 316–337). New York: Blackwell.

Laughlin, P. R. (1999). Collective induction: Twelve postulates. *Organizational Behavior and Human Decision Processes, 80,* 50–69.

Laughlin, P. R., Vanderstoep, S. W., & Hollingshead, A. B. (1991). Collective versus individual induction: Recognition of truth, rejection of error, and collective information processing. *Journal of Personality and Social Psychology, 61,* 50–67.

Lee, M. D., & Cummins, T. D. R. (2004). Evidence accumulation in decision making: Unifying 'take the best' and 'rational' models. *Psychonomic Bulletin and Review, 11,* 343–352.

Lichtenstein, S., & Fischhoff, B. (1977). Do those who know more also know more about how much they know? *Organizational Behavior and Human Performance, 20,* 159–183.

Lichtenstein, S., Fischhoff, B., Phillips, L.D. (1982). Calibration of probabilities: The state of the art to 1980. In D. Kahneman, P. Slovic, & A. Tversky (Eds.), *Judgment under uncertainty: Heuristics and biases* (pp. 306–334). Cambridge: Cambridge University Press.

Lichtenstein, S., & Slovic, P. (1971). Reversals of preference between bids and choices in gambling decisions. *Journal of Experimental Psychology, 89,* 46–55.

Lichtenstein, S., & Slovic, P. (1973). Response-induced reversals of preference in gambling: An extended replication in Las Vegas. *Journal of Experimental Psychology, 101,* 16–20.

Lichtenstein, S., Slovic, P., Fischhoff, B., Layman, M., & Coombs, B. (1978). Judged frequency of lethal events. *Journal of Experimental Psychology: Human Learning and Memory, 4,* 551–578.

Lindell, M. K., & Stewart, T. R. (1974). The effects of redundancy in multiple cue probability learning. *American Psychologist, 87,* 393–398.

Lindley, D. V. (1985). *Making decisions* (2nd ed.). Chichester, UK: John Wiley and Sons.

Lindsey, S., Hertwig, R., & Gigerenzer, G. (2003). Communicating statistical DNA evidence. *Jurimetrics Journal, 43,* 147–163.

Lipshitz, R., Klein, G., Orasanu, J., & Salas, E. (2001). Taking stock of naturalistic decision making. *Journal of Behavioral Decision Making, 14,* 331–352.

List, J. A. (2002). Preference reversals of a different kind: The 'more is less' phenomenon. *American Economic Review, 92,* 1636–1643.

Loewenstein, G. (1987). Anticipation and the valuation of delayed consumption. *Economic Journal, 97,* 666–684.

Loewenstein, G. (1988). Frames of mind in intertemporal choice. *Management Science*, *34*, 200–214.

Loewenstein, G. (1996). Out of control: Visceral influences on behavior. *Organizational Behavior and Human Decision Processes*, *65*, 272–292.

Loewenstein, G., & Angner, E. (2003). Predicting and indulging changing preferences. In G. Loewenstein, D. Read, & R. Baumeister (Eds.), *Time and decision: Economic and psychological perspectives on intertemporal choice* (pp. 351–391). New York: Russell Sage Foundation.

Loewenstein, G., Weber, E., Hsee, C., & Welch, N. (2001). Risk as feelings. *Psychological Bulletin*, *127*, 267–286.

Loomes, G., Starmer, C., & Sugden, R. (1992). Are preferences monotonic: Testing some implications of regret theory. *Economica*, *59*, 17–33.

Loomes, G., & Sugden, R. (1982). Regret theory: An alternative theory of rational choice under uncertainty. *Economic Journal*, *92*, 805–824.

Lorge, I., & Solomon, H. (1958). Two models of group behavior in the solution of eureka-type problems. *Psychometrika*, *29*, 139–148.

Louie, T. A. (1999). Decision makers' hindsight bias after receiving favorable and unfavorable feedback. *Journal of Applied Psychology*, *84*, 29–41.

Lovallo, D., & Kahneman, D. (2003). Delusions of success. *Harvard Business Review*, *81*, 57–63.

Løvborg, L., & Brehmer, B. (1991). *NEWFIRE – a flexible system for running simulated fire-fighting experiments*. Risö National Laboratory, Roskilde, Denmark.

Lovibond, P. F., & Shanks, D. R. (2002). The role of awareness in Pavlovian conditioning: Empirical evidence and theoretical implications. *Journal of Experimental Psychology: Animal Behavior Processes*, *28*, 3–26.

Luce, R. D., & Raiffa, H. (1957). *Games and decisions*. New York: Wiley.

MacCrimmon, K. R., & Larsson, S. (1979). Utility theory: Axioms versus 'paradoxes'. In M. Allais and O. Hagen (Eds.), *Expected utility and the Allais paradox* (pp. 333–409). Dordrecht: D. Reidel Publishing.

Maddox, W. T., & Ashby, F. G. (2004). Dissociating explicit and procedural-learning based systems of perceptual category learning. *Behavioural Processes*, *66*, 309–332.

Maia, T. V., & McClelland, J. L. (2004). A reexamination of the evidence for the somatic marker hypothesis: What participants really know in the Iowa gambling task. *Proceedings of the National Academy of Sciences*, *101*, 16075–16080.

Maier, N., & Solem, A. (1952). The contribution of a discussion leader to the quality of group thinking: The effective use of minority opinion. *Human Relations*, *5*, 277–288.

Malenka, D. J., Baron, J. A., Johansen, S., Wahrenberger, J. W., & Ross, J. M. (1993) The framing effect of relative and absolute risk. *Journal of General Internal Medicine*, *8*, 543–548.

Mann, T., & Ward, A. (2004). To eat or not to eat: Implications of the attentional myopia model for restrained eaters. *Journal of Abnormal Psychology*, *113*, 90–98.

March, J. G., & Shapira, Z. (1987). Managerial perspectives on risk and risk taking. *Management Science*, *33*, 1404–18.

Markowitz, H. (1952). The utility of wealth. *Journal of Political Economy*, *60*, 151–158.

Marr, D. (1982). *Vision*. San Francisco, CA: H. Freeman and Co.

Marschak, J. (1954). Towards an economic theory of organization and information. In R. M. Thrall, C. H. Coombs, & R. L. Davis (Eds.), *Decision processes* (pp. 187–220). New York: Wiley.

Martignon, L., & Hoffrage, U. (1999). Why does one-reason decision making work? A case study in ecological rationality. In G. Gigerenzer, P. M. Todd, & the ABC Research Group (Eds.), *Simple heuristics that make us smart* (pp. 119–140). New York: Oxford University Press.

Martignon, L., & Hoffrage, U. (2002). Fast, frugal and fit: Lexicographic heuristics for paired comparison. *Theory and Decision, 52*, 29–71.

Maule, J., & Villejoubert, G. (2007). What lies beneath: Reframing framing effects. In D. A. Lagnado & D. Read (Eds), Judgment and choice: Perspectives on the work of Daniel Kahneman. *Thinking and Reasoning* (Special Issue), *13*, 25–44.

McClelland, J. L. (1998). Connectionist models and Bayesian inference. In M. Oaksford & N. Chater (Eds.), *Rational models of cognition* (pp. 21–53). Oxford: Oxford University Press.

McClelland, J. L., & Rumelhart, D. E. (1986). *Parallel distributed processing: Explorations in the microstructure of cognition. Vol. 2. Psychological and biological models.* Cambridge, MA: MIT Press.

McClure, S. M., Laibson, D. I., Loewenstein, G., & Cohen, J. D. (2004). Separate neural systems value immediate and delayed monetary rewards. *Science, 306*, 503–507.

McKenzie, C. R. M. (2004). Framing effects in inference tasks – and why they are normatively defensible. *Memory and Cognition, 32*, 874–885.

McNeil, B. J., Pauker, S. G., Sox, H. C., & Tversky, A. (1982). On the elicitation of preferences for alternative therapies. *New England Journal of Medicine, 306*, 1259–1262.

Medin, D. L., & Edelson, S. M. (1988). Problem structure and the use of base-rate information from experience. *Journal of Experimental Psychology: General, 117*, 68–85.

Medin, D. L., & Schaffer, M. M. (1978). Context theory of classification learning. *Psychological Review, 85*, 207–238.

Meehl, P. E. (1954). *Clinical versus statistical prediction: A theoretical analysis and a review of the evidence.* Minneapolis: University of Minnesota Press.

Muchinsky, P. M., & Dudycha, A. L. (1975). Human inference behavior in abstract and meaningful environments. *Organizational Behavior and Human Performance, 13*, 377–391.

Murphy, A. H., & Winkler, R. L. (1974). Subjective probability forecasting experiments in meteorology: Some preliminary results. *Bulletin of the American Meteorological Society, 55*, 1206–1216.

Murphy, A. H., & Winkler R. L. (1977). Reliability of subjective probability forecasts of precipitation and temperature. *Applied Statistics, 26*, 41–47.

Murphy, G. L., & Ross, B. H. (1994). Predictions from uncertain categorizations. *Cognitive Psychology, 27*, 148–193.

Mussweiler, T., Strack, F., & Pfeiffer, T. (2000). Overcoming the inevitable anchoring effect: Considering the opposite compensates for selective accessibility. *Personality and Social Psychology Bulletin, 26*, 1142–1150.

Myers, J. L., & Cruse, D. (1968). Two-choice discrimination learning as a function of stimulus and event probabilities. *Journal of Experimental Psychology, 77*, 453–459.

Neimark, E. D., & Shuford, E. H. (1959). Comparison of predictions and estimates in a probability learning situation. *Journal of Experimental Psychology, 57*, 294–298.

Newell, B. R. (2005). Re-visions of rationality? *Trends in Cognitive Sciences, 9*, 11–15.

Newell, B. R. & Fernandez, D. (2006). On the binary quality of recognition and the inconsequentiality of further knowledge: Two critical tests of the recognition heuristic. *Journal of Behavioral Decision Making, 19*, 333–346.

Newell, B. R. & Lagnado, D. (2003). Think-tanks, or think *tanks*? *The Psychologist*, *16*, 176.

Newell, B. R., Mitchell, C. J. & Hayes, B. K. (2005). Imagining low probability events: Contrasting exemplar cuing and frequency format accounts. In B. Bara, L. Barsalou, & M. Bucciarelli (Eds.), *Proceedings of the 27th Annual Conference of the Cognitive Science Society* (pp. 1630–1635), Mahwah, NJ: Lawrence Erlbaum Associates Inc.

Newell, B. R., Rakow, T., Weston, N. J., & Shanks, D. R. (2004). Search strategies in decision making: The success of success. *Journal of Behavioral Decision Making*, *17*, 117–137.

Newell, B. R., & Shanks, D. R. (2003). Take-the-best or look at the rest? Factors influencing 'one-reason' decision making. *Journal of Experimental Psychology: Learning, Memory, and Cognition*, *29*, 53–65.

Newell, B. R., & Shanks, D. R. (2004). On the role of recognition in decision making. *Journal of Experimental Psychology: Learning, Memory, and Cognition*, *30*, 923–935.

Newell, B. R., Weston, N. J., & Shanks, D. R. (2003). Empirical tests of a fast and frugal heuristic: Not everyone 'takes-the-best'. *Organizational Behavior and Human Decision Processes*, *91*, 82–96.

Nosofsky, R. M., & Johansen, M. K. (2000). Exemplar-based accounts of 'multiple-system' phenomena in perceptual categorization. *Psychonomic Bulletin & Review*, *7*, 375–402.

Nosofsky, R. M., & Kruschke, J. K. (1992). Investigations of an exemplar-based connectionist model of category learning. In D. L. Medin (Ed.), *The psychology of learning and motivation* (Vol. 28, pp. 207–250). San Diego, CA: Academic Press.

Nosofsky, R. M., Kruschke, J. K., & McKinley, S. C. (1992). Combining exemplar-based category representations and connectionist learning rules. *Journal of Experimental Psychology: Learning, Memory, and Cognition*, *18*, 211–233.

Nunes, A., & Kirlik, A. (2005). An empirical study of calibration in air traffic control expert judgment. *Proceedings of the 49th Annual Meeting of the Human Factors and Ergonomics Society* (pp. 422–426). Santa Monica, CA: HFES.

Olds, J., & Milner, P. (1954). Positive reinforcement produced by electrical stimulation of the septal area and other regions of the rat brain. *Journal of Comparative and Physiological Psychology*, *47*, 419–427.

Oppenheimer, D. M. (2003). Not so fast (and not so frugal!): Rethinking the recognition heuristic. *Cognition*, *90*, B1–B9.

Orasanu, J., & Connolly, T. (1993). The reinvention of decision making. In G. A. Klein, J. Orasanu, R. Calderwood, & C. E. Zsambok (Eds.), *Decision making in action: Models and methods* (pp. 3–20). Norwood, CT: Ablex.

Ortmann, A., Gigerenzer, G., Borges, B., & Goldstein, D. (in press). The recognition heuristic: A fast and frugal way to investment choice? In C. R. Plott & V. L. Smith (Eds.), *Handbook of results in experimental economics*. Amsterdam: North-Holland/Elsevier.

Pascal, B. (1670). *Pensees*. (A. J. Krailsheimer, Intro & Trans. In Penguin Classics series. Harmondsworth: Penguin Books, 1995)

Payne, J. W. (1976). Task complexity and contingent processing in decision making: An information search and protocol analysis. *Organizational Behavior and Human Performance*, *16*, 366–387.

Payne, J. W., Bettman, J. R., & Johnson, E. J. (1993). *The adaptive decision maker*. New York: Cambridge University Press.

Payne, J., Bettman, J. R., & Luce, M. (1998). Behavioral decision research: An overview. In M. Birnbaum (Ed.), *Measurement, judgment and decision making* (pp. 303–359). San Diego, CA: Academic Press.

Pearl, J. (1988). *Probabilistic reasoning in intelligent systems: Networks of plausible inference.* San Mateo, CA: Morgan Kaufman Publishers.

Pearl, J. (2000). *Causality: Models, reasoning, and inference.* Cambridge: Cambridge University Press.

Peters, E., Västfjäll, D., Gärling T., & Slovic, P. (2006). Affect and decision making: A 'hot' topic. *Journal of Behavioral Decision Making, 19,* 79–85.

Peterson, C. R., Hammond, K. R., & Summers, D. A. (1965). Optimal responding in multiple-cue probability learning. *Journal of Experimental Psychology, 70,* 270–276.

Peterson, C. R., & Ulehla, Z. J. (1965). Sequential patterns and maximizing. *Journal of Experimental Psychology, 69,* 1–4.

Pidgeon, N. F., & Gregory, R. (2004). Judgment, decision making and public policy. In D. Koehler & N. Harvey (Eds.), *Blackwell handbook of judgment and decision making* (pp. 604–623). New York: Blackwell.

Pieters, R., Baumgartner, H., & Bagozzi, R. (2006). Biased memory for prior decision making: Evidence from a longitudinal field study. *Organizational Behavior and Human Decision Processes, 99,* 34–48.

Pirolli, P., & Card, S. (1999). Information foraging. *Psychological Review, 106,* 643–675.

Pitz, G. F. (1968). Information seeking when available information is limited. *Journal of Experimental Psychology, 76,* 25–34.

Plous, S. (1993). *The psychology of judgment and decision making.* New York: McGraw-Hill.

Pruitt, D. G. (1961). Informational requirements in decision making. *American Journal of Psychology, 74,* 433–439.

Pruitt, J. S., Cannon-Bowers, J. A., & Salas, E. (1997). In search of naturalistic decisions. In R. Flin, E. Salas, M. Strub, & L. Martin (Eds.), *Decision making under stress: Emerging themes and applications* (pp. 29–42). Aldershot, UK: Ashgate.

Purchase, I., & Slovic, P. (1999). Quantitative risk assessment breeds fear. *Human and Ecological Risk Assessment, 5,* 445–453.

Rachlin, H. (2000). *The science of self-control.* Cambridge, MA: Harvard University Press.

Raiffa, H. (1968). *Decision analysis.* Reading, MA: Addison-Wesley.

Rakow, T., Newell, B. R., Fayers, K. & Hersby, M. (2005). Evaluating three criteria for establishing cue-search hierarchies in inferential judgment. *Journal of Experimental Psychology: Learning, Memory, and Cognition, 31,* 1088–1104.

Ramsey, F. P. (1931). *The foundations of mathematics and other logical essays.* London: Routledge & Kegan Paul.

Read, D., & Lowenstein, G. (1995). Diversification bias: Explaining the discrepancy between combined and separate choices. *Journal of Experimental Psychology, 1,* 7–59.

Read, D., & van Leeuwen, B. (1998). Predicting hunger: The effects of appetite and delay on choice. *Organizational Behavior and Human Decision Processes, 76,* 189–205.

Reber, P. J., Knowlton, B. J., & Squire, L. R. (1996). Dissociable properties of memory systems: Differences in the flexibility of declarative and nondeclarative knowledge. *Behavioral Neuroscience, 110,* 861–871.

Redelmeier, D. A., Katz, J., & Kahneman, D. (2003). Memories of colonoscopy: A randomized trial. *Pain, 104,* 187–194.

Redelmeier, D., Koehler, D., Liberman, V., & Tversky, A. (1995). Probability judgment in medicine: Discounting unspecified possibilities. *Medical Decision Making, 15,* 227–230.

Redelmeier, D. A., & Shafir, E. (1995). Medical decision making in situations that offer multiple alternatives. *Journal of the American Medical Association, 273,* 302–305.

Rehder, B. (2003). Categorization as causal reasoning. *Cognitive Science, 27,* 709–748.

Rescorla, R. A., & Wagner, A. R. (1972). A theory of Pavlovian conditioning: Variations in the effectiveness of reinforcement and nonreinforcement. In A. H. Black & W. F. Prokasy (Eds.), *Classical conditioning II: Current theory and research* (pp. 64–99). New York: Appleton-Century-Crofts.

Rettinger, D. A., & Hastie, R. (2001). Content effects on decision making. *Organizational Behavior and Human Decision Processes, 85,* 336–359.

Rettinger, D. A., & Hastie, R. (2003). Comprehension and decision making. In S. L. Schneider & J. Shanteau (Eds.), *Emerging perspectives on judgment and decision research* (pp. 165–200). Cambridge: Cambridge University Press.

Richter, T. & Späth, P. (2006). Recognition is used as one cue among others in judgment and decision making. *Journal of Experimental Psychology: Learning, Memory, and Cognition, 32,* 150–162.

Rieskamp, J., & Hoffrage, U. (1999). When do people use simple heuristics and how can we tell? In G. Gigerenzer, P. M. Todd, & the ABC Research Group (Eds.), *Simple heuristics that make us smart* (pp. 141–167). Oxford: Oxford University Press.

Rieskamp, J., & Otto, P. (2006). SSL: A theory of how people learn to select strategies. *Journal of Experimental Psychology: General, 135,* 207–236.

Ross, M. (1989). Relation of implicit theories to the construction of personal histories. *Psychological Review, 96,* 341–357.

Ross, M., & Buehler, R. (2001). Identity through time: Constructing personal pasts and futures. In A. Tesser & N. Schwarz (Eds.), *Blackwell handbook in social psychology: Vol. 1. Intra-individual processes* (pp. 518–544). Oxford: Blackwell.

Rottenstreich, Y., & Hsee, C. K. (2001). Money, kisses, and electric shocks: On the affective psychology of risk. *Psychological Science, 12,* 185–190.

Rottenstreich, Y., & Tversky, A. (1997). Unpacking, repacking, and anchoring: Advances in support theory. *Psychological Review, 104,* 406–415.

Rumelhart, D. E., & McClelland, J. L. (1986). *Parallel distributed processing: Explorations in the microstructure of cognition: Vol. 1. Foundations.* Cambridge, MA: MIT Press.

Samuelson, W., & Zeckhauser, R. J. (1988). Status quo bias in decision making. *Journal of Risk and Uncertainty, 1,* 7–59.

Savage, L. J. (1954). *The foundations of statistics.* New York: John Wiley & Sons.

Sawyer, J. (1966). Measurement and prediction: Clinical and statistical. *Psychological Bulletin, 66,* 178.

Schmitt, N., & Dudycha, A. (1975). A reevaluation of the effect of cue redundancy in multiple-cue probability learning. *Journal of Experimental Psychology: Human Learning and Memory, 1,* 307–315.

Schultz, W., & Dickinson, A. (2000). Neuronal coding of prediction errors. *Annual Review of Neuroscience, 23,* 473–500.

Schwarz, N., & Vaughn, L. A. (2002). The availability heuristic revisited: Ease of recall and content of recall as distinct sources of information. In T. Gilovich, D. Griffin, & D. Kahneman (Eds.), *Heuristics and biases* (pp. 103–119). Cambridge: Cambridge University Press.

Sedikides, C., Ariely, D., & Olsen, N. (1999). Contextual and procedural determinants of partner selection: Of asymmetric dominance and prominence. *Social Cognition, 17*, 118–139.

Sedlmeier, P. (1999). *Improving statistical reasoning: Theoretical models and practical implications.* Mahwah, NJ: Lawrence Erlbaum Associates, Inc.

Sedlmeier, P., & Betsch, T. (Eds.) (2002). *Etc. Frequency processing and cognition.* Oxford: Oxford University Press.

Shanks, D. R. (1990). Connectionism and the learning of probabilistic concepts. *Quarterly Journal of Experimental Psychology, 42A*, 209–237.

Shanks, D. R. (1991). A connectionist account of base-rate biases in categorization. *Connection Science, 3*, 143–162.

Shanks, D. R. (1992). Connectionist accounts of the inverse base-rate effect in categorization. *Connection Science, 4*, 3–18.

Shanks, D. R., Tunney, R. J., & McCarthy, J. D. (2002). A re-examination of probability matching and rational choice. *Journal of Behavioral Decision Making, 15*, 233–250.

Sides, A., Osherson, D., Bonini, N., & Viale, R. (2002). On the reality of the conjunction fallacy. *Memory and Cognition,* 30, 191–198.

Simon, H. A. (1955). A behavioral model of rational choice. *Quarterly Journal of Economics, 69*, 99–118.

Simon, H. A. (1956). Rational choice and the structure of environments. *Psychological Review, 63*, 129–138.

Simonson, I. (1990). The effect of purchase quantity and timing on variety seeking behavior. *Journal of Marketing Research, 27*, 150–162.

Skolbekken, J. A. (1998). Communicating the risk reduction achieved by cholesterol reducing drugs. *British Medical Journal, 316*, 1956–1958.

Sloman, S. A. (1996). The empirical case for two systems of reasoning. *Psychological Bulletin, 119*, 3–22.

Sloman, S. A. (2005). *Causal models.* New York: Oxford University Press.

Sloman, S. A., & Lagnado, D. A. (2004). Causal invariance in reasoning and learning. In B. Ross (Ed.), *The psychology of learning and motivation* (Vol. 44, pp. 287–325). San Diego, CA: Elsevier Science.

Sloman, S. A. & Lagnado, D. A. (2005). Do we 'do'? *Cognitive Science, 29*, 5–39.

Sloman, S. A., & Over, D. E. (2003). Probability judgment: From the inside and out. In D. E. Over (Ed.), *Evolution and the psychology of thinking: The debate* (pp. 145–169). Hove, UK: Psychology Press.

Sloman, S. A., Over, D., Slovak, L., & Stibel, J. M. (2003). Frequency illusions and other fallacies. *Organizational Behavior and Human Decision Processes, 91*, 296–309.

Sloman, S. A., Rottenstreich, Y., Wisniewski, E., Hadjichristidis, C., & Fox, C. R. (2004). Typical versus atypical unpacking and superadditive probability judgment. *Journal of Experimental Psychology: Learning, Memory, and Cognition, 30*, 573–582.

Slovic, P. (1974). Hypothesis testing in the learning of positive and negative linear functions. *Organizational Behavior and Human Performance, 11*, 368–376.

Slovic, P., Fischhoff, B., & Lichtenstein, S. (1980). Facts and fears: Understanding perceived risk. In R. Schwing & W. A. Albers, Jr (Eds.), *Societal risk assessment: How safe is safe enough?* (pp. 181–214). New York: Plenum Press.

Slovic, P., & Lichtenstein, S. (1971). Comparison of Bayesian and regression approaches to the study of information processing in judgment. *Organizational Behavior and Human Performance, 6*, 649–744

Slovic, P., Monahan, J., & MacGregor, D. M. (2000). Violence risk assessment and risk communication: The effects of using actual cases, providing instructions, and employing probability vs. frequency formats. *Law and Human Behavior, 24*, 271–296.

Slovic, P., & Tversky, A. (1974). Who accepts Savage's axiom? *Behavioral Science, 19*, 368–373.

Sniezek, J. (1986). The role of variable labels in cue probability learning tasks. *Organizational Behavior and Human Decision Processes, 38*, 141–161.

Sniezek, J. A. (1989). An examination of group process in judgmental forecasting. *International Journal of Forecasting, 5*, 171–178.

Sniezek, J. A., & Henry, R. A. (1989). Accuracy and confidence in group judgment. *Organizational Behavior and Human Decision Processes, 43*, 1–28.

Sniezek, J. A., & Henry, R. A. (1990). Revision, weighting, and commitment in consensus group judgment. *Organizational Behavior and Human Decision Processes, 45*, 66–84.

Soll, J. B., & Klayman, J. (2004). Overconfidence in interval estimates. *Journal of Experimental Psychology: Learning, Memory, and Cognition, 30*, 299–314.

Starmer, C. (2000). Developments in non-expected utility theory: The hunt for a descriptive theory of choice under risk. *Journal of Economic Literature, 38*, 332–382.

Starmer, C., & Sugden, R. (1993). Testing for juxtaposition and event-splitting effects. *Journal of Risk and Uncertainty, 6*, 235–254.

Starmer, C., & Sugden, R. (1998). Testing alternative explanations of cyclical choices. *Economica, 65*, 347–361.

Steiger, J. H., & Gettys, C. F. (1972). Best-guess errors in multistage inference. *Journal of Experimental Psychology, 92*, 1–7.

Steyvers, M., Tenenbaum, J. B., Wagenmakers, E. J., & Blum, B. (2003). Inferring causal networks from observations and interventions. *Cognitive Science, 27*, 453–489.

Stigler, G. J. (1961). The economics of information. *The Journal of Political Economy, 69*, 213–225.

Stone, E. R., Sieck, W. R., Bull, B. E., Yates, J. F., Parks, S. C., & Rush, C. J. (2003). Foreground:background salience: Explaining the effect of graphical displays on risk avoidance. *Organizational Behavior and Human Decision Processes, 90*, 19–36.

Stone,. E. R., Yates, J. F., & Parker, A. M. (1997). Effects of numerical and graphical displays on professed risk taking behaviour. *Journal of Experimental Psychology: Applied, 3*, 243–256.

Stone, G. O. (1986). An analysis of the delta rule and the learning of statistical associations. In D. E. Rumelhart, J. L. McClelland, & the PDP Research Group (Eds.), *Parallel distributed processing: Explorations in the microstructure of cognition: Vol. 1. Foundations* (pp. 444–459). Cambridge, MA: MIT Press.

Strack, F., & Mussweiler, T. (1997). Explaining the enigmatic anchoring effect: Mechanisms of selective accessibility. *Journal of Personality and Social Psychology, 73*, 437–446.

Surowiecki, J. (2005). *The wisdom of crowds: Why the many are smarter than the few.* London: Abacus.

Tentori, K., Crupi, V., Bonini, N., & Osherson, D. (2007). Comparison of confirmation measures. *Cognition, 103*, 107–119.

Thaler, R. (1980). Towards a positive theory of consumer choice. *Journal of Economic Behavior and Organization, 1*, 39–60.

Thompson, W. C., & Schumann, E. L. (1987). Interpretation of statistical evidence in criminal trials: The prosecutor's fallacy and the defense attorney's fallacy. *Law and Human Behavior, 11*, 167–187.

Todd, P. M., & Hammond, K. R. (1965). Differential effects of feedback in two multiple-cue probability learning tasks. *Behavioral Science, 10*, 429–435.

Tucker, L. R. (1964). A suggested alternative formulation in the developments by Hursch, Hammond, and Hursch, and by Hammond, Hursch, and Todd. *Psychological Review, 71*, 528–530.

Turner, M., & Pratkanis, A. (1998). Twenty-five years of groupthink theory and research: Lessons from the evaluation of a theory. *Organizational Behavior and Human Decision Processes, 73*, 105–115.

Tversky, A. (1972). Elimination by aspects: A theory of choice. *Psychological Review, 79*, 281–299.

Tversky, A., & Edwards, W. (1966). Information versus reward in binary choices. *Journal of Experimental Psychology, 71*, 680–683.

Tversky, A., & Fox C. R. (1995). Weighing risk and uncertainty. *Psychological Review, 102*, 269–283.

Tversky, A., & Kahneman, D. (1973). Availability: A heuristic for judging frequency and probability. *Cognitive Psychology, 5*, 207–232.

Tversky, A., & Kahneman, D. (1974). Judgment under uncertainty: Heuristics and biases. *Science, 185*, 1124–1131.

Tversky, A., & Kahneman, D. (1981). The framing of decisions and the psychology of choice. *Science, 211*, 453–458.

Tversky, A., & Kahneman, D. (1983). Extensional versus intuitive reasoning: The conjunction fallacy in probability judgment. *Psychological Review, 90*, 293–315.

Tversky, A., & Kahneman, D. (1992). Advances in prospect theory: Cumulative representation of uncertainty. *Journal of Risk and Uncertainty, 5*, 297–323.

Tversky, A., & Koehler, D. J. (1994). Support theory: A nonextensional representation of subjective probability. *Psychological Review, 101*, 547–567.

Tversky, A., Sattath, S., & Slovic, P. (1988). Contingent weighting in judgment and choice. *Psychological Review, 95*, 371–384.

Ubel, P. A. (2002). Is information always a good thing? Helping patients make 'good' decisions. *Medical Care, 40*, 39–44.

Usher, M., & McClelland, J. L. (2001). On the time course of perceptual choice: The leaky competing accumulator model. *Psychological Review, 108*, 550–592.

Van Wallendael, L. R., & Guignard, Y. (1992). Diagnosticity, confidence, and the need for information. *Journal of Behavioral Decision Making, 5*, 25–37.

Varey, C., & Kahneman, D. (1992). Experiences extended across time: Evaluation of moments and episodes. *Journal of Behavioral Decision Making, 5*, 169–185.

Villejoubert, G., & Mandel, D. R. (2002). The inverse fallacy: An account of deviations from Bayes's theorem and the additivity principle. *Memory and Cognition, 30*, 171–178.

von Neumann, J., & Morgenstern, O. (1947). *Theory of games and economic behavior* (2nd ed.). Princeton, NJ: Princeton University Press.

von Winterfeldt, D., & Edwards, W. (1986). *Decision analysis and behavioral research.* Cambridge: Cambridge University Press

Vulkan, N. (2000). An economist's perspective on probability matching. *Journal of Economic Surveys, 14,* 101–118.

Ward, A., & Mann, T. (2000). Don't mind if I do: Disinhibited eating under cognitive load. *Journal of Personality and Social Psychology, 78,* 753–763.

Wason, P. C. (1960). On the failure to eliminate hypotheses in a conceptual task. *Quarterly Journal of Experimental Psychology, 12,* 129–140.

Wedell, D. H., & Böckenholt, U. (1990). Moderation of preference reversals in the long run. *Journal of Experimental Psychology: Human Perception and Performance, 16,* 429–438.

Weiss, D. J., & Shanteau, J. (2003). Empirical assessment of expertise. *Human Factors, 45,* 104–116.

Welsh, I. (1996). *Trainspotting.* New York: Norton.

Wendt, D. (1969). Value of information for decisions. *Journal of Mathematical Psychology, 6,* 430–443.

Werner, P. D., Rose, T. L., & Yesavage, J. A. (1983). Reliability, accuracy, and decision-making strategy in clinical predictions of imminent dangerousness. *Journal of Consulting and Clinical Psychology, 51,* 815–825.

White, C. M., & Koehler, D. J. (2006). Assessing evidential support in an uncertain environment. In K. Fiedler & P. Juslin (Eds), *Information sampling and adaptive cognition* (pp. 261–298). Cambridge: Cambridge University Press.

Wicklund, R. A., & Brehm, J. W. (1976). *Perspectives on cognitive dissonance.* Hillsdale, NJ: Lawrence Erlbaum Associates, Inc.

Widrow, B., & Hoff, M. E. (1960). *Adaptive switching circuits.* 1960 IRE WESCON Convention Record, Pt. 4, 96–104.

Wirtz, D., Kruger, J., Scollon, C. N., & Diener, E. (2003). What to do on spring break? The role of predicted, on-line, and remembered experience in future choice. *Psychological Science, 14,* 520–524.

Wolford, G., Newman, S. E., Miller, M. B., & Wig, G. S. (2004). Searching for patterns in random sequences. *Canadian Journal of Experimental Psychology, 58,* 221–228.

Wu, G., & Gonzalez, R. (1996). Curvature of the probability weighting function. *Management Science, 42,* 1676–1690.

Yamagishi, K. (1997). When a 12.86 per cent mortality is more dangerous than 24.14 per cent: Implications for risk communication. *Applied Cognitive Psychology, 11,* 495–506.

Yates, J. F. (1990). *Judgment and decision making.* Englewood Cliffs, NJ: Prentice Hall.

Yates, J. F., Veinott, E. S., & Patalano, A. L. (2003). Hard decisions, bad decisions: On decision quality and decision aiding. In S. L. Schneider & J. Shanteau (Eds.), *Emerging perspectives on judgment and decision research* (pp. 13–63). New York: Cambridge University Press.

Yechiam, E., & Busemeyer, J. R. (2005). Comparison of basic assumptions embedded in learning models for experience-based decision making. *Psychonomic Bulletin and Review, 12,* 387–402.

Zajonc, R. (1980). Feeling and thinking: Preferences need no inferences. *American Psychologist, 35,* 151–175.

Zsambok, C. E. (1997). Naturalistic decision making: Where are we now? In C. E. Zsambok & G. A. Klein (Eds.), *Naturalistic decision making* (pp. 3–16). Mahwah, NJ: Lawrence Erlbaum Associates, Inc.

Author index

Subject index